Resource Mana

SCHOOL LEADERSHIP AND MANAGEMENT SERIES

Series Editors: Brent Davies and John West-Burnham

Other titles in the series:

Effective Learning in Schools
by Christopher Bowring-Carr and John West-Burnham

Managing Quality in Schools
by John West-Burnham

Middle Management in Schools
by Sonia Blandford

Reengineering and Total Quality in Schools
by Brent Davies and John West-Burnham

Strategic Marketing for Schools
by Brent Davies and Linda Ellison

Forthcoming titles:

Human Resource Management for Effective Schools
by John O'Neill and John West-Burnham

Management Development
by John West-Burnham

Strategic Development Planning in Schools
by Brent Davies and Linda Ellison

Resource Management in Schools

■ ■ ■

Effective and Practical Strategies for the Self-managing School

SONIA BLANDFORD

London · Hong Kong · Johannesburg · Melbourne · Singapore · Washington DC

For Susan, Emma and Melissa

PITMAN PUBLISHING
128 Long Acre, London WC2E 9AN
Tel: +44 (0) 171 447 2000
Fax: +44 (0) 171 240 5771

A Division of Pearson Professional Limited

First published in Great Britain in 1997

© Pearson Professional Limited 1997

The right of Sonia Blandford to be identified as author of this work
has been asserted by her in accordance with the Copyright, Designs
and Patents Act 1988.

ISBN 0 273 62411 3

British Library Cataloguing in Publication Data
A CIP catalogue record for this book can be obtained from the British Library

10 9 8 7 6 5 4 3 2 1

Typeset by Phoenix Photosetting, Chatham, Kent
Printed and bound in Great Britain by Redwood Books, Trowbridge, Wiltshire

The Publishers' policy is to use paper manufactured from sustainable forests.

Contents

■ ■ ■

The Impact of Labour Government Initiatives

■ ■ ■

Resource managers need to be aware of the proposed changes to the management of schools that will be implemented from September 1998. The new government aims to raise standards in education, as well as introducing transparency and simplicity to the allocation of resources to schools. More specifically, the government intends to review the LMS framework in order to move away from the diversity of practice that currently exists. A revised framework will build on good practice, and allow for local differences as required. The principles underpinning the government's intentions are:

- to provide nursery places for all 4 year olds and to set targets for the expansion of provision for 3 year olds;
- to reduce class sizes for 5–7 year olds, using money saved from the phasing out of the assisted places scheme;
- to introduce a major literacy drive to ensure that all pupils leaving primary schools have a reading age of at least 11;
- to set targets by which schools and LEAs will improve key stage and examination results;
- to improve school buildings through public/private partnership;
- to increase parental involvement in decision-making about the future of local grammar schools.

The new government intends to revise the structure of schools by creating three kinds of school:

- *Community* – based on existing county schools, but with an increased parental representation on the governing body.
- *Aided* – based on existing church schools, with increased parental representation on the governing body and a majority of church governors, they will continue to employ staff, develop an admissions policy in partnership with the LEA and hold the school assets in trust.
- *Foundation* – will hold their own assets, employ their own staff and retain charitable status. The governing body will have two LEA representatives and at least five parent governors.

Prior to the implementation of the above policies, a wide ranging consultation process is to take place from which changes to practice and the structure of schools will be formed.

Preface

■ ■ ■

Resources are a means of supply or support that assist school managers in the achievement of goals. The allocation and management of resources – fiscal, material, time and human – are critical to effective school management and should relate to pupil need. Self-management has led schools to the point where resource managers with knowledge and understanding of education, financial and human resource management are required if schools are to be economic, efficient and effective.

Central to this book is the notion that school resource management should be the responsibility of a resource manager who, by definition, has knowledge, experience and understanding of educational practice, and the skill and ability required to manage resources in schools. As we approach the new millennium, with the proposals in the White Paper *Self-Government for Schools* (DFEE, 1996c) such a position is required in all schools – primary, secondary, special and sixth-form colleges. Resource management is integral to effective school management and is, therefore, a position within the management structure not dissimilar to that of a curriculum or pastoral manager in terms of status and influence.

This book is written for primary and secondary school governors, school leaders, subject leaders, classroom teachers, higher education lecturers, local education authority officers and inspectors, and education consultants. Each chapter provides an insight into the principles and practices of resource management for practitioners with limited knowledge and experience. Examples of good practice are incorporated to illustrate key processes.

In sum, a resource manager should be an experienced and trained practitioner, able to participate effectively as a member of the school senior management team. Resource managers are responsible for the management of personnel, fiscal, material and building matters, as determined by the 1988 Education Reform Act (ERA). In practice, resource management requires knowledge and understanding of financial and human resource management and the development of skills and abilities previously associated with the private sector.

Chapter 1 introduces the notion that each school should have a resource manager with practitioner experience who will be responsible for the management of fiscal, material, human and time resources as determined by government Acts and initiatives since 1979 and according to need. A framework for practice focuses on the need for resource managers to have knowledge and understanding of education, schools and resource management. This chapter describes the relationship between resource management and management accounting, a system adopted in other areas of public sector resource management. The chapter concludes with a summary of key issues.

Chapter 2 describes local management of schools (LMS) and grant-maintained (GM) schools. This provides details of the process by which funds are allocated to schools, from central government to local education authorities (LEAs) and the school governing body. The chapter also includes details of the process by which LEAs report the distribution of resources to schools within their authority. The chapter concludes with a summary of the structure of funding and accountability.

Chapter 3 details the roles and responsibilities of those involved in the resource management of schools. This includes central government, local government, LEAs, the Funding Agency for Schools (FAS), headteachers, senior management teams, middle managers (budget holders), class teachers and special needs co-ordinators. The chapter describes the function of each player in the process of resourcing effective schools. The chapter concludes with a summary of the management of funds and resources within education.

Management is about getting things done through people. Chapter 4 focuses on the management skills and abilities required for resource management in primary and secondary schools. These encompass communication, participation and delegation, and decision-making. Models of good practice are described and the chapter concludes with a summary of the key skills required for effective resource management.

Chapter 5 describes the purpose of planning and the planning process, relating resource management to school development plans and key stage or department development plans. Examples of good practice are shown and discussed within the context of resource procurement and allocation. The chapter concludes with a summary of the key stages in educational planning.

The management of resources involves managing priorities as determined by the school development plan. Within the context of funding staff, materials and buildings Chapter 6 examines pupil–teacher ratios, staff mix, non-contact time, part-time staff and temporary contracts, non-teaching staff, supply and services, premises and insurance. The chapter concludes with a review of compulsory competitive tendering.

Chapter 7 introduces resource managers to the purpose and function of budgets. Several budgeting designs are examined within the context of school financial and resource management: programme budgeting, incremental budgeting, zero-based budgeting, rolling budgets and fixed and flexible budgets. The chapter reviews the idea of schools as cost-centres and concludes with guidance on planning for budgets.

Chapter 8 explains how to build and manage a budget, from starting to plan to budget implementation. Models of good practice are shown. Budget control is considered and guiding principles are given. The role of budget holders in building and controlling a budget encompassing stock controls and audits is described. The chapter concludes with a summary of key principles and practice.

Chapter 9 describes the use of information technology in the administration of resources. Practical advice is presented on the use of spreadsheets in the process of planning budgets. The chapter concludes with an introduction to systems designed for monitoring and controlling budgets.

Chapter 10 considers the importance of measuring performance in the management of resources. The monitoring and evaluation of educational practice is described, as is the possible introduction of performance indicators within the context of resource management. The chapter also encompasses a discussion focusing on equity, examining the disparity that exists in the allocation of resources at national and local levels. The chapter concludes with a summary of practical points and issues relevant to resource management in schools.

Chapter 11 describes the impact of open enrolment on schools and the need for resource managers to develop marketing strategies and practices. Models from business are examined and advice given on the marketing process. The chapter concludes with a summary of good practice as appropriate to schools.

Chapter 12 looks at the opportunities available to schools for generating their own income. Key issues are addressed and guidance given on how to approach the management of fund-raising opportunities from school raffles to lottery bids. The chapter introduces sources of income and advice that can be developed by resource managers and fund-raising groups. The chapter concludes with a summary of how to develop effective and appropriate fund-raising strategies.

Sonia Blandford

Acknowledgements

■ ■ ■

This book would not have been possible without the generous help and support of friends and colleagues. Primary and secondary practitioners and managers and local authority officers provided information which created the framework for the book. Because of the demands of confidentiality these teachers and officers cannot be named or thanked in person.

My thanks are to the 'team' who contributed to the process of creating the final copy, in particular: Rachel Soper, Charlie Eldridge and Sarah Stephens who word-processed each draft with speed and accuracy; Linet Arthur (School of Education, Oxford Brookes University), Dr Nicola McCormack (Bath and Wiltshire Health Trust), John Commack (School of Business, Oxford Brookes University), Paul Trembling (Royal Postgraduate Medical School) and John Howson (Teacher Training Agency) for their professional advice and support; and John Wood and Gill Fox for proofreading and their valuable comments.

My thanks also to John West-Burnham and Brent Davies for their faith and support.

Crown copyright is reproduced with the permission of the Controller of Her Majesty's Stationery Office.

Biographical Details

■ ■ ■

Sonia Blandford has taught in primary and secondary schools, and has held a variety of middle and senior management posts.

Sonia was among the first cohort to gain a taught doctorate in education (EdD) at the University of Bristol.

Sonia is currently a member of the Oxford Centre for Education Management, School of Education, Oxford Brookes University.

Sonia also conducts youth choirs and wind orchestras.

1
■ ■ ■

A framework for practice

Introduction

The management of schools has, for almost twenty years, embraced the 'five great themes' of educational change:

> Five great themes run through the story of educational change in England and Wales since 1979: quality, diversity, increasing parental choice, greater autonomy for schools and greater accountability.
>
> (DFE, 1992, p. 2; Crown copyright)

During this period of change and evolution there has emerged a body of education literature, within which guidance is given to practising and aspiring managers on how to manage and lead schools. In essence this book does not differ from established management literature in that it provides a framework for practice. However, the content relates to the position of resource manager, a role which requires knowledge and understanding of financial and human resource management and the development of skills and abilities previously associated with the private sector. Using examples from theory and practice the book defines resource management in the context of school management. Resource management is integral to effective school management and the resource manager is, therefore, a position within the management structure not dissimilar to that of a curriculum or pastoral manager in terms of status and influence, as Figure 1.1 indicates.

No school can avoid the issue of resources and resource management. As Thomas and Martin (1996, p. 3) explain:

> Resources matter. Those who work in schools as teachers and associate staff, school premises, furniture, books and equipment, all provide some of the means by which we transform our hopes and aspirations for children's education into daily learning opportunities and experiences and, beyond that, into the longer-term outcomes of schooling.

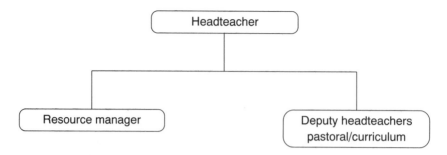

Figure 1.1: Position of resource manager in senior management team: primary/secondary/special

Central to this book is the notion that school resource management should be the responsibility of a resource manager who, by definition, has knowledge, experience and understanding of educational practice, and the skill and ability required to manage resources in schools. Such a position would be found in all schools – primary, secondary, special and sixth-form colleges. A resource manager should be an experienced practitioner and trained resource manager, able to participate effectively as a member of the school senior management team. Resource managers are responsible for the management of personnel, fiscal, material and building matters as determined by the 1988 Education Reform Act (ERA).

An outcome of government legislation has been a dramatic change in the management of schools. There has been a polarisation of power to the government and schools, away from the local education authority (LEA). As Esp and Saran (1994, p. 11) state:

> *The full force of the consumerist ideology hit the education service for the first time in the ERA.*

The first prerequisite for quality in any organisation is leadership – creating a sense of purpose and direction, aligning people behind it and inspiring people to make it a reality. The reality is then managed by planning, budgeting, monitoring, identifying problems, resolving them and evaluating the outcomes. Effective management is central to school effectiveness.

Resource management is not a value-free zone. Government, unions, school governors, senior management teams, budget holders and class teachers are all players in the field of school resource management. Parents also have an interest.

The National Association of Headteachers (NAHT) (1989) points out that, under local management of schools (LMS), schools have far more responsibility for their own survival. Critically, all schools now need to have a clear idea of the direction in which they are moving, and are no longer in a position to blame the LEA for ineffective management. Glatter (1996, p. 1) comments:

The term 'new public management' [. . .] has been used to cover a wide range of often rather different approaches [. . .] the driving force of all these various initiatives has been a determination to improve the quality of our public services as defined by clients and that should surely be the driving force for all of us involved in education management and delivery as we approach a new millennium.

Developments in LMS and grant-maintained (GM) programmes have created the need for schools to appoint resource managers. Prerequisites for such posts would be:

1 knowledge of education and public sector initiatives
2 understanding of resource management and education
3 management skills and experience
4 the ability to plan and implement a budget.

Resource managers should be members of senior management teams (SMTs), able to support and guide headteachers and governing bodies. In addition, resource managers should not be 'controllers of the school purse'; they should perceive resource management as integral to school management. Resource managers also need to have knowledge and understanding of recent legislation, as discussed in brief in the sections which follow.

The Education Reform Act 1988

The key elements of the 1988 Education Reform Act are described by the National Association of Headteachers (1989, p. 1/4) as follows:

- *Formula funding.* Each LEA's scheme of delegation must incorporate the formula for distributing its budget as determined by pupil numbers and pupil needs. Formula funding aims to make governors responsible for delivering central policy according to local need. Interestingly there was no virement before LMS.
- *Staff.* While LEAs continue to employ teaching and non-teaching staff, the power and responsibility of central management areas has been passed to school governors and the headteacher.
- *Admission* of pupils to county and voluntary schools – open enrolment or parental choice. Parents are able to enrol their children at any school that has the physical capacity to accept them, provided this is appropriate for the age and aptitude of the child. As the NAHT (1989, p. 1/4) explain:

    Physical capacity is interpreted as meaning 'the standard number' which in turn usually means the number admitted in 1979. Obviously changes which have taken place in the accommodation at a school since 1979 must be taken into account which means that LEAs and governors can agree to increase the admission limit. In the event of a disagreement, or if they want to reduce the limit, they must apply to the Secretary of State for a decision.

Where a school is oversubscribed, LEAs and governors have to establish criteria on which parents are to have preference.

- *Publication of schemes.* The 1986 Education Act required LEAs to publish annual statements setting out budget, or outturn, information on capital and recurrent expenditure for each school, itemised as the LEA deemed appropriate. These provisions were carried forward by the ERA. LEAs are required to publish:

  - statements of both budget and outturn expenditure to be provided in respect of each year, to allow comparisons
  - information on indirect as well as direct expenditure on schools
  - an indication of the basis on which this information is derived
  - comparative information for all schools to enable governors, staff and parents to consider the level of provision at their schools.

As shown, through the 1988 Education Reform Act, the government created a funding structure which enables spending decisions to be made by those most closely involved with a school: governors and the headteacher. The assumption was that they would have the necessary understanding and expertise to manage school resources. Prior to the ERA, many LEAs had already given governors responsibility for the management of large sums of money, which the NAHT (1989) considered to be a healthy trend.

In practice, this involves each LEA consulting with all school governing bodies, then publishing the allocation of its total resources among the schools in its area. Funds are shared between schools largely on the basis of pupil numbers, while (in theory) making allowances for factors such as a high proportion of children with special needs. The aim of LMS is to ensure that all schools get a fair share of the available funds. LMS involves the following, as the NAHT (1989, p. 1/2) explains:

The governors will take responsibility for expenditure on staff salaries, books and equipment, heat and light, cleaning, rates [...] indeed almost everything [...] managed by the education authority. The authority will continue to be responsible for capital expenditure, for home to school transport, for providing advisory, inspection, welfare and other services and for taking care of pay, tax and superannuation. Governors will be able to provide school meals if they can offer as good a service as the authority, at the same or lower cost.

In essence the funding framework established by the ERA still remains today. However, the current government has presented further measures to extend LMS in its recent White Paper *Self-Government for Schools* (DFEE, 1996c). Further details of the proposed changes to the LMS process are given in Chapters 2 and 3.

In addition to LMS, the ERA provided the opportunity for parents and the local community to run their own schools, whereby funds are paid direct from the central government. Schools which opt out of LEA control are known as grant-maintained (GM) schools. This element of the ERA aimed to increase choice of education within the state sector and to improve standards in schools. The government believes that where parents are dissatisfied with existing standards, they will be able to act so that their schools develop in ways best suited to the needs of their children. Further information on GM schools is provided in Chapter 2.

As stated, the ERA aimed to improve standards for pupils, increase choice and diversity for parents and increase central government and school management control of funding and resources. In sum, the education reforms which began with the 1988 ERA embody a strategy designed to pursue the government's 'five great themes' as Simkins (1995, p. 221) explains:

> *Taken together these reforms represent a radical and multi-faceted attempt to address concerns about the quality of schooling in England and Wales. How far they will succeed depends on a number of complex factors.*

The School Act 1992

The Act established the Office for Standards in Education (OFSTED) thus changing the role of the long-established Her Majesty's Inspectors of Schools (HMI). OFSTED's function is to appoint and train inspectors who will inspect schools every four years (five in Wales). This process began in 1993 for secondary schools and 1994 for primary schools. In brief, teams of inspectors tender for the contract and OFSTED selects which team will inspect a particular school. The team of OFSTED inspectors assesses the school's performance against predetermined criteria, set out in the *Framework for School Inspection* written by HMI (DFEE, 1996). The results of the inspection are made public and the school governors are required to draw up an action plan to address the issues raised by the inspectors.

The Education Act 1993

Further changes in the control of education were contained in the 1993 Act in which a new funding authority for GM schools only – the Funding Agency for Schools (FAS) – was created. As Esp and Saran (1995, p. 12) state:

> *This provided that the Secretary of State should promote standards, diversity and choice. When the percentage of grant-maintained (opted-out) school provision in an area in either primary or secondary schools reaches 10%, the strategic powers of the*

5

LEA are shared with a new funding authority appointed by the Secretary of State. This funding authority is also responsible for grants to the opted-out sector, and can establish new grant-maintained schools. When the proportion reaches 75% the funding agency takes over all the strategic powers formerly exercised by LEAs, and it can take the initiative in securing a change of character in any grant-maintained school.

1997 Labour government initiatives

The election of the Labour Party to government will have a direct impact on the management of schools. The new government aims to raise standards in education; it also aims to introduce transparency and simplicity to the allocation of resources to schools. More specifically, the government intends to review the LMS framework in order to move away from the diversity of practice that currently exists. A revised framework will build on good practice and allow for local differences, as required.

The principles underpinning the government's intentions are:

- the provision of nursery places for all 4 year olds and setting targets for the expansion of provision for 3 year olds;
- the reduction of class sizes for 5–7 year olds using money saved from the phasing out of the assisted places scheme;
- the introduction of a major literacy drive to ensure that all pupils leaving primary schools have a reading age of at least 11;
- the setting of targets by schools and LEAs to improve key stage and examination results;
- the improvement of school buildings through public/private partnership;
- the increase of parental decision-making on the future of local grammar schools.

The Labour government intends to create three kinds of school:

- *Community* – based on existing county schools, but with an increased parental representation on the governing body.
- *Aided* – based on existing church schools. Together with increased parental representation on the governing body and a majority of church governors, they will continue to employ staff, develop an admissions policy in partnership with the LEA and hold the school assets in trust.
- *Foundation* – will hold their own assets, employ their own staff and retain charitable status. They will have two LEA representatives on the governing body and at least five parent governors.

In effect, aided and foundation schools will own their assets and community schools are not dissimilar to existing local authority schools. The allocation of funds will be based on this structure.

In practice the only schools that will change in any significant way are the 1,100 in the GM sector. The urgency with which this will occur will be dependent on transitional arrangements and the speed with which the Funding Agency for Schools will be dismantled. This will create problems for those authorities where the majority of schools have opted out.

Prior to any implementation of the above policies, a wide ranging consultation process is to take place from which changes to practice and the structure of schools will be formed.

The timetable for developing and implementing education policy is as follows:

- **14 May 1997, Queen's Speech:** The government presents a broad outline for forthcoming education legislation.
- **Early Summer 1997, Education Summit:** Leading educationalists meet with the government's education team to discuss key issues.
- **Mid-Summer 1997, White Paper:** Details of intended legislation for consultation with leading professionals.
- **Before Summer 1997 Recess, Short Education Bill:** Legislation to stop assisted places before September to release funds for the reduction of class sizes.
- **Autumn 1997, Major Education Bill:** Main issues are the raising of standards, creation of the General Teaching Council, identification of education action zones, setting targets and reducing class sizes.

The timetable for change in schools will be:

- **Summer 1997, Consultation:** Practitioners asked to review White Paper.
- **September 1997, Implementation of Short Bill 1997:** Pupil–teacher ratio for 5–7 years olds reduced to 30 or less; assisted places scheme to end; grant-maintained programme to be reviewed.
- **September 1998, Implementation of Autumn Bill 1997:** Transitional arrangements for GM schools; further funding for primary schools – focus on literacy; lottery funding for INSET and extra-curricular activities.
- **September 1999, Restructuring of Schools:** Introduction of aided, foundation and community schools; increase of LMS 90% of LEA budget delegated to schools.

LMS – developing the model

Changes to LMS will be guided by practitioners following the government White Paper and subsequent consultation processes. The outcome of this process will also determine the extent to which schools will have increased funding. In addition, the Secretary of State for Education and Employment has advised LEAs of the need to undergo a comprehensive evaluation of LMS. This evaluation and review will reveal differing practices and may release more resources for the direct provision of educational services by the LEA in the raising of standards in schools. The evaluation will be by the Audit Commission, DFEE, Local Government Association and LEAs. During the evaluation process the Audit Commission will also review the role of LEAs in terms of efficiency and effectiveness.

The government intends to benchmark best practice within LEAs so as to advise authorities on how to deliver high quality services within their budgets. A common formula for all LEAs has been suggested. The government has stated that 90 per cent of every LEA's school budget will be delegated to schools, thus extending the management of funds at a local level.

Grant maintained schools – integration

The government proposes that the GM programme, which allows schools to opt out of local authority control and run their own affairs, is to be ended. As stated, the Autumn Bill will provide for foundation, community and aided schools. Where GM schools are aided, for example by the Church, they are likely to retain control of their admissions policies. The non-aided GM schools that decide not to return to the local authority will become foundation schools and set their admission policy in consultation with the LEA. Foundation schools may lose funds if the share of central resources allocated to buy services returns to LEAs.

Immediate changes

Assisted places = reduction in class sizes

Within 24 hours of the general election the Labour Secretary of State for Education was implementing plans for the reduction of class sizes for 5–7 year olds. The Local Government Association was asked to show how funds from the assisted places scheme could be redirected to reduce class sizes, to start in September 1997. While full implementation may take several years, immediate changes will be based on allocation of funds according to the number of pupils aged 5–7 in each authority.

Additional funds

The Secretary of State for Education and Employment has pledged an increase in funds for extra-curricular activities in schools and for the in-service training of teachers. Funds will be generated by the National Lottery.

Essentially, future changes to the status of schools and funding arrangements will impact on the relationship between central government, local government and schools. An understanding of the management of delegation is critical to the management of effective schools.

Managing delegation

The implementation of LMS/GM status raised several issues concerning the management of delegation.

Positive outcomes

These are summarised as Jones and Pendlebury (1996, p. 3) comment:

> A further development in recent years, having a profound impact on the management of public services, is that of 'devolved management' [...]. A prime example is the local management of schools, whereby the head and governors of a school are given an operating costs budget that is based largely on the number of students enrolled, and are then required to operate the school and control their costs against the budget.

While resources may be limited, the majority of school management teams have embraced financial delegation with enthusiasm. Arnott, Bullock and Thomas (1992), in a study for the National Association of Headteachers (NAHT) on the impact of local management on 800 primary and secondary schools, found that headteachers welcomed delegation and would not wish to return to full LEA control. Further, GM managed schools found that independence from LEAs was one of the main benefits of GM status (Bush *et al.*, 1993). Hirst (1996) also believes that there have been some positive outcomes of LMS, including a greater understanding of the costs of the education service, within a school, LEA and across the country. There have also been incentives to cut out waste, leading to a better management of premises. Education managers now have an understanding of cost-benefit analysis or value for money. School leaders have an incentive to increase direct income through the letting of premises, sponsorship, merchandising, fund-raising and developing an entrepreneurial flair. Thomas and Martin (1996, p. 26) comment:

> Clearly, at the level of public reporting, delegated resource management has been a great success.

However, Thomas and Martin are cautious and balance this with the HMI's (DFE, 1992, p. 11) assessment of locally managed schools:

> There is little evidence yet of LMS having any substantial impact on educational standards, although specific initiatives have led to improvement in the targeting of resources and staff, and so to improvements in the quality of educational experiences.

Areas of weakness

While educationalists agree that the management of resources is central to the improvement of educational experiences there are those that question the effectiveness of LMS/GM initiatives. Hirst (1996) considers that there are areas of weakness in LMS which include:

- lack of rigorous evaluation – does LMS improve educational outcomes?
- difficulty of spreading the LMS culture across the whole school community – response of staff, response of pupils?
- continuing tensions between LEAs and schools – accounting systems, bank accounts, central hold-backs on service contracts
- the frustration of competitive tendering – site-based incoherence
- administrative costs – more accountants at school level and still as many in the LEA?

Hirst (1996) also believes that LMS is being abused by those who drive down expenditure and are putting the blame on somebody else, e.g. passing the buck. LMS also places an excessive emphasis on competition by placing education in the market place. In addition Hirst (*ibid.*) considers that in the context of choice and diversity, grant-maintained schools have created fragmentation and incoherence, rivalry, bitterness and chaos.

Limited funding since LMS is an issue that has affected the whole school community. TES *Opinion* (1996, p. 16) comments on the contribution made by parents to school funds:

> [...] *there is no doubt that, overall, parents are paying more for what is still ostensibly a free state education service.*

Department for Education and Employment figures show that spending per pupil dropped by 3.3 per cent in real terms between 1992–3 and 1994–5. Class sizes have risen for the sixth year running; approximately 5000 teachers were made redundant in 1994–5 and another 4000 lost their jobs in 1995–6. LEAs estimate that there is now a £3.2 billion backlog of school building repairs and improvements, 750 000 children are being taught in mobile classrooms, 600 primary schools still have outside toilets and many primary schools are spending less than £5 a year per pupil on books. Education authorities are also continuing to reduce discretionary awards for music tuition, adult and community education and youth work. There is a need for internal controls which can be identified by auditors.

John Atkins (1996, p. 13) believes that schools are being torn by the conflicting demands of what they can spend and what they can deliver. He focuses on five pupil-related questions:

- Why should more money be spent on some pupils than on others?
- Which pupils should these be?

- What is to be achieved by this?
- How should the number of these pupils in any one authority be assessed?
- How much extra should they receive?

A way forward is suggested by Michael Barber (1996, p. 128) who considers that school improvement is the key to an increase in government funding on education:

> *Education needs more money [. . .]. The emphasis on school improvement from both government and opposition has been a welcome step forward. It is surely right to expect schools to take responsibility for improving themselves and to make the most of what they have. The real potential of school improvement will, however, only be achieved if schools are working within a resource framework which helps rather than hinders their efforts.*

As Hirst states, political leaders will need to consider two issues:

- Education – a drain on the public purse or an essential investment?
- Education – better for some or better for all?

School leaders (LEAs, headteachers and governors)

In practice there are challenges for school leaders arising from the management of shrinking resources. LEA and school leaders will need to resolve conflicts arising from the pressure of autocracy. The moral dilemma is: *education for the public good or as a marketable commodity?*

LEA officers and school leaders need to establish a relationship with schools and between schools within their local education authority. They also need to target scarce resources within education and prioritise education over social services. In addition LEA officers need to enter the debate concerning the distribution of resources across the country. LMS has created an industry for LEA accountants and advisors.

School leaders (headteachers and governors) now have an increased sense of autonomy, accountability and ownership, having been weaned off dependency on the LEA. Senior management teams have an enhanced leadership role with increased flexibility to use resources appropriately with the better use of technology and employment of non-teaching staff. Managers now have an insight into the national picture and greater democratic accountability.

However, headteachers have an insecurity about financial management which has to be accommodated with all other changes to their professional lives. Key problems have been: preparing a budget, controlling a budget (avoiding overspending and underspending) and review and monitoring in preparation for the next year. Headteachers have suffered from lack of training and expertise – the introduction of the Headteachers' Leadership and Management Programme (HEADLAMP) has had limited effect. The Teacher Training

Agency's (TTA) National Professional Qualification for Headteachers (NPQH) may improve the quality of training. Meanwhile, some LEAs have appointed an accountant to advise school senior management teams.

Management accounting and control

The appointment of resource managers, with knowledge and understanding of education and the skill and ability to manage resources, would resolve many of the above issues. Resource managers require a model on which to base their practice – management accounting and control provide a model that has been adopted in other areas of the public sector.

The model is based on the premise that all organisations have objectives. Decisions need to be taken on which strategies to pursue to achieve the objectives and which to reject, i.e. the *planning* process. Plans then have to be implemented and systems are needed to ensure that the plans are followed and the objectives achieved. This is the *control* process, as Jones and Pendlebury (1996, p. 17) explain:

> [The] *processes of planning and control are two of the most important tasks undertaken by the managers of an organisation and together they form the nucleus of the overall management system. In order to carry out these tasks, managers require information. It is with the provision of such information that management accounting is primarily concerned.*

In practice, resource managers in schools are responsible for gathering information. The role of a resource manager is, therefore, not dissimilar to that of a management accountant. The Chartered Institute of Management Accountants (1994, p. 13) defines management accounting as:

> *An integral part of management concerned with identifying, presenting and interpreting information used for:*
>
> *(a) formulating strategy*
>
> *(b) planning and controlling activities*
>
> *(c) decision taking*
>
> *(d) optimising the use of resources*
>
> *(e) disclosure to shareholders and others external to the entity*
>
> *(f) disclosure to employees*
>
> *(g) safeguarding assets.*

This definition relates accounting information directly to the key elements of the overall management system, as Figure 1.2 indicates.

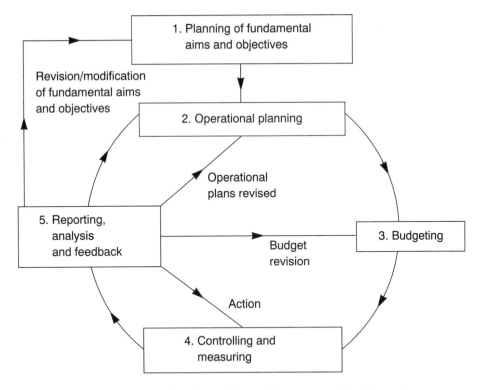

Figure 1.2: The managerial planning and control processes of public sector organisations
(*Source:* Jones and Pendlebury, 1996, p. 19; reproduced by permission of the authors)

As shown, the basic role of management accounting in public sector organisations is to provide managers with the accounting information they need to carry out the planning and control functions (Jones and Pendlebury, 1996, p. 21). An effective managerial planning and control system is therefore an essential requirement of public sector organisations. In sum (p. 22):

> *Management accounting has a crucial part to play in providing the information needed to operate such a system. Information is needed at the planning stage to decide which activities to undertake and the resources that will be required. Information is needed at the control stage to measure how effective the organisation is in achieving its objective and how efficient it was in the use of resources.*

Resource managers also need to build on the strengths of middle managers who develop their skills as budget holders. Staff should be rewarded for their professional expertise as an incentive to save in the public sector.

A framework for resource management in schools? Management accounting, as with other management practices from the business world, can help to inform and guide education managers.

13

Human Resource Management

In addition to management accounting and control, resource management also encompasses human resource management (HRM). A range of possible models is available from outside education. West-Burnham (1990, pp. 66–7) comments:

> The changing context of educational management requires schools to adopt proactive staff management strategies in order to come to terms with a range of complex issues.

In brief, these include:

- appraisal
- LMS and increased institutional autonomy
- equal opportunities
- institutional improvement and quality management
- the need to manage morale and motivation
- [development] of good staff interpersonal relationships
- [inclusion of] non-teaching staff into all [...] effective institutional management
- need to develop [planning mechanisms]
- develop[ment of] management procedures
- the need to recognise and treat adults as adults.

In Figure 1.3, West-Burnham (1990, p. 87) presents a structure for performance management in schools.

West-Burnham (p. 91) concludes that human resource management in schools requires a total approach which has the following components:

1 Headteachers being leaders and not teachers with extra jobs.

2 Senior staff and middle managers having an explicit management role and being trained and developed to do it.

3 A vision which is translated into genuine aims and attainable objectives which inform job design, delegation, the creation of work teams and operating procedures.

4 Recognising that management structures and procedures exist to facilitate action and are not ends in themselves.

5 Making time and releasing creative energy by incorporating the community and children into management processes so that they can contribute to, rather than be subjects of school management.

6 Recognising that the integrity of the learning process applies as much to adults in schools as it does to children.

Resource managers need to consider human resource management issues when determining their framework for practice. Resource managers also need

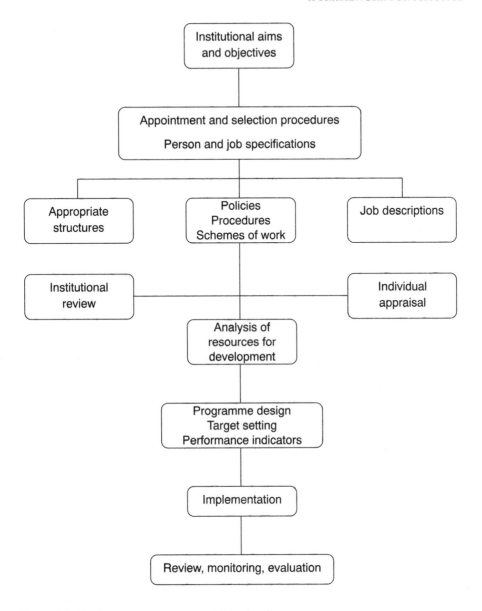

Figure 1.3: Performance management in schools
(*Source:* West-Burnham, 1990, p. 87)

to understand that central to school resource management is the belief that schools function in order that:

- pupils learn, and
- teachers teach.

Summary

No school can avoid the issue of resources and resource management. Central to this book is the notion that school resource management should be the responsibility of a resource manager who, by definition, has knowledge, experience and understanding of educational practice, and the skill and ability required to manage resources in schools. A resource manager should be an experienced practitioner and trained resource manager, able to participate effectively as a member of the school senior management team.

Developments in LMS and GM programmes have created the need for schools to appoint resource managers. Prerequisites for such posts would be:

1 knowledge of education and public sector initiatives
2 understanding of resource management and education
3 management skills and experience
4 the ability to plan and implement a budget.

As shown, through the 1988 Education Reform Act, the government created a funding structure which enables spending decisions to be made by those most closely involved with a school: the governors and the headteacher. The assumption was that they would have the necessary understanding and expertise to manage school resources.

In practice, this involves each LEA consulting with all school governing bodies, then publishing the allocation of its total resources among the schools in its area. Funds are shared between schools largely on the basis of pupil numbers, while (in theory) making allowances for factors such as a high proportion of children with special needs. The aim of LMS is to ensure that all schools get a fair share of the available funds. Further changes in the control of education were contained in the 1993 Act in which a new funding authority for GM schools only – the Funding Agency for Schools (FAS) – was created.

While resources may be limited, the majority of school management teams have embraced financial delegation with enthusiasm. Limited funding since LMS is an issue that has affected the whole school community. In practice there are challenges for school leaders arising from the management of shrinking resources. LEA officers and school leaders need to establish a relationship with schools and between schools within their local education authority. They also need to target scarce resources within education and prioritise education over social services.

The appointment of resource managers, with knowledge and understanding of education and the skill and ability to manage resources, would resolve many of the above issues. Resource managers require a model on which to base their practice – management accounting and control provide a model that has been adopted in other areas of the public sector.

2
■ ■ ■

Delegation principles

Introduction

Resource managers require knowledge and understanding of delegation principles. This chapter focuses on the evolution of the LMS/GM initiatives and describes the principles on which delegation is practised.

Since the 1988 Education Reform Act (DES, 1988a) there have been radical and dramatic changes to school management and the education of pupils (Maychell, 1994; Gilbert, 1990a). The ERA introduced fundamental alterations to the power structure of the education system which had previously been determined by the 1944 Education Act. Essentially, the ERA increased the powers of the Secretary of State for Education, thus strengthening the role of central government. Local education authority roles and responsibilities were decreased while the power and functions of governing bodies and head-teachers were increased. The main ERA provisions relating to schools concern:

1 the establishment of a national curriculum
2 the open enrolment of pupils
3 the delegation of staffing responsibilities
4 the establishment of grant-maintained schools.

Gilbert (1990b, p. 13) states:

> [. . .] these four elements should be seen as part of a coherent government package designed explicitly to improve the quality of education by reinforcing the accountability and responsiveness of schools and their local education authorities.

The government's aim was to improve standards in education by increasing market forces and competition. The assumption and rationale of the ERA was accountability. As Gilbert (1990b, p. 14) comments, educational quality would be strengthened by:

- teachers striving to improve the results of national curriculum assessments and public examinations to make the school attractive to parents

- *increasing pupil numbers, attracting funds and thereby securing staff jobs.*

These assumptions do not consider socio-political factors which inevitably influence the effectiveness of schools. The background to the ERA may illuminate the process which led to the notion that schools can be market-led.

Background

Britain has a tradition of strong, well-developed and effective local government. The system of administering central and local government education and other policies dates back to mediaeval England. During the nineteenth century, the provision of services for the community reflected the increasing needs of the rapidly expanding towns and cities. In brief, the Local Government Acts of 1888 and 1894 created a structure of counties, districts and county boroughs which continued until 1965. Then local government in Greater London was reorganised, followed by reorganisations in Northern Ireland in 1973, the rest of England and Wales in 1974 and Scotland in 1975 (Burgess and Travers, 1980). Education and social services were the responsibility of the county councils in the non-metropolitan areas and of the districts in the metropolitan areas and outer London boroughs. In inner London there was a single Inner London Education Authority (ILEA). Further changes occurred with the dissolution of the Greater London Council and ILEA (1989) and the creation of unitary authorities in 1996.

As the above indicates, at no time in the history of education has provision in the United Kingdom been uniform (Howson, 1982, p. 187). Prior to the ERA, local government managed over 80 per cent of the spending on education, although there was recognition of the need for monitoring expenditure (HMI, 1981). Howson (pp. 187–92) concluded that variations in levels of provision were recognised as early as 1926. Not all variations in education are due to provision; socio-economic factors will impact on education at all levels and across all phases.

As an example, although the 1944 Education Act should have ensured that secondary education was available to all, lack of resources in post-war Britain and the use of existing school buildings meant that many pupils continued to receive their education in 'all-age' schools. In 1958 the government paper *Secondary Education for All – A New Drive* (Ministry of Education) set the parameters for a determined effort to replace the remaining 'all-age' schools with primary and secondary schools. The five-year building programme cost the government £300 million; however, this did not include those schools where primary and secondary pupils shared the same building. By 1968, 24 years after the 1944 Act, over 7000 pupils were still receiving their education in the remaining 32 'all-age' schools (DES, 1968).

The provision of school buildings has, inevitably, varied across the country and has been closely linked to areas of population growth. As Howson (1982) indicated, most improvements in school buildings have been as a result of capital spending from the minor works programme, and have not been designed to replace whole schools but to allow for adaptations such as converting classrooms into specialist accommodation.

Disparity of provision in education extends beyond school buildings – comparative studies of county boroughs (Ashford, 1974; Boaden, 1971) reveal widely differing levels of provision for all services (Howson, 1982, p. 188). County boroughs were abolished in the reorganisation of local government following the Maud Committee Report (1969) which led to a decrease in the number of LEAs.

The change in government in 1970 did not alter the emerging pattern of central government control. Howson (1982, p. 193) reflected on central government's desire to control local government spending. Fundamentally, the government was determined that schools should be more effective (and efficient) institutions for learning and believed that transferring funding from LEAs to schools would:

1 enable governing bodies and headteachers to direct resources to the needs and priorities of their schools
2 make schools more responsive to their clients – parents, pupils, employers and community
3 improve the quality of teaching and learning within the available resources.

In practice, central government was to devolve much of the responsibility for resource management directly to headteachers and school governing bodies. This followed a pilot programme experiment known as local financial management (LFM).

Local financial management

In 1982 Cambridgeshire established the first pilot scheme for LFM. Six secondary schools and one primary school were included in the initial pilot scheme. Derek Nightingale, one of the headteachers participating in the pilot project, reports (1990, p. 1):

> Cambridgeshire for some years had been moving towards giving schools greater control of various issues affecting management. Throughout the 1980s the theme of the headteacher as manager was consistently advocated despite the resistance of many heads. Whilst this was thought to be applicable to large secondary schools, it was not thought to be the style for primary schools. The authority pursued their belief in local management by devolving more responsibility to schools.

At the end of the scheme, Cambridgeshire County Council (1985) stated that:

> The scheme is essentially one of delegation of management and not simply financial administration. It allows real decisions to be taken locally about the shape of the education service in a school, albeit within the policy parameters of the Authority.

The three-year pilot project proved to be successful. By 1986 all Cambridgeshire secondary schools and also 11 primary schools were introduced to LFM. As an exemplar of good practice, Nightingale and his school governing body decided not to make any decisions about redeploying resources until they had become familiar with the financial information and its implications (Nightingale, 1990, p. 7).

The day-to-day administration of the scheme could only be undertaken by the headteacher and school secretary. A finance subcommittee of the governing body had responsibility for the management of the delegated budget. The purpose of the finance subcommittee was to examine the budget, to look at the school's needs and to recommend decisions accordingly. As the subcommittee became more confident, it was able to make decisions concerning resources. The two biggest problems which arose early in the scheme were related to supply cover and community education. However, Nightingale (p. 21) concluded that LFM had been of benefit to the school, as it was more about managing than accounting. In sum, Nightingale (p. 22) found:

1 *There was a need to establish a clear system of record keeping.*
2 *Time was needed to understand the scheme, and this was difficult without any real training.*
3 *The scheme brought benefits to the school not only in terms of resources but also in involvement of people.*
4 *The scheme brought about an adaptation of management style.*
5 *There are problems, but these are best seen as challenges to be overcome.*

Nightingale (pp. 33–4) believes that the disadvantages of LFM were outweighed by the advantages, as follows:

Advantages
1 *Local decision-making*
2 *Finance deployed to meet the identified needs of the school*
3 *Understanding of school finances*
4 *Accountability of authority to schools*
5 *Ability to vire resources*
6 *Control of the supply teacher budget*
7 *Identification of anomalies*
8 *Less interference by 'the Office'* [LEA administrators]

9 *Clarification of management planning*

10 *Improved resources available to school.*

Disadvantages

1 *Temptation to employ cheap staff*

2 *Who really controls the budget?*

3 *How planned can understanding be?*

4 *Danger of raising expectations of sustaining 'extras'*

5 *What happens if a school overspends?*

6 *Vulnerability to political decisions*

7 *Vulnerability of headteacher (particularly to media)*

8 *Difference in primary and secondary resources*

9 *Mismatch of educational year and financial year.*

The above lists raise the following issues, pertinent to resource management in schools:

1 training – roles and responsibilities
2 knowledge and understanding – budgets
3 management
4 planning – strategic and operational
5 comparisons between primary and secondary schools
6 priorities – capital and revenue expenditure
7 opportunities to improve resources.

Local management of schools

As stated, LMS is an outcome of the ERA. Davies and Braund (1989) explain:

> *[. . .] most of the school expenditure previously allocated by the Local Education Authority will now be allocated by the school governors in consultation with the headteacher. Thus the LEA will determine the total amount of money a school will receive (its budget) but how this is spent [. . .] will be left for the school to decide, as long as it keeps its spending within the overall budget limit.*

The principles on which financial management was based are described in Circular 7/88 – *Local Management of Schools* (DES, 1988b; Crown copyright):

> *Local management represents a major challenge and a major opportunity for the education service. The introduction of a needs-based formula funding and delegation of financial, managerial responsibilities to governing bodies are key elements in the Government's overall policy to improve the quality of teaching and learning in*

schools. Local management is concerned with far more than budgeting and accounting procedures. Effective schemes of local management will enable governing bodies and head teachers to plan to use their resources – including their most valuable resource, their staff – to maximum effect in accordance with their own needs and priorities, and to make schools more responsive to their clients – parents, pupils, the local community and employers.

In the context of resource management, schools are given responsibility for finance and staffing. Based on a formula devised by each LEA, LMS delegates the schools' financial budgets to governors. LMS also delegates related managerial authority and responsibility for staff. Thomas *et al.* (1989, p. 1) state:

1   *LMS means that each school will have more control over its own affairs. A requirement of the Education Reform Act (1988), it has two main parts:*

   (i)   *The Act requires each school within a Local Education Authority (LEA) to be given a budget. This budget will cover most of the school's costs; its calculation will be based mainly on the number of pupils in the school (referred to as the formula). The 'formula' must apply to each school within the LEA.*

   (ii) *Control over how to spend its budget must be given to each secondary school and to each primary school with more than 200 pupils; this control can be given to other schools too. Schools will be 'delegated' power under the Act.*

2   *The aims are:*

   ● *to enable schools to adjust to the needs of their pupils and community;*

   ● *to enable schools to make the best use of the money available and to report on their achievements.*

Since April 1993, all schools have been included in the LMS scheme, with the exception of special schools which were included from April 1994. However, LEAs have sufficient discretion to ensure that there will be almost as many schemes as there are LEAs (Knight *et al.*, 1993).

Legislation

The 1988 Education Reform Act details the framework for the local management of schools. Circular 7/88 (DES, 1988b) describes the principles on which LMS was based. The government White Paper, *Self-Government for Schools* (DFEE, 1996c, p. 10) describes how LMS works now (*see* Figure 2.1).

In practice, the LMS process is as follows.

General Schools Budget

Determined by the LEA, this represents the total financial resources available in any one financial year to all schools covered by a scheme of delegation. These total resources include the planned direct and indirect spending at school, central government and LEA level. From the total resources, *excepted items* are deducted – *mandatory and discretionary.*

- Each year every LEA decides the total amount it will be spend on its schools – the General Schools Budget (GSB).

- From that it holds back money for 'excepted items' which it manages centrally, such as building projects, home-to-school transport, premature retirement costs, and the educational psychology service.

- The total amount left after taking away these 'excepted items' is called the Potential Schools Budget (PSB).

- The LEA can hold centrally money for further items within the PSB, such as central administration, some elements of special educational needs, library and music services. But it cannot hold back more than 15% of the PSB – so at least 85% of the PSB must be delegated to schools (90% in Wales).

- The total amount delegated to schools is called the Aggregated Schools Budget (ASB). Each school's share of the ASB must be worked out by a formula based on the objective measures of need, particularly the number of pupils on the school register.

- Each school's governing body has the right to decide how to spend its delegated budget to meet the school's needs.

Figure 2.1: How LMS works now
(*Source:* DFEE, 1996c, Box 2.1; Crown copyright)

The amount of money that an LEA spends on schools, therefore, is called the GSB. The items that remain under LEA control are called *mandatory deductions* and have to be taken from the GSB. Mandatory deductions are to be returned centrally by all LEAs and not delegated to schools. These include:

1 capital spending
2 debt charges
3 spending taken into account in determining specific grants, e.g.
   - education support grants
   - LEA training grants
   - travellers' children grants
   - section 11 grants
   - European Community grants.

With some items the LEA can choose either to retain control or to delegate. These must not be more than 15 per cent of the GSB and are called *discretionary exceptions*. These include:

1 central administration

2 inspectors/advisors

3 premature retirement and severance

4 school meals

5 home–school transport

6 governors' insurance

7 transitional arrangements involving existing contracts (e.g. grounds maintenance)

8 structural repairs and maintenance

9 premises and equipment insurance

10 children with special educational needs in ordinary schools

11 special units serving statemented or non-statemented pupils

12 educational psychologists

13 educational welfare officers

14 peripatetic and advisory teachers

15 pupil support (e.g. clothing grants)

16 special staff costs:

   – 'safeguarded' incentive allowances

   – supply cover (e.g. for long-term absence)

   – cover for teachers who are magistrates, local councillors or senior officers of teachers' associations

17 school library and school museum services

18 LEA policy initiatives (e.g. 'pump-priming' for aspects of curriculum development)

19 contingencies (individual school or LEA wide).

Guidelines issued by central government to LEAs allow them to pass on, as appropriate, *earmarked funds* related to any mandatory or discretionary excepted item. To ensure maximum delegation the DFEE places limits over LEAs on the extent of discretionary exceptions. Apart from the first seven items listed above, an LEA has to keep its costs of all excepted items within an agreed limit of the GSB.

Potential Schools Budget

The function of the PSB is to provide an indication of the proportion of the GSB that will be allocated to schools once mandatory and discretionary exceptions have been deducted, as determined by central government legislation and the LEA (responsible for identifying local needs). The final amount delegated to schools is the Aggregated Schools Budget (ASB).

Aggregated Schools Budget

This is the amount remaining after deducting all mandatory and discretionary exceptions. The school budget share of the ASB is determined primarily by the number of pupils in each school weighted for differences in age-weighted pupil units (AWPUs). This will take into consideration the objective needs of the school rather than previous practice. This is shared among schools on the basis of a *formula* developed by each LEA, as determined by the Secretary of State. Circular 7/88 states that the formula must allocate the ASB summarised as follows:

1　At least 85 per cent on the basis of numbers of pupils in each school. Weighting is given for differences in age, sixth-form and, possibly, subjects. This percentage is an average across the LEA, therefore the proportion allocated for individual schools may vary.

2　Up to 15 per cent for other factors, e.g.
   - special educational needs
   - socio-economic needs
   - small schools
   - premises-related costs.

The application of the LEA's formula to the ASB produces each school's budget share. This must be determined on an annual basis. In those schools which have delegated budgets, control of expenditure rests with the governing body. In those which do not have delegated budgets, control still rests with the LEA. By far the most important factor in the allocation formula is the number of children in the school and their relative ages. Figure 2.2 illustrates the formula funding process.

LEAs must produce the funding formula and provide a detailed explanation by 31 March of each year as required under section 42 of the ERA. Failure to produce a financial statement could result in the GM schools in an area being given unallocated funds. The basic format of the financial statement has been determined by the Secretary of State and must be made available for public inspection at LEA offices and public libraries (*see* Figure 2.3).

One advantage of increased control is that school management teams are now able to vire from one budget heading to another. Virement is the transfer of a budgetary provision from one expenditure heading to another. Viring is most likely to take place when there is underspend or overspend in particular areas. In practice, accounts must be kept up to date and constantly reviewed if the possibility of viring money is to be considered.

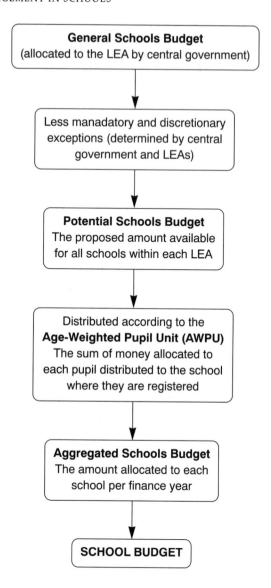

Figure 2.2: Allocation of funds – formula funding

Grant-Maintained Schools

The ERA provides schools and parents with an alternative to local authority control. As the National Association for Headteachers (NAHT, 1989, p. 5/1) states:

Basic Format of the Funding Formula Statement

Part 1 Details of the overall planning expenditure (direct or indirect) on primary and secondary schools, i.e. the General Schools Budget (GSB), details of expenditure not devolved to schools.

Part 2 Analysis of expenditure and details of the school's budget share.

Part 3 Explanation of the formula used to calculate a school's budget share, giving details of amount per pupil, which varies according to age. This also includes a block sum depending on school size (providing protection for small schools) in terms of premises-related costs, special needs and salaries, etc. There may also be an element for enabling the transition of schools to delegated budgets; this may only last for four years from the inception of the LMS scheme.

Part 4 Demonstrate how the formula has been applied for each school within the LMS.

Education Budget

less non-school items

General Schools Budget (GSB)

less mandatory exceptions

Potential Schools Budget (PSB)

less discretionary exceptions (10% limit 1996 onwards)

Aggregated Schools Budget (ASB)

divided amongst schools by formula

Budget Share of each School

From April 1995 at least 90% of the PSB will have to be delegated to all schools.

Figure 2.3: Formula funding statement
(*Source:* adapted from Knight *et al.*, 1993, pp. 13–14)

Subject to endorsement by the parents of its pupils, the governing body of any eligible maintained school may apply to opt out of [. . .] LEA control and to become a grant-maintained school in receipt of direct funding from the Secretary of State.

Schools can opt out by balloting parents. If over 50 per cent of parents vote, then a majority in favour of grant-maintained status will ensure the school can opt-out. If fewer than 50 per cent vote, a second ballot must be held within 14 days and a majority vote in favour of opting out will then prevail irrespective of the number of parents voting. As the NAHT (1989, p. 5/5) comments:

Such a ballot may be initiated in one of two ways:

- *the governing body may resolve to hold a ballot [. . .]*
- *the governing body may be mandated to hold a ballot by virtue of a written request from a number of parents [. . .] equal to at least 20% of the number of pupils [. . .].*

The Secretary of State will then decide whether to approve the proposal. Significantly, once a school becomes grant-maintained it cannot apply to go back to the LEA system. The government (DFEE, 1996c, p. 21; Crown copyright) considers grant-maintained status to be:

[. . .] the most advanced form of self-government for state schools, GM governing bodies have full responsibility for running their schools – for deciding how to spend their budgets, for employing their staff and (in most cases) owning the school premises, and for deciding what changes to propose to the school's character and admission arrangements.

GM status has been available to larger primary (over 300 on roll) and secondary schools since 1988, to smaller primary schools since 1991 and to special schools since 1994. Between 1988 and 1994 the method of financing grant-maintained schools was, broadly speaking, the same as for local management of schools, the difference being the source of funding. Central government provides the same amount for current spending that each school would have received from the relevant LEA. GM schools would also be able to obtain more favourable capital spending grants, not least in the areas of large-scale equipment and repairs/improvement.

In April 1994, the Funding Agency for Schools (FAS) was established under the 1993 Education Act. The role of the agency is to support GM schools in England and Wales.

Summary

Resource managers require knowledge and understanding of delegation principles. Essentially, the ERA increased the powers of the Secretary of State for Education, thus strengthening the role of central government. LEA roles and responsibilities were decreased while the power and functions of governing bodies and headteachers were increased. The main ERA provisions relating to schools concern:

1   the establishment of a national curriculum
2   the open enrolment of pupils

3 the delegation of staffing responsibilities

4 the establishment of grant-maintained schools.

The government's aim was to improve standards in education by increasing market forces and competition. The assumption and rationale of the ERA was accountability. In practice, central government was to devolve much of the responsibility for resource management directly to headteachers and school governing bodies. This followed a pilot programme experiment known as local financial management (LFM).

In 1982 Cambridgeshire established the first pilot scheme for LFM. The three-year pilot project proved to be successful. By 1986 all Cambridgeshire secondary schools and also 11 primary schools were introduced to LFM.

LMS is an outcome of the ERA. Based on a formula devised by each LEA, LMS delegates the schools' financial budgets to governors. LMS also delegates related managerial authority and responsibility for staff. LEAs must produce the funding formula and provide a detailed explanation by 31 March of each year as required under section 42 of the ERA. One advantage of increased control is that school management teams are now able to vire from one budget heading to another. Virement is the transfer of a budgetary provision from one expenditure heading to another.

The ERA provides schools and parents with an alternative to local authority control. Schools can opt out by balloting parents. The Secretary of State will then decide whether to approve the proposal. Central government provides the same amount for current spending that each school would have received from the relevant LEA. GM schools will also be able to obtain more favourable capital spending grants, not least in the areas of large-scale equipment and repairs/improvement.

In April 1994, the Funding Agency for Schools was established under the 1993 Education Act. The role of the agency is to support GM schools in England and Wales.

The funding mechanism for LMS/GM schools in England and Wales is given in Figure 2.4.

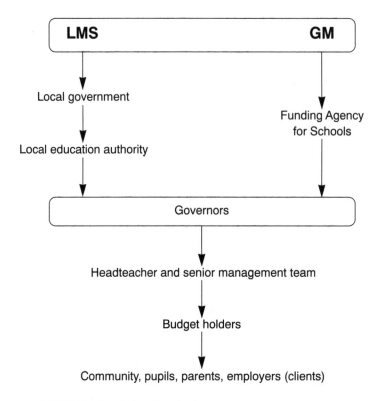

Figure 2.4: LMS/GM schools funding structure

3
■ ■ ■

Roles and Responsibilities

Introduction

Critical to the effectiveness of a school are the people who share the responsibility of resource management, their knowledge and understanding of specific roles. Local management of schools (LMS) has impacted on the roles of key personnel in schools (Levačić, 1995, p. 108). If governors, school managers, resource managers and class teachers are to develop skills and abilities associated with resource management, there is a need to know and understand their roles and responsibilities. This chapter defines the roles and responsibilities of key players in the resource management of schools. These include:

1 central government
2 local government
3 local education authorities
4 the Funding Agency for Schools
5 school governing bodies
6 governing body subcommittees
7 headteachers
8 senior management teams
9 middle managers – budget holders
10 class teachers
11 special educational needs co-ordinators.

Central government

Glynn (1993, p. 132) describes the process for reporting financial information on the government's activities and plans. This includes five major documents:

- *Financial Statement and the Budget Report* – issued by the Treasury on Budget Day, it sets out the budget, the short-term economic forecast and the medium-term financial strategy which provides the financial framework for economic policy. This is different from, but occurs at the same time as, the Autumn Statement (below).

- *The Autumn Statement* – sets out the Treasury's latest economic forecast and the planning totals for the next three years and provides the broad departmental allocation of expenditure, as agreed during the Public Expenditure Survey (PES).

- *Departmental Reports* – which describe in some detail each department's spending plans, its aims and objectives and various output measures against which performance is assessed.

- *Supply estimates* – the government's formal request to Parliament for cash to finance the major part of central government's expenditure.

- *Appropriate accounts* – audited by the Comptroller and Auditor General (C&AG), published in the autumn following the end of the financial year.

Funding

The funding of education is determined by central government policy and local government management, as Coopers & Lybrand (1996, p. 6) state:

> *The original principle behind the funding of statutory education was that local authorities would raise finance through local taxation to provide local schools. However, it was recognised as long ago as 1835 that local authorities could not raise sufficient funds to deliver all their responsibilities [. . .] increasingly from 1927 the function of central government intervention was seen not only as supporting local authorities' powers to raise revenue but also as equalising them.*

The Coopers & Lybrand report *Funding of Education* (1996) explains that there have been various attempts to standardise government grants to local authorities, the most recent being the Standard Spending Assessment (SSA) – established practice since 1990. SSA calculations are based on how much should be spent on local authority services in the coming year as determined by Total Standard Spending (TSS). Education is one of the seven areas in which, once grants have been allocated from central government, local authorities have total control over their expenditure. The others are: social services, police, fire and civil defence, highway maintenance, other services and capital finances. Coopers & Lybrand (p. 8) comment:

> *Neither the choice of a TSS figure or the way in which [. . .] totals are arrived at is transparent; as might be expected, both sets of decisions are highly politicised.*

Once the TSS has been allocated the government's SSA methodology paper divides education into sub-blocks. The education sub-blocks are: under 5, primary, secondary, post-16 and other. The sub-block totals are then allocated pro rata to local authorities according to population figures, e.g. for primary education the population is the number of pupils aged 5–10. The government considers that funding is allocated according to need – an equalisation of each population's funding which balances need with the LEA's own revenue-raising capabilities. The exact amount of money paid to the local authority takes account of the authority's own revenue-raising capabilities. The government therefore equalises resources available to each sub-block within education as Figure 3.1 illustrates.

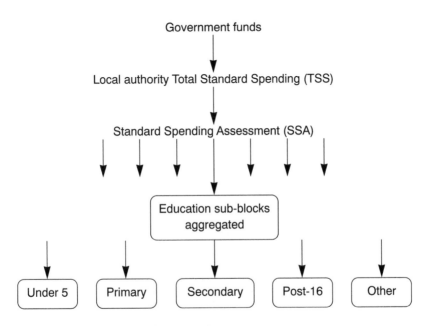

Figure 3.1: Government funding mechanism

Control of public money

All government departments are responsible for the control of public funds, as Jones and Pendlebury (1996, p. 5) state:

The proper control of public money is, of course, a fundamental requirement of any public sector organisation. As far as central government's own activities are concerned, the framework of control has been developed over many years.

The framework of control involves (adapted from Pendlebury *et al.*, 1992):

1 *The use of vote accounting.* All revenues and payments go into and out of the central fund, and spending can only take place if specifically authorised, or voted, by Parliament.

2 *The gross budget principle.* All revenues are paid in gross without deducting expenditure [...].

3 *Annuality.* All spending is authorised (voted) on an annual basis, and unspent balances at the end of the year are returned to the central fund.

4 *Specification.* Spending is authorised (voted) for specific purposes and virement [...] must be approved by Parliament.

Audit

Public funds are audited as Jones and Pendlebury (1996, p. 209) comment:

The auditor of government is a unique institution [...]. The principal Acts of Parliament which set down the audit requirements of central government are the Exchequer and Audit Department Acts 1866 and 1921 and the National Audit Act 1983.

Central government's accounts are, in practice, audited by the Comptroller and Auditor General (C&AG).

Accountability

Each of the above – funding, control and auditing – is determined by government policies as defined in Acts of Parliament. In addition, each central government department is accountable to a Minister, the Treasury, the Public Accounts Committee, the Accounting Officer and Parliament as Figure 3.2

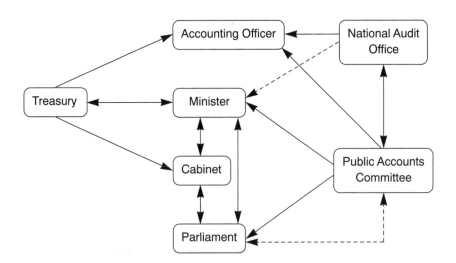

Figure 3.2: Formalised accountability to Parliament
(*Source:* Glynn, 1993, p. 27; reproduced by permission of the publisher, Blackwell)

illustrates (the broken lines indicate where information can be requested on an *ad hoc* basis).

While systems of control and accountability are evident, there is a lack of transparency as to the way in which funds are allocated to local government (Coopers & Lybrand, 1996, p. 8).

Local government

The origins of local government can be traced back to the Anglo-Saxons, though the basic structure of current practice was first introduced at the end of the nineteenth century (Glynn, 1993, p. 147). As CIPFA (1990a, p. 1) comments, *local authorities are created by Acts of Parliament.*

All local authority spending has to be authorised by statute or subordinate legislation. Local authorities account for 25 per cent of central government expenditure. In practice, central government policies severely restrict the rights of local authorities to manage their own affairs.

A main function of local authorities is to manage the provision of education as determined by central government; this responsibility is delegated to the local education authority. The LEA is managed by officers and elected members of the local authority education subcommittee. Glynn (1993, p. 30) comments:

> *Local authorities probably face the most complex set of responsibilities. Certain services, such as education, have minimum standards imposed by government.*

In terms of accountability, local authorities have a complex system of internal and external committees to which to report, as shown in Figure 3.3.

Each local government office is accountable to central government and external auditors, as indicated in Figure 3.3.

Education

The relationship between local authorities and education is changing. Local authority financial control over education has been reduced in three main ways (Jones, 1995, p. 9):

1 *Polytechnics (1989) and colleges of further education (1993) have been removed from local authority control and are now funded through funding councils with central government money.*

2 *Local (financial) management of schools has been introduced.*

3 *Schools have been given the option to move to grant-maintained status.*

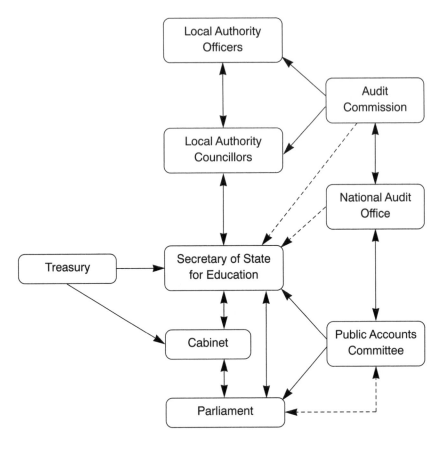

Figure 3.3: Local authority – accountability
(*Source:* Glynn, 1993, p. 27; reproduced by permission of the publisher, Blackwell)

Value for money

As indicated local authority elected members, officers and auditors are responsible for securing value for money. This has been defined in terms of the three Es – economy, efficiency and effectiveness. The LMS Initiative (1990, p. 103) and Jones (1995, pp. 120-1) provide the following definitions:

- **Economy** – maximising the non-cash resource which we can purchase with our available cash resource, i.e. buying goods and services cheaply and minimising waste.

- **Efficiency** – converting non-cash resource into the maximum volume of service, i.e. making sure that staff work hard and use their time and materials to maximise output.

- **Effectiveness** – ensuring that the services offered are appropriate to the needs of the client.

The Audit Commission plays a role in ensuring efficiency and effectiveness. Local branches scrutinise the work of the local authorities. More recently, local authorities have introduced performance indicators in order to indicate the status of their economy, efficiency and effectiveness. Performance indicators are of use to management and external control/audit agencies. They can also be used as bargaining levers in discussions concerning the allocation of resources (Jones, 1995, p. 124).

Local education authorities

The relationship between local education authorities and schools has changed as a consequence of LMS/GM status. However, cost-centre budget control does not mean that the LEA abdicates all responsibility. Under LMS, an LEA has statutory obligations as Armstrong *et al.* (1993, p. 43) describe:

- *Within the overall local authority structure, the education division must compete with other services for funding, i.e. the General Schools Budget.*
- *The authority must allocate funds according to the 'scheme' it has put forward under LMS year by year.*
- *Schools must be inspected and standards monitored regularly.*
- *The authority must accept responsibility for the financial management of a school if the Governing Body fails to run it satisfactorily.*
- *The administration of government grants takes place centrally.*
- *The authority has responsibility for the way in which education is organised in the area.*
- *[...] The authority continues to oversee capital expenditure and the external structure of premises.*

In practice, LEAs remain responsible for a number of key matters:

1 creation of local policies
2 offering support to schools
3 advising schools
4 monitoring performance.

In the recent DFEE White Paper *Self Government for Schools* (DFEE, 1996c, p. 49; Crown copyright), the government considered that the main functions which LEAs should, or may, undertake are:

a. *Organising forms of education which take place outside schools.*
b. *Planning the supply of school places, handling complaints and other regulations.*

   c. *Allocation and monitoring of school budgets.*

   d. *Organising services to support individual pupils.*

   e. *Supplying support services for schools to buy if they wish.*

   f. *Promoting quality in schools, complementing the responsibility of the national inspectorates for inspecting and reporting on that performance.*

   g. *Co-ordinating school networks and developing good practice, particularly in carrying out national initiatives.*

Essentially, LEAs are responsible for the allocation of the overall education budget. LEA administrators continue to make decisions on staff/pupil ratios, curriculum, advisory support and special educational needs. LEAs are able to offer support and advice to schools which lack management skills. LEAs can also provide specialist advice from lawyers, architects and other local authority services. LEAs are also available to monitor school effectiveness through OFSTED.

Financial delegation

As described in Chapter 2, each LEA is responsible for determining the exact form of each individual school's delegated budget within its authority, based on a formula designed by the LEA within guidelines set by central government. Detailed guidelines are given in the Education Reform Act and Circular 7/88 (DES, 1988a/1988b), although there are exceptions which, being mandatory or discretionary, will differ from one LEA to another. Interpretation of the legislation will vary according to local factors. Key tasks for LEAs as identified by Davies and Braund (1989, p. 63) are:

- *Determining the total resources available to schools.*
- *Deciding the scope of delegation within the framework of the Act.*
- *Establishing the basis for allocating resources to individual schools.*
- *Setting out the conditions and requirements within which governing bodies operate.*
- *Monitoring the performance of schools and giving advice or taking corrective action.*
- *Operating sanctions, including withdrawal of delegation if required.*

In brief, LEAs are required to delegate to school governors the majority of funds (85–90 per cent) available to resource schools. These include:

1 employee costs
2 premises-related costs
3 establishment-related expenses
4 supplies and services
5 miscellaneous expenses.

Managing employee costs

The LEA decides on what percentage of the total schools budget will be allocated to staffing; however, LEAs cannot force this point. Once the school has received its budget governors can allocate funds according to their own policies based on local needs. LEAs, governors and senior managers have to stay within the parameters set by the *School Teachers' Pay and Conditions Document* (DES, 1987), revised in 1993 (*A Guide to the Law for Governors*, DFE, 1993).

The extent of staffing responsibilities delegated to schools is dependent on each LEA's policy. Staff appointments, recruitment and selection practices will also vary from LEA to LEA, and school to school. Decisions about whom to select for appointments rest with the governors, subject to advice from the headteacher and chief education officer (CEO). Governing bodies are also required to adhere to statutory regulations on race and gender discrimination. However, LEA recruitment and selection policies are non-statutory.

In practice, the CEO, or representative, has a duty to offer advice to school management teams and should attend relevant meetings of each school's staff selection panel. Both the selection panel and governing body must consider the CEO's advice before reaching a decision. Critically, an LEA is no longer able to safeguard a teacher's employment by insisting on redeployment from one school to another within that LEA. The LEA is only able to nominate teacher employees for consideration for any position by a particular governing body.

Schools have responsibility for deciding whom to employ. LEAs administer the process, i.e. maintaining payrolls for teaching and non-teaching staff, although this can be contracted out. Governors are responsible for appointments, discipline and grievance procedures, and dismissals within the school. LEAs have an advisory role on all staff appointments, i.e.:

1   headteacher/deputy headteacher appointments
2   teaching staff appointments
3   non-teaching staff appointments.

Each school governing body may decide to ignore LEA advice. Once appointed the employee becomes an employee of the LEA, not the school. Gilbert (1990b, pp. 28–9) states that the guidance offered to governing bodies by LEAs, summarised as follows, is likely to emphasise that:

- the post should be fairly and clearly advertised;
- all applicants should receive a full job description, person specification and relevant information on the school, together with a standard form which does not ask questions about family or marital status;
- shortlisting and interviewing should involve more than one person;
- shortlisting should be carried out on the basis of a previously agreed person specification detailing the qualifications, experience and skills necessary to do the job;

- shortlisting should be done by the interviewing panel;
- the interviewing panel should meet before the formal interview to discuss the relevant criteria based on the job description and person specification and to agree areas of questioning;
- all candidates should be asked broadly similar questions, but not about their:
  - age
  - sexual orientation
  - marital status
  - family commitments
  - ethnic background
  - political or religious beliefs
  - membership of trade unions
- candidates should be informed of the outcome as soon as possible.

LEA guidelines should be objective. LEAs have a responsibility to inform schools of all legislation regarding conditions of service for teaching and non-teaching staff. It is important to note that an LEA is not empowered to set a staff complement for a school operating under full delegation and is not able to determine staffing plans for teaching or for other school staff. However, LEA and government policies on curriculum matters will, inevitably, impinge on staff numbers.

In addition to costs there are a number of human resource management issues to consider; e.g. LEAs should also advise schools on employee discipline and grievance procedures. As there are no nationally agreed procedures for discipline, each governing body determines its own practice. The governing body must inform the LEA if someone is to be suspended. It is only the governing body which can end a suspension.

Where staff express a grievance, governors and headteachers should draw on advice for implementing various stages of their procedure. If there are grievances against the LEA, these should follow LEA procedures.

In the case of a dismissal, governing bodies must provide LEAs with a written statement on the reasons for dismissal of anyone employed for over six months. Dismissal arrangements, set up by the governing body, must involve a representative of the CEO. Costs of dismissal should be met by the LEA outside the school's budget share from excepted funds, unless there is a justifiable reason for taking these from the school's budget share.

LEA formulae have to take into consideration the cost of supply teachers, whose salaries fall upon the school in the first instance. LEAs have discretionary powers over this item. In practice, some have decided to keep the money centrally while others include this within the delegated budget of schools.

Managing premises-related costs

The relationship between schools and LEAs is similar to that of landlord and tenant. Schools are responsible for rates and rent on non-LEA property. Circular 7/88 (DES, 1988b) suggests how LEAs might divide responsibility for the maintenance of school buildings. This is a discretionary area and, as such, can create difficulties for LEAs and schools. For example, there may be situations where poor external maintenance affects the internal decoration of a building. In these cases, the school would have to claim compensation from the LEA. In practice, difficulties may arise, e.g. in the event of a broken window the responsibility of replacing the window is divided between school and LEA. The school would replace the window, while the LEA would paint any external fabric.

Maintaining school premises is a specialist area. LEAs have expertise which may be bought by school managers. However, the 1988 Local Government Act put school cleaning, catering and grounds maintenance out to competitive tendering, and schools can choose whether or not to employ local authority services.

Managing establishment expenses

LEAs may delegate educational supplies and office materials, telephone bills and cleaning equipment. In practice, insurance has been retained by LEAs. LEAs may also develop new services that could be attractive to schools, for example marketing and transport.

Managing supplies and services

LEAs do not have a specific responsibility for capitation, i.e. allowance for books and equipment. However, LEAs are in a position to provide expertise in planning and management. Schools may also purchase time and expertise from LEA services, e.g. music teachers, advisory teachers and support staff.

Miscellaneous expenses

LEAs can advise schools on the cost of planning and management. LEAs and governors need to be aware of headteachers who are likely to overspend or underspend significantly.

Operating delegated budgets

Under the ERA, LEAs are empowered to impose certain conditions under which schools can operate delegated budgets. These conditions (LMS Initiative, 1990, p. 93) can relate to:

- *arrangements to be made for the management of expenditure, [. . .]*

- *the keeping and auditing of accounts and records with respect to expenditure and transactions*
- *the accounts, records and information to be supplied to the LEA by the school.*

Information requirements

The ERA empowered the Secretary of State to make regulations on the publication of schemes. This followed the 1986 Education Act which required LEAs to publish annual statements setting out budget or outturn information on capital and recurrent expenditure for each school, itemised as the LEA thinks appropriate.

All local authorities have to submit draft schemes for financial delegation to the government. LEAs are required to publish annual statements covering all schools in the scheme, containing specified information in comparative form on the following:

1 the amount of the General Schools Budget
2 the amount of the Aggregated Schools Budget
3 prescribed details of the formula
4 an indication of the basis on which excepted expenditure is attributed to schools
5 planned expenditure per pupil in each school to be met from its delegated budget
6 planned expenditure per pupil in each school to be met by the LEA from its budget for mandatory and discretionary exceptions.

At the end of each financial year the LEA has to prepare a statement giving information of outturn expenditure on each school covered by its scheme, as well as for the LEA as a whole.

Financial regulations

Local authorities have standard procedures for financial administration to ensure that decisions affecting the use of public money are properly authorised. A possible list of financial regulations is given in Figure 3.4.

In essence, financial regulations devised by schools and governing bodies have to comply with accepted practice. For example, contracts for large items such as cleaning or grounds maintenance require competitive tendering. The 1988 Local Government Act sets out legal requirements for competitive tendering of services if they are to be provided by the local authority's own staff.

Financial regulations also need to specify administration procedures. Schools are free to set up their own systems, which must comply with the Data

Possible LEA Financial Regulations

1 Duties of the treasurer and chief officers

2 Revenue budget preparation

3 Revenue budget control

4 Authority to incur revenue expenditure

5 Preparation of the capital programme

6 Authority to incur capital expenditure

7 Accounting procedures

8 Petty cash interest accounts

9 Internal audit arrangements

10 Banking arrangements and use of bank accounts

11 Contracts

12 Income

13 Insurance

14 Inventories

15 Investments and borrowing

16 Orders for goods and services

17 Payment of accounts

18 Protection of private property

19 Salaries, wages and pensions

20 Stocks and stores

21 Travel and subsistence

22 Security

23 Unofficial funds

24 Carryover of savings/deficits

25 Charging/payment of interest

26 Financial interests of government

Schools drawing up their own financial regulations should check against this to see that they are comprehensive in their coverage.

Figure 3.4: Possible LEA financial regulations
(*Source:* CIPFA, LMS Initiative, 1990c, p. 97; reproduced by permission of CIPFA)

Protection Act 1984. LEAs should advise on the requirements of the Act and how they apply to school records.

Schools may also enter into commitments which extend beyond a single financial year. The LEA needs to set regulations about the extent of any such provisions – particularly to ensure that any net deficit incurred by schools will not adversely affect the authority's overall financial position.

Auditing

LEAs are responsible for the stewardship of delegated funds. As shown in the previous section, the local authority treasurer has a duty to ratepayers/council tax payers under the Local Government Act 1972 and the Local Government Finance Act 1988 to monitor all local authority expenditure, including education. This is important as financial years and academic years do not run simultaneously.

The local authority treasurer maintains an internal audit of all authority activities, including schools. External auditors may also visit schools. The role of auditors is to ensure that resources are managed safely and effectively, that public money is spent wisely and that value for money is secured (LMS Initiative, 1990, p. 96). This involves the routine examination of records and accounts. Auditors also have the responsibility of detecting and reporting any evidence of fraud.

The Funding Agency for Schools

The existence of grant-maintained schools is a key component in the policy of increased parental choice and improvement of standards. The Funding Agency for Schools was established in 1994 to support GM schools in England. The Agency's key functions are to:

- calculate and pay recurrent, special purpose and capital grants to GM schools
- financially monitor GM schools
- carry out value for money studies as the Agency determines or as directed by the Secretary of State
- ensure the provision of sufficient school places in specified local authority areas
- provide information and advice to the Secretary of State in connection with any education function and any other information and advice that the Agency thinks fit
- carry out other activities in connection with the discharge of its key functions including the undertaking of research functions.

The way the FAS relates to GM schools is part of the new framework for the service. The FAS ensures that schools meet national requirements relating to the curriculum, while standards of achievement are determined by the Secretary of State on the advice of the Schools Curriculum and Assessment Authority (SCAA) and the Office for Standards in Education (OFSTED). The FAS is accountable to the Secretary of State for Education and Employment and through this route to Parliament. GM schools are accountable directly to parents and the local community. The FAS also monitors financial resources and management in schools, and plans school places in certain areas, ensuring public accountability for the expenditure of public monies.

Governors

Since the 1980 Education Act central government has legislated that all schools should have their own governing bodies, including elected parent governors and elected teacher governors. Thomas and Martin (1996, p. 11) state:

> *The constitution and functions of governing bodies were set out in Instruments and Articles of Government and model articles which dated back to 1944.*

The 1986 Education Act determined the type and number of governors according to the size and status of the school. Governing bodies of maintained schools are to include representatives of the LEA, parents, teachers and members of the local business community.

Financial delegation

Governors in England and Wales enjoy considerably more power than their equivalents elsewhere in Western Europe. The role of the governing body in the resource management of a school is determined by the 1988 Education Reform Act, and the governing body is responsible for creating a management plan incorporating resources. Having gained new powers of authority, these powers must be exercised accountably. Governors are required to account for the activities within their schools.

Specifically, governors must get value for the expenditure they authorise. As stewards of local education funds, governors have to account for their spending through annual reports and meetings with parents and their local communities; they will also have to provide information for LEAs and central government. There is an emphasis on providing quantitative evidence on the quality of education provided by schools.

Headteachers receive their delegated powers over spending of the budget via governing bodies. For budget management, the governing body is accountable to:

1 **the providers of the funds** – the LEA in maintained schools and funding authorities in GM schools
2 **the parents of pupils of the school** – a financial statement must be provided with the annual report to parents, prior to the parents' annual meeting, and is required by law
3 **the wider public** – through auditors of public money who ensure priority and value for money.

The ultimate responsibility for the management of school finances therefore rests with the governing body. The governing body has formal responsibility for managing the school and approving budgets. In practice, many governing bodies are unlikely to meet more than twice a term and are therefore likely to delegate major planning powers to the headteachers or subcommittees. The delegation of powers to such committees is governed by regulations issued to all schools.

Membership

Gilbert (1990a, p. 47) found that governors come from very different backgrounds and experience. Levels of management expertise will differ, as will levels of commitment. Nightingale (1990, p. 51) commented:

As governors become more aware of the responsibilities they are taking on, there is a possibility that recruiting governors will become more difficult.

Pupil Enrolment

Following the 1993 Education Act, governors must publish their admission and appeals arrangements and information about individual schools. Governors have to admit up to the standard number – based on the number of pupils registered on each school's pupil roll in September 1979. Should the number of pupils at any school decline to a point where it becomes difficult for it to provide a curriculum of the desired range and diversity, the governors and LEA should consider whether to bring forward proposals either to cease to maintain the school or amalgamate it with another school.

Governing body subcommittees

For maintained schools, there is no legal requirement to establish a finance subcommittee. In GM schools the articles of government require the governing body to appoint a finance subcommittee. Schools may wish to have other committees for other areas of governance, e.g. curriculum, admissions and exclusions, and premises. A working model for primary school governing subcommittees is described by Nightingale (1990) following his LFM experience. He comments on the need for subcommittees to meet the demands of the work of the governing body. While it is the responsibility of each governing body to define the role of its committees, Nightingale (1990, p. 58) suggests the following:

Finance Committee	1. *3 governors (including teacher governor)*
	2. *3 teaching staff (including deputy headteacher)*
	3. *1 parent nominated by PSA*
	4. *headteacher*
	5. *school secretary*
	6. *community representative*
Curriculum Committee	1. *3 governors*
	2. *2 parents nominated by PSA*
	3. *headteacher or deputy headteacher*
	4. *teaching staff – 1 per year group plus others if issues particularly relevant to their responsibilities*
Premises Committee	1. *2 governors*
	2. *teacher (health and safety representative)*
	3. *caretaker*
	4. *community representative*
	5. *headteacher and chair, as required*
Staffing Committee	1. *3 governors (including chair)*
	2. *headteacher*
	3. *deputy headteacher*
	4. *teacher representing teacher associations*
	5. *[support staff representative].*

Finance subcommittee

Committees may be given delegated powers to take action on certain matters and have to follow legislation and guidance given by central government. The terms of reference for the finance subcommittee are determined by the governing body and should be reviewed annually. Knight (1993, p. 10) advises that, in deciding the terms of reference, the governing body should have regard to two principles:

1 *to allow the head to get on with the job of the day-to-day running of the school*

2 *to ensure the control and monitoring of the school budget.*

Knight *et al.* (1993, pp. 10–11) believe that terms of reference for the finance subcommittee should include all of the following:

1   *To consider and advise the governing body on the financial implications of adopting certain policies, especially those with long-term budget implications.*

2   *To interpret and implement the broad policies of the governing body in so far as they involve financial matters.*

3   *To take decisions on financial matters that need to be dealt with between meetings of the governing body which may be cash limited.*

4   *To provide information and reports so as to enable the governing body to comply with financial regulations set down by the providers of the funds to the school.*

5   *To monitor the progress of expenditure during the year. The Audit Commission recommends that governors should receive, at least on a termly basis, a report on expenditure and the budget.*

6   *To prepare a draft budget, with recommendations as necessary, on projections of income and expenditure for the governing body as a whole to consider and decide upon.*

The finance subcommittee should meet more often than the governing body and produce minutes for examination by the whole governing body. The involvement of governors will depend on the degree of interest. The finance subcommittee almost always involves the headteacher. In practice, Earley (1994) found that in the majority of cases the headteacher and finance officer (deputy headteacher) planned the budget on their own.

Headteachers

The role of the headteacher in relation to governing bodies was defined by Davies and Braund (1989, p. 47) as *chief executive*. Pugh (1990, pp. 81–8) suggests that governors, headteachers and staff should work together in partnership to improve their school. Maychell (1994, p. 89) found that LMS has had an impact on the role and responsibilities of the headteacher. Several studies (Bullock and Thomas, 1994a; Taylor, 1990) have shown that headteachers and staff have to acquire the skill of working with governors. In particular, headteachers have to understand that it does not diminish their status and professional authority if they share the decision-making with the governing body. However, this does not mean that school governors should have day-to-day involvement. Only about half the headteachers in the Bullock and Thomas survey welcomed increased governor involvement (Levačić, 1995, p. 135).

The following summary (NAHT, 1989, p. 4/36) indicates the range of responsibilities delegated to headteachers as determined by the ERA (DES, 1988a):

● All headteachers of county and voluntary schools in an authority must be consulted by their LEA before it formulates the scheme submitted to the Secretary of State.

- Governors of schools with delegated budgets may delegate their power to spend any sum forming part of the school's budget share to the headteacher as they think fit for the purposes of the school.

- A headteacher is to receive a copy of any notice of suspension of a governing body's right to a delegated budget. The LEA must allow the headteacher to make representations when any such suspension is being reviewed and must give the headteacher written notification of any decision reached on that review.

- Advisory rights given to CEOs in the case of aided schools may relate to the appointment and dismissal of headteachers.

- Governors may delegate to headteachers of schools not covered by delegated budgets their powers in relation to spending the sum allocated.

Specifically, there are 23 professional duties for headteachers detailed in *A Guide to the Law for Governors* (DFE, 1993). These include:

1 formulating the overall aims and objectives of the school and policies for their implementation

2 deploying and managing all teaching and non-teaching staff

3 advising and assisting the governing body of the school in the exercise of its functions, including (without prejudice to any rights s/he may have as a governor of the school) attending meetings of the governing body and making such reports to it in connection with the discharge of his/her functions as it may properly require

4 allocating, controlling and accounting for those financial and material resources of the school which are under the control of the headteacher.

The NFER study (Maychell, 1994, p. 91) found that changes to headteachers' duties following LMS have mainly been attributed to the increase in financial administration. Headteachers have entered the world of business, responding to market forces through open enrolment and management of enterprise income. These issues will be discussed in Chapters 11 and 12.

In brief, headteachers now have to manage, which conflicts with their traditional role as the leading professional (Nightingale, 1990, p. 83). Bullock and Thomas (1994a) found that headteachers involved in resource management responded positively to their new role. They reported that the majority of headteachers surveyed would not welcome a return to the previous system.

Maychell (1994, p. 93) commented that approaches of individual headteachers to their new roles were a matter of personal preference and attitude. Her study found that the ability of headteachers to act as resource managers also differed according to their knowledge and understanding of the role.

In essence the main elements of the headteacher's role in locally managed schools are closely related to the components of the open systems model of the school (Levačić, 1995, p. 110). These are:

Boundary management: this is important for resource management, because it is central to the acquisition of resources.

Resource management: this embraces budget management and the creation and maintenance of as good a learning environment as possible with the resources available. It encompasses the connection between the allocation of financial and physical resources and the resulting educational outputs and outcomes.

Instructional leadership: managing the technical core of the school, i.e. its processes of teaching and learning, and embracing both curriculum and human resource management.

In sum, as Thomas and Martin (1996, p. 180) imply, good schools with good headteachers will allocate resources according to learning priorities. The process of managing resources should be collaborative, and decisions communicated to staff as appropriate. Critical aspects of school management will be discussed in Chapter 4.

Deputy headteachers

Following LMS, many schools reviewed their management structure. As headteachers developed their management skills, management responsibilities were delegated to senior staff. In addition school management teams needed to consider the involvement in decision-making by other teaching and non-teaching staff. Maychell (1994, p. 95) found that the roles of deputy headteachers were affected by LMS. *A Guide to the Law for Governors* (DFE, 1993; Crown copyright) defines the professional duties of a deputy headteacher as follows:

A person appointed deputy headteacher in a school will:

(1) *assist the headteacher in managing the school or such part of it as may be determined to him/her by the headteacher*

(2) *undertake any professional duty of the headteacher which may be delegated to him/her by the headteacher*

(3) *undertake, in the absence of the headteacher and to the extent required by him/her or his/her employers, the professional duties of the headteacher*

Levačić examined the role of deputy headteachers as finance officers and found that clarity of roles is relevant to the successful fulfilment of the post. Specifically, Levačić (1995, p. 119) found that *delegating the budget manager role still leaves unresolved the question of how best to allocate these tasks.* The appointment of an experienced practitioner with knowledge and understanding of resource management would resolve these issues.

Budget holders

Within the framework of collaborative management (Caldwell and Spinks, 1988) teachers should develop professionally through further involvement in resource management. Maychell (1994, pp. 101–2) found that in the majority of her study schools some teachers were budget holders. The role of a budget holder involved responsibility for a sum of money which was to be spent on a particular subject, year group or for some specific purpose, such as pupils with special educational needs (SEN) or in-service training (INSET). In practice, budget holders are responsible for ensuring that classroom teachers have the required materials to teach each pupil the National Curriculum. In resource management terms this means:

1 recording used stock (including consumables)
2 planning curriculum needs, e.g. examination courses
3 producing a budget for each classroom/subject area
4 bidding for capitation
5 ordering stock.

As budget holders are essentially practitioners, they would require support and training for this function. Curriculum and pastoral leaders should work with their teams to determine a budget for their area which relates to the school development plan (SDP). It is the headteacher's/senior manager's responsibility to consult with budget holders as to the amount they would need for the next academic year.

Class teachers

In a collaborative environment, class teachers may wish to increase their involvement in the decision-making process. However, as Chapman (1990, p. 213) notes:

The influence of the headteacher remains fundamental in determining the extent, nature and pattern of teacher participation in the decision-making of schools.

Fundamental to the effectiveness of schools are teachers' knowledge and understanding, skills and abilities in resource management. Teachers are resources, as are the classrooms they teach in; without collaboration teachers are limited in their professional practice. Therefore teachers have a role as resource managers within the management structure of their schools. Thomas and Martin (1996, p. 29) comment:

An emphasis on collaboration and a focus upon the practice of teaching is [. . .] evident in studies of school effectiveness [. . .].

Specifically, Thomas and Martin (p. 31) urge researchers to include resource management in the context of school improvement and staff development.

Special educational needs co-ordinators

The role of a special educational needs co-ordinator (SENCO) is complex, compounded by the hybrid legislation specific to this area of practice and more general legislation concerning LMS, GM schools and the National Curriculum. The 1993 Education Act introduced a new national Code of Practice on the Identification and Assessment of Special Educational Needs.

In brief, the Act required the Secretary of State to issue a Code of Practice which provides guidance to LEAs and schools on their responsibilities towards children with SEN. Schools, and therefore SEN co-ordinators, are responsible for assessing and meeting the needs of pupils at Stages 1–3 of the Code (there are five stages). LEAs are responsible for delegating the relevant funding; LMS formulae may include factors that reflect the number of SEN pupils in schools. As the government White Paper *Self Government for Schools* (DFEE, 1996c, p. 13; Crown copyright) advises:

> Schools should know what funds for SEN are included in their budgets, and how they have been calculated.

SEN co-ordinators need to manage the integration of support staff within the school and the use of expensive equipment. In some cases LEAs may centrally hold contingency funds for specific schemes. When these funds are allocated the SEN co-ordinator should be able to decide how to spend them on pupils at Stages 1 to 3.

Pupils who have been statutorily assessed at Stages 4 and 5 will require significant expenditure beyond that already included in schools' budgets. The DFEE (1996c, p. 15; Crown copyright) comments:

> The Government intends that spending on the educational psychology service and the administration of SEN statementing should continue to be outside the Potential Schools Budget. LEAs will still be able to choose, in consultation with schools, to delegate funds for the extra support needed to fulfil pupils' statements, or to devolve earmarked funds to schools.

The White Paper (p. 13) advises that in the future schools' budgets should generally include all the funding to meet pupils' needs at Stages 1 to 3. The management of these funds will be the responsibility of the SEN co-ordinator.

Accountability

Central to resource management is the structure of accountability as shown in Figure 3.5 for LMS schools, and in Figure 3.6 for GM schools. The structures of accountability for LMS and GM schools provide an overview of the key players and a means of summarising roles and responsibilities.

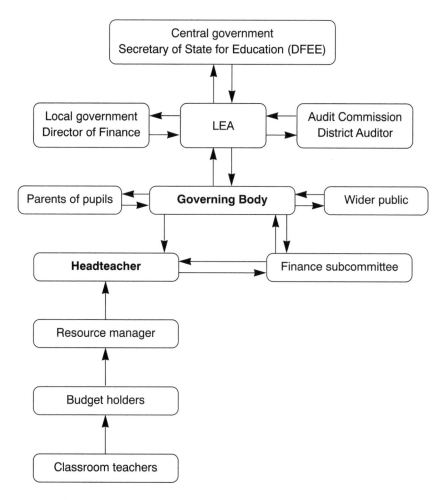

Figure 3.5: Structure of accountability (LMS)

53

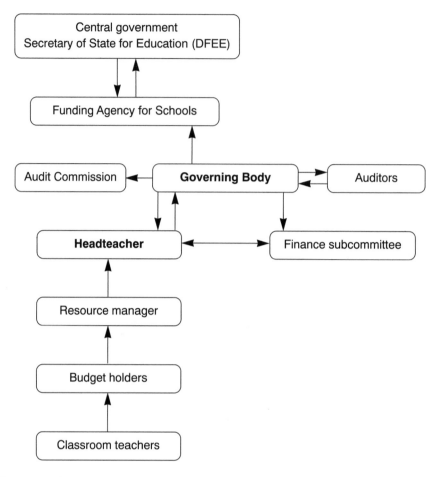

Figure 3.6: Structure of accountability (GM)

Summary

Critical to the effectiveness of a school are the people who share the responsibility of resource management, and their knowledge and understanding of specific roles. If governors, school managers, resource managers and class teachers are to develop skills and abilities associated with resource management, there is a need to know and understand their roles and responsibilities.

The funding of education is determined by central government policy and local government management. The origins of local government can be traced back to the Anglo-Saxons, though the basic structure of current practice was first introduced at the end of the nineteenth century. All local authority spending has to be authorised by statute or subordinate legislation. Local authorities account for 25 per cent of central government expenditure. In practice, local and central government policies severely restrict the rights of local authorities to manage their own affairs. The relationship between local authorities and education is changing.

Local authority elected members, officers and auditors are responsible for securing value for money. This has been defined in terms of the three Es – economy, efficiency and effectiveness. The Audit Commission plays a role in ensuring efficiency and effectiveness. Local branches scrutinise the work of the local authorities.

The relationship between local education authorities and schools has changed as a consequence of LMS/GM. However, cost-centre budget control does not mean that the LEA abdicates all responsibility. Essentially, LEAs are responsible for the allocation of the overall education budget. Local authorities have standard procedures for financial administration to ensure that decisions affecting the use of public money are properly authorised.

The existence of grant-maintained schools is a key component in the government's policy of increased parental choice and improvement of standards. The Funding Agency for Schools was established in 1994 to support GM schools in England. The FAS also monitors financial resources and management in schools, and plans school places in certain areas, ensuring public accountability for the expenditure of public monies.

Governors in England and Wales enjoy considerably more power than their equivalents elsewhere in Western Europe. The role of the governing body in the resource management of a school is determined by the 1988 Education Reform Act, and the governing body is responsible for creating a management plan incorporating resources. Having gained new powers of authority, these powers must be exercised accountably. Governors are required to account for the activities within their schools. For maintained schools, there is no legal requirement to establish a finance sub-committee. In GM schools the articles of government require the governing body to appoint a finance subcommittee. Schools may wish to have other committees for other areas of governance, e.g. curriculum, admissions and exclusions, and premises.

The governors' finance subcommittee should meet more often than the governing body and produce minutes for examination by the whole governing body. The involvement of governors will depend on the degree of interest. The finance subcommittee almost always involves the headteacher. In practice, Earley (1994) found that in the majority of cases the headteacher and finance officer (deputy headteacher) planned the budget on their own.

55

Headteachers now have to manage, which conflicts with their traditional role as the leading professional (Nightingale, 1990, p. 83). Bullock and Thomas (1994a) found that headteachers involved in resource management responded positively to their new role. They reported that the majority of headteachers surveyed would not welcome a return to the previous system.

In sum, as Thomas and Martin (1996, p. 180) imply, good schools with good headteachers will allocate resources according to learning priorities. The process of managing resources should be collaborative, and decisions communicated to staff as appropriate.

Following LMS, many schools reviewed their management structure. As headteachers developed their management skills, management responsibilities were delegated to senior staff. In addition school management teams needed to consider the involvement in decision-making by other teaching and non-teaching staff. Within the framework of collaborative management (Caldwell and Spinks, 1988) teachers should develop professionally through further involvement in resource management.

In practice, budget holders are responsible for ensuring that classroom teachers have the required materials to teach each pupil the National Curriculum. As budget holders are essentially practitioners, they would require support and training for this function.

In a collaborative environment, class teachers may wish to increase their involvement in the decision-making process. The role of a special educational needs co-ordinator (SENCO) is complex, compounded by the hybrid legislation specific to this area of practice and more general legislation concerning LMS, GM schools and the National Curriculum. Fundamental to the effectiveness of schools are teachers' knowledge and understanding, and skills and abilities in resource management. Teachers are resources, as are the classrooms they teach in; without collaboration teachers are limited in their professional practice.

4

■ ■ ■

Management

Introduction

This chapter places resource management within the context of management theory and practice and encompasses the changes to school organisational structure which have occurred as a consequence of LMS/GM initiatives.

Historically, the leader of a school was, as the headteacher, a senior colleague with expert teaching skills who led a team of teachers by example. Today, this concept has ceased to exist. Although headteachers may reject the notion of corporate management, their position can now be compared to that of the managing director of a corporate company, whose product is education and whose clients are pupils (and parents). School management is influenced by the owners or patrons of the school: governors, parents, the government and/or LEAs.

The impact of LMS on schools has also affected classroom practice. As a result of resource constraints decisions taken by LEAs, governors and senior managers may have led to larger classes and a reduction in non-contact time (Moisan, 1990, pp. 55–69). However, as Moisan found, LMS may also have the potential for improving the quality of teaching and learning. He concluded that in an open style of management, 'teacher involvement' is critical in establishing an effective school. However, legislation does not require teachers to be involved in the decision-making process.

The process by which teachers become decision-makers and managers is unclear, yet many teachers are now managers. In essence, teachers are managers of their classes and classrooms, but management priorities change when teachers become managers of other teaching and non-teaching staff. Central to management and teaching in schools is learning. There is an ongoing need to develop teachers as managers, as Foster (1996, p. 4) comments:

> British government in the 1980s and 1990s has promoted a climate of uncertainty for professional training, both in its pre-service and in-service modes [. . .]. With such

major changes in the ground rules for provision of training underway it is important to retain a vision of important issues governing the continued education of the teaching force.

Within this context it is important to note the problems of definition and measurement of management skills. Collaboration between government agencies, higher education institutions and schools is required for the development of appropriate training.

As Oldroyd and Hall (1990, p. 35) suggest, understanding what a manager does is a necessary prerequisite to doing it effectively. In essence, managers lead, manage and administrate. Managers keep things going, cope with breakdown, initiate new activities and bring teams and activities together (Blandford, 1997, p. 1).

A manager is someone who gets the job done through people. Everard (1986) defined a manager as someone who:

- *knows what he or she wants to happen and causes it to happen*
- *is responsible for controlling resources and ensuring that they are put to good use*
- *promotes effectiveness in work done, and searches for continual improvement*
- *is accountable for the performance of the unit he or she is managing, of which he or she is a part*
- *sets a climate or tone conducive to enabling people to give of their best.*

Bush and West-Burnham (1994) provide a definition of the principles of management which encompass planning, resourcing, controlling, organising, leading and evaluating. In brief, these involve:

- **leadership**   *values, missions and vision*
- **management**   *planning, organisation, execution and deployment*
- **administration**   *operational details.*

Central to school management is Caldwell and Spinks' (1988) model of collaborative management which identifies six phases in the management of a school. Spinks (1990, p. 123) states:

*These phases relate to **where** the school is going and **why**, **how** it is going to get there and then checking very carefully to see **if** and **when** it has arrived.*

The six key phases are summarised as follows:

1 goal-setting
2 policy-making
3 curriculum planning
4 resource provision
5 implementation of the learning programme
6 evaluation.

A further consideration in this process is that of personal relationships. Managers are in a position where their relationship with their team is critical to its effectiveness. Resource management is now a key function of school management. It has been defined by Davies as shown in Figure 4.1.

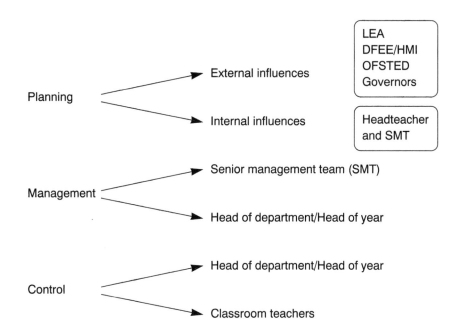

Figure 4.1: Levels of resource management
(*Source:* Davies, 1990, p. 49)

Resource managers need to work closely with the headteacher, school governors and senior management team (SMT). The resource manager should be a member of the SMT and function as a key adviser to the governors' finance subcommittee.

A resource manager should also have a close working relationship with the LEA. This will encompass the provision of financial/resource information and advice to facilitate effective management and policy-making decisions. All relevant committees, management teams and classroom teachers need to be aware of the financial/resource implications of each policy. An example of good management practice from other areas of the public sector is management accounting. Jones and Pendlebury (1996, p. 21) describe the role of management accounting as follows:

The basic role of management accounting in public sector organisations is to provide managers with the accounting information they need to carry out the planning and *control functions. The information **requirement** will, of course, depend to some extent on the nature of the organisation.*

While resource managers require knowledge and understanding of resource management models, it is also necessary to look at different aspects of school management. The following sections present an overview of whole-school, faculty and department management.

Whole-school management

A resource manager will be required to have knowledge and understanding of whole-school issues and of all operational aspects of the school, which encompass:

- curriculum issues
- pastoral issues
- policy and practice
- monitoring and evaluation.

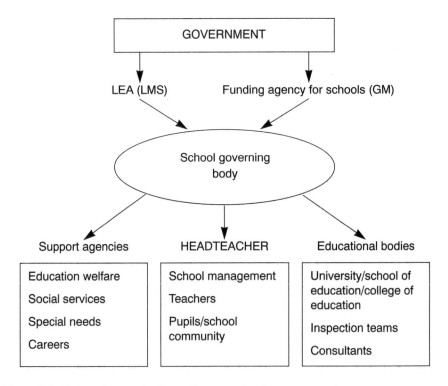

Figure 4.2: External agencies impacting on school management

Schools do not stand alone; there are a number of agencies that are participant players in the management of schools. Figure 4.2 illustrates the diversity of external agencies which impact on the management of schools.

Department/faculty management

The size of the department or faculty accommodating each subject area will be determined by the size of the school. Formula funding through the LMS determines the amount of income for each school and therefore the number of staff; for example, while it might be desirable to employ a drama specialist, this may not be affordable in all schools. For a resource manager responsible for a department or faculty, the number of staff within each academic team will reflect the number of pupils attending the school. The size of the academic team will also determine the financial incentive allocated to the post and the level of delegation possible.

In contrast, the tasks of each academic team will not differ according to size. At each key stage, teachers are required to deliver the National Curriculum. Each pupil is to be assessed; recording and reporting criteria are to be met. Curriculum support teams, special needs, language support and peripatetic music staff have to be managed.

Roles

Areas of responsibility should be well-defined within the management structure of the school. This is occasionally a neglected area within school management. A framework for the practice of resource management should:

- be workable
- recognise the needs of the school
- be understood and acknowledged by all staff
- relate to the school's vision and mission
- allow middle and senior managers to develop knowledge and under-standing, skills and abilities.

Being a resource manager does not mean being 'all things to all people'. Resource managers must adopt their own management style which fulfils the requirements of the post. Knowing what is required is the key. It is essential for resource managers to identify their role in terms of:

- tasks
- responsibilities
- relationships
- working conditions
- external influences.

Resource managers should also have an understanding of their role in relation to others, to avoid management dilemmas. As Thomas and Martin (1996, p. 171) comment:

> *The schools we have studied exhibit a sense of purposeful leadership in their management of resources [. . .]. There was little difficulty in identifying decisions on resources which were consistent with a wider and coherent framework of aims and priorities for the school [. . .].*

Decision-making and participation

Management involves decision-making, individually and collaboratively. If resource management is to be effective, managers will need to understand how to prioritise and make decisions.

Management involves people. In order to be effective decisions have to be made. Analysing the design of the job, applying this in practice and reflecting on failures and successes are central to management (Blandford, 1997).

A resource manager needs to develop the skills and abilities required to determine when to act on his/her own and when to collaborate with others. Adopting a structured approach to decision-making will aid the process. This involves:

1 Clear analysis of the learning purpose:
   – context
   – resources
   – outcomes.
2 Clear specification of the criteria for the budget plan as determined by:
   – the school development plan
   – the LEA
   – government initiatives.
3 Systematic research.
4 Testing decisions against likely outcomes to the quality of teaching and learning.

Oldroyd and Hall (1990, p. 16) advise that *decision-making is intimately bound up with every individual manager's personal values, personal goals and management style.* In order to make quality decisions, Oldroyd and Hall (p. 16) suggest that managers should have:

- *clear personal values*
- *clear personal goals*
- *problem-solving skills*

- *high creativity*
- *high influence.*

Resource management is linked to educational needs and therefore does involve consulting colleagues. Effective management will encourage participation. Effective management will also enable staff to relate departmental plans to school development plans (SDPs). Deciding when to consult others will affect the quality of the decision, staff's acceptance of the decision and the amount of time involved in the decision-making process.

As Fidler *et al.* (1991, p. 5) state:

Participation in decision-making has two major benefits:

(a) an improvement in the quality of the decision

(b) improved motivation and commitment of those involved.

However, *participation is not without its drawbacks*. These include:

1 *It is slower than autocracy.*

2 *It consumes a great deal of staff time.*

3 *The pattern of decision-making is less predictable.*

4 *The pattern of decision-making is less consistent.*

5 *The location of accountability may be less clear.*

6 *Some decisions are expected to be taken by senior managers and participation may be seen as abdication.*

As the above indicates, a sudden change to full staff participation in decisions relating to resource management is not possible. In order to facilitate a gradual transition, managers should be developing classroom teachers' management skills within the context of continuous professional development (CPD). The transition should be supported by appropriate training, and a climate where risk-taking is accepted. Monitoring and evaluation of such processes are necessary for success.

Maychell (1994, pp. 95–105) examined the process of participation in resource management. In brief:

- **Governors' involvement in financial decision-making.** School governors have a major responsibility in the financial management of the school. However, the majority of governors delegate this to the finance sub-committee or headteacher. The NFER (1994) study found that the extent to which governors are involved in the financial planning process reflects the skills and interests of individual governors.

- **Teachers' involvement in spending decisions.** Although the NFER study did not focus on this area, information gathered through the research allowed for some examination of this issue. In general, teachers' involvement in financial planning was confined to decisions relating to their own curriculum area or year group. Whole-school decisions, such as premises or staffing, were in the domain of the headteachers or governors. Teachers did have access to governors' papers and budget statements. Generally head-teachers and senior managers felt that teachers did not wish to be involved in financial matters, and this was substantiated by the teachers interviewed in the study.

- **Curriculum/departmental budget decisions.** In the majority of the schools in the study there were budget holders responsible for a sum of money to be spent on a particular subject, year group or specific purpose. Any money left unspent at the end of the year in these budgets was returned to the school's budget. Maychell found that this was to ensure that budget holders used the money for the purpose for which it was allocated, rather than treating budgets as bank accounts. Budget holders were consulted on the amount they would need for the coming financial year. The amount requested was expected to reflect specific plans for the area, as identified in the SDP. By this process a clear link had been established between financial and school development planning.

- **The emerging role of school finance staff in spending decisions.** The study found that the appointment of financial staff to senior posts in schools (particularly secondary schools) represents a critical shift in school manage-ment approaches. In several cases schools employed a bursar or finance manager who subsequently became a member of the senior management team. None of the financial staff had a background in teaching. One school had replaced a deputy headteacher with a bursar, which indicated a business approach to resource management.

Organisational structure

Decision-making, as a process, is dependent on the organisational structure of a school. Appropriate organisational design, or structure, is essential for efficient and effective management. Mullins (1993) describes organisational structure as follows:

> *Structure is the pattern of relationships among positions in the organisation and among members of the organisation. The purpose of structure is the organisation and the co-ordination of their activities so they are directed towards achieving the goals and objectives of the organisation. The structure defines tasks and responsibilities, work roles and relationships, and channels of communication.*

There are several possible pictorial representations of school organisational structures (*see* Figures 4.3 to 4.7 below). The participants in school management differ according to phase and school culture. However, in order to encompass the above, a framework for practice should be similar to one of the following examples of a school management structure.

Nursery/Primary/Small Secondary School

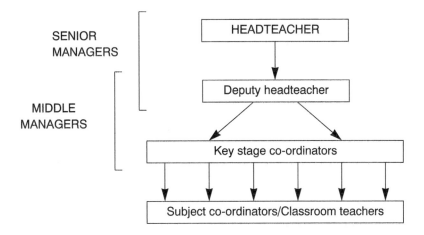

Figure 4.3: School management structure: nursery, primary and small secondary schools

In Figure 4.3, pastoral and academic issues are integrated. Differences in practice would be determined not by organisational structures, but by professional practice, i.e. a classroom teacher would have pastoral and curriculum responsibilities for the pupils in his/her class and a key stage co-ordinator would be responsible for the management of all pastoral and academic issues. Figure 4.3 illustrates the different levels of responsibility between teachers who focus on their classroom activities and key stage co-ordinators who have whole-school responsibilities. This differs from current practice in many secondary schools whereby the management of key stage initiatives is the responsibility of a member of a curriculum or pastoral team. In contrast, Figure 4.3 emphasises the need for a key stage co-ordinator with full responsibility for all academic and pastoral issues.

This view is endorsed by the Teacher Training Agency (TTA) which is currently developing a model for the training of subject leaders, the National Professional Qualification for Subject Leaders (NPQSL). Further enhancement of management responsibilities focuses teachers on the need to develop management skills.

The organisational structure shown in Figure 4.3 may not require each position to be filled by a separate individual. In reality teachers may have shared responsibilities, or have more than one responsibility. The allocation of posts will be determined by local needs, staff availability and financial resources. Within this model resource management is the responsibility of the head-teacher with support from the deputy headteacher. Key stage co-ordinators have delegated responsibility as budget holders for their designated areas. Classroom teachers are responsible for the allocation of materials required to deliver the National Curriculum.

Figure 4.4 indicates the need for resource managers within larger primary and secondary schools. In practice the headteacher has overall responsibility for the management of their school. A resource manager is responsible for all fiscal, material and personnel matters. Deputy headteachers with responsibility for academic and pastoral issues work with key stage co-ordinators to ensure that central government and local initiatives are implemented in the classroom. Heads of year and heads of academic teams have responsibility for managing the delivery of the National Curriculum and assessment, recording and reporting procedures. They are also budget holders responsible for the budget and management of materials allocated to their area. Classroom teachers are responsible for the management of learning.

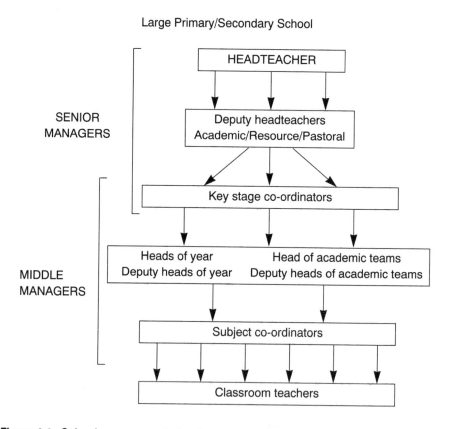

Figure 4.4: School management structure: large primary or secondary schools

As a tall structure, Figure 4.5 is hierarchical in practice. Within this model resource managers would be providers of information, not key decision-makers. The resource manager's role would be that of a business manager ensuring that administrative tasks were completed and resource targets met. This is not a collaborative structure and does not reflect the need for middle managers and classroom teachers to become decision-makers.

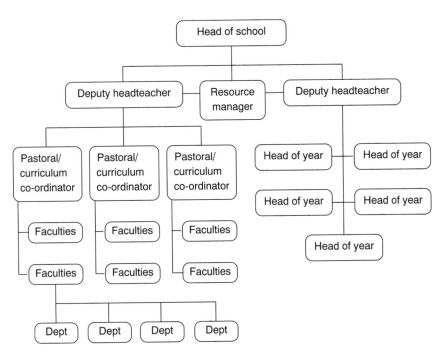

Figure 4.5: School management structure: tall model

The antithesis of a tall structure is a flat structure shown in Figure 4.6. This limits the need for pastoral and academic managers, thus reducing the number of senior managers employed. Resource management would be the respon-sibility of the headteacher. As a model, a flat structure may be more representative of primary school practice. In recent years, models of school management have tended to become flatter, largely due to the reduction in the number of deputy headteachers and increased responsibility for middle managers and classroom teachers. In practice this can avoid the problems of tall structures, where there are too many layers of management and there is a tendency for needless bureaucracy. Flatter organisations can change and react more quickly in the increasingly dynamic and ever changing working environment of education. Flatter organisations have a tendency to force managers into delegation, because of the enlarged managerial span of control.

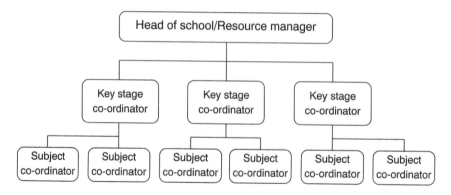

Figure 4.6: School management structure: flat model

Larger primary schools and secondary schools should consider the advantages of the interlinked model shown in Figure 4.7. A development of the flatter model, this is the most effective collaborative structure for the management of schools: work is interlinked, therefore management of tasks, control and direction is clearly defined. The resource manager's position is central to this

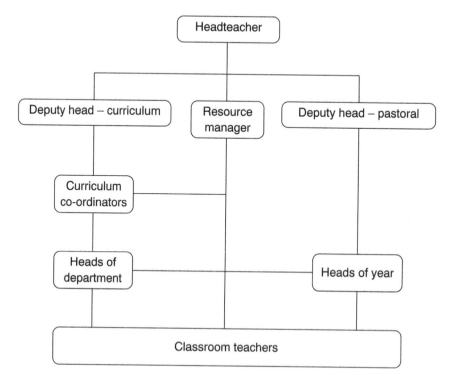

Figure 4.7: School management structure: interlinked model

model. The principles of collaboration are reflected in it: teams are created according to academic and pastoral need, and school administration is managed by those qualified and trained for the role. Resource managers are placed in a senior position providing support for the whole school, headteacher and governors.

Collaboration

As indicated, in practice participation in the decision-making process in schools is dependent on the relationships between staff. Structures may be needed to provide a framework for collaboration, such as the established model designed by Caldwell and Spinks (1988) as shown in Figure 4.8.

In the context of school management structures, Caldwell and Spinks' model (Figure 4.8) is more flexible and would be appropriate to the majority of schools. As Spinks (1990, p. 145) stated, *the model [. . .] is just a starting point*. If managers are to make it work they need knowledge and skills related to 'learning and teaching', curriculum design and development, the gathering of information for programme evaluation and the capacity to exercise leadership. The specific purposes to be achieved in collaborative decision-making at school level are (Spinks, 1990, p. 122):

1 *To provide an approach to school management which clearly focuses on learning and teaching (the central issues of any school).*

2 *To facilitate sharing in the decision-making processes and the involvement of all possible participants in appropriate ways.*

3 *To identify clearly the management tasks and to provide direct and easily understood links between them and information about them.*

4 *To identify clearly responsibilities for decision-making and activities and to demonstrate lines of accountability.*

5 *To provide a means to relate resource allocations of all kinds to learning priorities for students.*

6 *To facilitate evaluation and review processes with the emphasis on further improving opportunities for students.*

7 *To limit documentation to simple, clear statements that can easily be prepared by those involved in their already busy schedules.*

School management is focused on creating a learning environment. Managers need to consider what effect their actions and decisions have on the school as a centre for learning. Collaboration within a recognised structure is critical to an effective school. As part of the collaborative process communication is the means by which collaboration occurs.

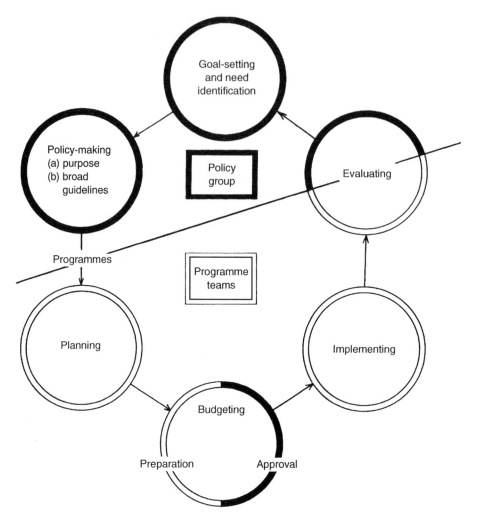

Figure 4.8: The collaborative school management framework
(*Source:* Caldwell and Spinks, 1988, p. 37; reproduced by permission of the publisher, Falmer Press)

Communication

Communication, written or oral, is essential for the success of the team. A resource manager will need to be a gatherer and disseminator of information, acting as the 'gate-keeper'. In the majority of cases teachers will want to be informed of policies that affect their practice. This means that resource managers should try not to be too protective; there will be a need to know about available resources.

The complexities of resource management are often compounded by limited communication between participants in the planning and implementation process. Communication is central to effective school operations. In education, LEAs, governors, teachers and management use different methods of communication for different purposes. An open and supportive communication climate will promote co-operative working relationships where staff will feel valued, trusted, secure and confident. Resource managers need to ensure that the process of managing resources is transparent. Resource managers need to adopt a model of practice that enables all members of the school community to know and understand the origins of their practice. There is little to be gained from creating an air of mystery – this leads to mistrust and bad practice. Teachers and managers need to feel secure that the management of resources within their institution is equitable within the parameters set by external agents, i.e. central and local government.

Communication is the exchange of information, which can range from an informal discussion with a colleague to a full report to governors or the LEA. Verbal and non-verbal communication involves listening and observing. Being an effective listener is a skill that can be developed and practised in each new situation. Problems that arise during the communication process are generally focused on the message, encoding the setting, transmission, decoding and feedback (Blandford, 1997). Some people appear to have an innate ability to communicate; many others acquire skills through study and practice.

Networking

Networking, the activity of developing personal contacts, is the most acceptable form of politicking in organisations. Networks offer support and a means to share information. Hoy and Miskel (1991) state:

> [. . .] communication underlines virtually all organisational and administrative situations, and is essential to decision-making and effective leadership. [. . .] At the heart of communication lies the opportunity to resolve contradictions, quell rumours, provide reassurance, and, ultimately, instil meaning in the complex but engaging task of education.

Networking is a legitimate means of communicating and can be time-saving. Resource managers need to identify with whom to network among local government, LEA and school colleagues in order to procure and allocate resources, as appropriate to achieve the school's aims and objectives.

Information technology

Information technology, as will be discussed in detail later in Chapter 9, is increasingly making information easier to access and share, enabling resource managers and budget holders to engage in the communication chain in schools. Resource managers and budget holders require adequate training in order to access and process information. There is also a responsibility for those designing and contributing to the site network to comply with relevant legislation.

Meetings

A significant difference in governor and management practice since the ERA is the importance of meetings. Governors, resource managers and budget holders are now required to plan, lead and participate in meetings. As Thomas and Martin (1996, p. 172) found:

> [...] regular departmental meetings are forums for all staff to participate in discussions on resource choices related to learning materials [...].

Understanding the culture and style of meetings will help governors and managers to make better use of opportunities. All participants in the resource management process should aim to become valued members of meetings: prepare, think and listen, then speak and encourage others. It is essential to know your audience. With good leadership, meetings can be effective.

Teams

It is axiomatic that teams are necessary within the context of schools as organisations and that schools as organisations should value effective team-work. Everard and Morris (1990, p. 172) state:

> A team is a group of people that can effectively tackle any task which it has been set to do. The contribution drawn from each member is of the highest possible quality, and is one which could not have been called into play other than in the context of a supportive team.

Teams need to work together on a common task, therefore resource mangers need to focus governors, senior managers and budget holders on specific tasks within the management cycle, as defined by John West-Burnham (1994b, p. 157), shown in Figure 4.9.

West-Burnham (1994a, p. 79) explains:

> Strategy, policy and planning are inextricably related management activities in that each requires the others in order to translate aspiration into action.

Bell (1992, p. 45) defined teamwork as a group of people working together on the basis of:

- *shared perceptions*
- *a common purpose*

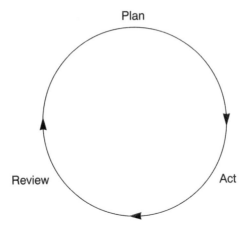

Figure 4.9: The management cycle
(*Source:* West-Burnham, 1994b, p. 157)

- *agreed procedures*
- *commitment*
- *co-operation*
- *resolving disagreements openly by discussion.*

More specifically, Handy (1993) suggested the following functions or purposes of teams which can be applied to resource management in schools:

- *distributing and managing work*
- *problem-solving and decision-making*
- *enabling people to take part in decision-making*
- *co-ordinating and liaising*
- *passing on information*
- *negotiating or conflict resolution*
- *increasing commitment and involvement*
- *monitoring and evaluation.*

Essentially, successful teamwork depends on a clearly defined set of aims and objectives, the personalities of team members and the team manager. Teamwork is, as with all aspects of effective management, time-consuming (Blandford, 1997). The following model, adapted from Tuckman (1965), defines the stages of team development as:

Forming: The team is not a team but a set of individuals. The focus is on the team purposes, composition, leadership and lifespan. Individuals are concerned to establish their personal identities in the team and make some individual impression.

73

Storming: Having reached a consensus on the team's purpose, conflict arises as assumptions are challenged. Personal agendas are revealed and some interpersonal hostility may be generated. Successful handling enables the team to reach fresh agreement on purpose, procedures and norms.

Norming: The team seeks to establish its norms and practices: when and how it should work. As working procedures are established there will be a communication of feelings, mutual support and sense of team identity.

Performing: Solutions to problems emerge, the team is mature and productive. Individuals and team are relaxed and confident.

Time is required if teams are to complete each of Tuckman's stages and function effectively. Schools, post ERA, need teams – governors, senior managers, middle managers and practitioners. Ultimately team decisions are expressed in terms of action. Each team member knows what has to be done, by whom and when (West-Burnham, 1992, pp. 121–4). A resource manager needs to know and understand the relationship he/she has with colleagues as a team leader and team member. Communication and trust are essential to good practice. Effective schools require effective teams.

Summary

Historically, the leader of a school was, as the headteacher, a senior colleague with expert teaching skills who led a team of teachers by example. Today, this concept has ceased to exist. Although headteachers may reject the notion of corporate management, their position can now be compared to that of the managing director of a corporate company, whose product is education and whose clients are pupils (and parents). School management is influenced by the owners or patrons of the school: governors, parents, the government and/or LEAs.

The process by which teachers become decision-makers and managers is unclear, yet many teachers are now managers. In essence, teachers are managers of their classes and classrooms, but management priorities change when teachers become managers of other teaching and non-teaching staff. Central to management and teaching in schools is learning.

A manager is someone who gets the job done through people. Resource managers need to work closely with the headteacher, school governors and senior management team (SMT). The resource manager should be a member of the SMT and function as a key adviser to the governors' finance subcommittee. A resource manager should also have a close working relationship with the LEA. This will encompass the provision of financial/resource information and advice to facilitate effective management and policy-making decisions.

While resource managers require knowledge and understanding of resource management models, it is also necessary to look at different aspects of school management. Participants in school management differ according to phase and school culture. The allocation of posts will be determined by local needs, staff availability and financial resources. In practice the headteacher has overall responsibility for the management of their school. A resource manager is responsible for all fiscal, material and personnel matters. Being a resource manager does not mean being 'all things to all people'. Resource managers must adopt their own management style which fulfils the requirements of the post. Knowing what is required is the key.

As indicated, in practice participation in the decision-making process in schools is dependent on the relationships between staff. Structures may be needed to provided a framework for collaboration, such as the established model designed by Caldwell and Spinks (1988) as shown in Figure 4.8. If managers are to make it work they need knowledge and skills related to 'learning and teaching', curriculum design and development, the gathering of information for programme evaluation and the capacity to exercise leadership.

School management is focused on creating a learning environment. Managers need to consider what effect their actions and decisions have on the school as a centre for learning. Collaboration within a recognised structure is critical to an effective school. As part of the collaborative process communication is the means by which collaboration occurs.

Resource managers need to ensure that the process of managing resources is transparent; they should adopt a model of practice that enables all members of the school community to know and understand the origins of their practice. There is little to be gained from creating an air of mystery – this leads to mistrust and bad practice. Teachers and managers need to feel secure that the management of resources within their institution is equitable within the parameters set by external agents, i.e. central and local government.

Networking is a legitimate means of communicating and can be time-saving. Resource managers need to identify with whom to network among local government, LEA and school colleagues in order to procure and allocate resources, as appropriate in order to achieve the school's aims and objectives.

Understanding the culture and style of meetings will help governors and managers to make better use of opportunities. All participants in the resource management process should aim to become valued members of meetings: prepare, think and listen, then speak and encourage others. It is essential to know your audience. With good leadership, meetings can be effective.

It is axiomatic that teams are necessary within the context of schools as organisations and that schools as organisations should value effective team-work. Essentially, successful teamwork depends on a clearly defined set of aims and objectives, the personalities of team members and the team manager. Teamwork is, as with all aspects of effective management, time-consuming (Blandford, 1997). A resource manager needs to know and understand the relationship he or she has with colleagues as a team leader and team member. Communication and trust are essential to good practice. Effective schools require effective teams.

5
■ ■ ■
Planning

The purpose of planning

If schools are to be effective, resource management has to be planned. Knowledge and understanding of the planning process is therefore central to resource management. Planning is a messy, repetitive and confusing aspect of a manager's life (Blandford, 1997). In resource management the critical element, finance, is not static. In addition, human resources and material resources are factors in the framework for resource management planning that change on a daily basis. Therefore the parameters for resource management, in practice, are identifiable but changing. Thomas and Martin (1996, p. 13) quote Caines (1992, pp. 15–16):

> *The 1988 Act [. . .] was about changing the way in which the delivery of education was to be managed [. . .] setting realistic goals and drawing up plans to achieve them. Those plans involve distinct phases: setting objectives, allocating resources, delivering results, evaluating the impact, resetting objectives in the light of evaluation.*

As a process, planning consists of the following three elements:

1 **Objectives:** goals which are to be achieved, in sufficiently detailed and precise terms to enable others to identify whether they have been achieved.

2 **Actions:** specification of the activities required to meet the objectives.

3 **Resources:** identification of what and who will be required to achieve the objectives and an indication of the timescale.

Planning may involve 'going around in circles' as managers consider the various combinations of objectives, actions and resources which will provide the way forward. However, this is a necessary stage to ensure that all elements are considered.

Consistency in resource management can be determined through strategic planning and operational planning. A strategy is a broad statement which relates to the overall approach and direction of the school towards the achievement of its mission. Developing and maintaining a strategy involves establishing a framework within which an operational plan can take place (Blandford, 1997).

Vision and mission statements are critical to the effectiveness of strategic and operational plans. A vision moves an organisation forward from where it is now to where it would like to be. A precise goal is more credible than a vague dream. As a condition, a vision should be more desirable in many important ways than that which currently exists. A specific definition of vision within the context of schools is reflected in the school's aims. These are notably achievement-orientated and, as such, should be shared by all members of the school community.

If a school is to be successful, it has to be effective. A measure of a school's effectiveness is the ability of the staff to work towards achieving the school's vision, i.e. working towards a shared set of values and beliefs. The vision statement should be succinct and should contain, within a few words, the philosophy underlying the professional practice within the school.

A vision must be clear and comprehensive to all: teachers, parents, pupils, governors, visitors, etc. A school's vision statement is not a party political statement – it does not require the fervour and charisma of political rhetoric. School vision statements should direct the school's population towards a common purpose. Identifying shared values is central to generating a vision for the school. Based on past and present practice they should reflect what is *good* within the school. A genuinely *good* school with characteristics of openness and trust, shared values and beliefs will be an effective school. An example of good practice is given in Figure 5.1.

Vision and mission statements provide a clear sense of direction and purpose. These are a means of creating school development plans – objectives or targets to be met by members of the school community. When determining objectives, be **SMART** (Tuckman, 1965):

Specific
Measurable
Attainable
Relevant
Timed.

Strategic planning is long-term planning, which takes into consideration the strengths and weaknesses of the school as an organisation, and external factors such as government directives. School managers have a critical role in articulating organisational goals. These reflect personal values, vision or mission for each area of responsibility, or the school as a whole (Oldroyd and Hall, 1990, p. 29). The headteacher has the responsibility for defining the

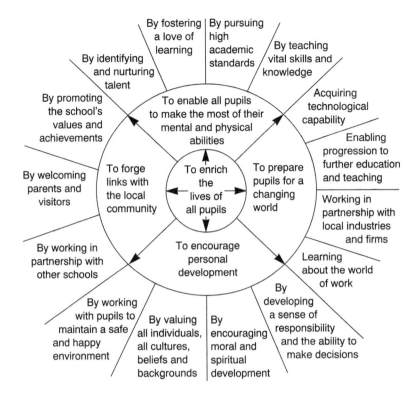

Figure 5.1: School vision statement
(*Source:* Blandford, 1997, p. 50)

school's vision or aims. Vision is fundamental to the success of the school. Strategic planning is therefore central to the process of managing resources.

Strategic planning in all schools will occur annually through the school development plan (SDP). The value of an SDP as an operational tool will rest with the senior management team. Within the content of the SDP, vision, mission and aims can be achieved. This process is defined by Davies and Ellison (1992, p. 16) as follows:

It involves a process of developing shared visions into activities so that the school's product and service match the clients' wants and needs [. . .]. By going through this process, clear objectives can be developed which relate to the achievement of the school's mission and aims.

This is illustrated in Figure 5.2.

Having determined the school development plan, managers need to consider how the plan will be put into operation. Operational planning is about tables and targets: who does what, when and how? Operational planning is detailed.

Figure 5.2: The planning process

It aims to achieve a particular set of objectives within a given time. As shown later in Table 5.2 (p. 90), a department development plan (DDP) is an operational plan.

Effective schools have a collaborative approach to planning involving the whole school community. Thomas and Martin (1996, p. 184) advise that developmental planning is a means of participatory management. They suggest (p. 30) that people other than teachers should also be involved in school planning. Governors have responsibility for approving the development plan and the school budget. Parents are also invited to the governors' annual general meeting and to participate in the school inspection process.

Resource managers need to develop the skills required to prepare a well constructed plan. Table 5.1 describes the eight stages involved in planning which develop the model defined in Figure 5.2. The process of developing a school's vision statement and development plan should be collaborative; managers who spend time planning on their own will feel resentful when other people become involved and spoil what was a good plan.

Table 5.1: Planning stages

Objectives	Stage 1	*Define the objectives*	What are you aiming to achieve?
	Stage 2	*Generate and evaluate objectives/actions*	What are the courses of action available? Which ones will best achieve your objectives?
Actions	Stage 3	*Identify the actions*	What is required to implement your objectives?
	Stage 4	*Sequence the actions*	What is the best order?
Resources	Stage 5	*Identify the resources*	What resources are required?
Review	Stage 6	*Review the plan*	Will it work? If not, return to Stage 2 or 3.
Preparation	Stage 7	*Prepare plans and schedules*	Who will do what and when?
Audit	Stage 8	*Monitor and evaluate*	Re-plan if necessary.

(*Source:* Blandford, 1997, Table 7.1, p. 132.)

Planning involves two aspects of practice that should be identified by a manager from the start:

1 **Analytical:** thinking things through involving calculation and individual reflection.

2 **Social:** motivating and drawing on the contributions and commitment from colleagues.

In sum, the purpose of planning is to operationalise the school's vision and mission within a strategic framework. Planning can be challenging, enjoyable even; it can also be difficult (LaGrave *et al.*, 1994, pp. 5–24). Planning can be constrained by environmental factors, in particular the need to meet deadlines.

School development plan

All schools should have a school development plan (Blandford, 1997). The SDP provides a framework for strategic planning in which the school can identify long- and short-term objectives to manage itself effectively. An SDP should relate clearly to the school's vision and mission (DES, 1991b; Crown copyright):

> *A School Development Plan is a plan of needs for development set in the context of the school's aims and values, its existing achievements and national and LEA policies and initiatives.*

It is critical that each school development plan should be unique. Skelton *et al.* (1991, pp. 166–7) state that the school development plan should:

- *demonstrate involvement*
- *provide a focus for action*
- *provide a means of presenting the plan*
- *provide a means of assessing progress.*

In order to produce the school plan the following process should be gone through (LMS Initiative, 1990, Summary, p. 6):

- *Establish the context in which the school is working including:*
  - *numbers of pupils in the area*
  - *pupil destinations*
  - *policies of neighbouring schools*
  - *any other major changes.*
- *Be clear about the aims and values of the school.*
- *Convert these aims and values into more concrete achievable objectives for the school.*
- *Set down strategies, priorities and plans for each school activity.*
- *Match plans to the resources available.*

An example of good practice is shown in Figure 5.3.

School Development Plan 1996/8

This is a two-year rolling plan which focuses the aims and objectives of the school following the completion of the five-year plan which preceded it. In this version of the plan, there is a deliberate concentration on short-term aims to achieve clarity on the immediate objectives of the school.

The plan will be monitored continuously and reviewed annually through the school's annual review process. External evaluation will be provided by the governing body, OFSTED inspection and monitoring by the LEA inspectorate.

AIM – RAISING ACHIEVEMENT: Improving standards of teaching and learning

Objectives:

- By the end of 1996, all subject departments will have placed <u>differentiation</u> at the head of their priorities, and plans for developing differentiation will have been <u>fully funded as priorities in the budget.</u>

- The <u>organisation of teaching groups in Year 8</u> will have been discussed and any changes implemented in the school timetable 1997/8.

- A policy statement on <u>Equal Opportunities</u> will have been written, disseminated and be reflected in practice.

- <u>Assessment and reporting</u> will have been reviewed to establish a system which shows progress, incorporates <u>target setting</u> and is motivating for pupils of all abilities.

- A whole-school policy on <u>language across the curriculum</u> will be developed in 1996/7, tied in with the partnership project to <u>raise reading standards</u> at all ages and levels of ability.

- The <u>curriculum at Key Stage 4</u> will have to be reviewed and any plans to <u>introduce vocational courses</u> implemented by 1997.

- The <u>curriculum in the Sixth Form</u> will have been reviewed and any plans to <u>extend GNVQ work to Advanced level</u> implemented by 1998.

- <u>IT facilities in the school will be upgraded</u> in the Library in 1996, and made more accessible to pupils by <u>extending opening hours</u> by 1997.

- A rolling programme of <u>updating and extending the book stock of the Library</u> will begin in 1996.

AIM – RAISING ACHIEVEMENT: Improving standards of behaviour

Objectives:

- The <u>Good Behaviour Policy</u> will be published and become the basis of practice for all staff.

- Training in <u>positive discipline</u> strategies will be made available to a range of staff and disseminated.

- <u>Anti-bullying</u> work will continue, advised by a group of parents, pupils and staff established in 1995.

- <u>Display areas</u> will be created throughout the school and pupils' work and records of activities put on exhibition to make corridors reflect the life and ethos of the school.

- Building and redecoration work will focus on <u>improving the physical conditions for pupils</u> in the school: cloakroom spaces converted into attractive social areas, lavatories and changing rooms refurbished and redecorated. The School Council will be able to recommend spending up to £1000 on the fabric of the building.

- Arrangements for <u>home/school transport</u> will be overhauled, with the emphasis on higher standards of behaviour on the buses and in the bus park.

- A <u>professional counselling</u> service will be made available to pupils in 1996.

AIM – RAISING ACHIEVEMENT: Improving school management and continuing staff development

Objectives:

- A new and <u>wider forum for discussion of the curriculum</u> will have been established by September 1996.

- Opportunities for <u>new responsibilities</u> will have been offered at middle management level within the school for fixed periods, to retain flexibility.

- Members of the <u>Senior Management Team will have been linked to all subjects</u> to provide a clear line of communication, monitor standards and offer support.

- All staff will have completed their first cycle of <u>appraisal</u> by July 1997, and meeting times will have been made available.

- A <u>revised pattern of meetings</u> will be introduced from September 1996, increasing the number of 'task groups' and increasing the number of whole-staff, subject and year team meetings.

- <u>Management training</u> courses for all interested teaching and support staff will have been arranged in 1996/7.

- The standards set by <u>Investors in People</u> will be used as a benchmark for the development of in-service training, planning and communication: the school should be ready for IIP assessment by the end of 1997.

Figure 5.3: School development plan

The example of good practice shown in Figure 5.3 reflects the advice given by the LMS Initiative (1990, Summary, p. 6), i.e. SDPs should be:

- *realistic;*
- *achievable;*
- *drawn up by methods involving the whole school community (governors, staff, parents and pupils).*

An SDP encompasses national, LEA and school initiatives, providing schools with a framework for strategic planning. The SDP will identify existing achievements and needs for development. Each school's aims – visions and missions – will be stated and reflected at every stage of the plan. The SDP enables schools to manage themselves in an effective, coherent manner within both local and national contexts.

The main purpose of an SDP should be to improve the quality of learning for pupils. In practice, all management activities should relate to the SDP if they are to have a central role in school life. Effective resource management will depend on the knowledge and understanding of the SDP in directing the school towards its vision. The LMS Initiative (1990, Summary, p. 7) also details how to draw up plans for each activity:

- *Break down all the functions of the school into activities and, where necessary, sub-activities (e.g. delivery of the curriculum subdivided by NC subject area).*
- *Set up planning units for each activity and sub-activity.*
- *Give them guidance, together with advice on priorities.*
- *Ask them to analyse existing strengths and weaknesses.*
- *In particular ask them to examine present activities and not just concentrate on new developments.*
- *Ask them to examine the resources they need for each activity (e.g. finance, staff, time, materials and space).*
- *Match the activity levels with the available resources to produce the School Plan.*

Critically:

- *The school should start out with a full School Plan but might only look in depth at some of its activities each year, say one third, so that in three years all activities have been reviewed.*
- *Planning should be a continuous process so that the evaluation of one year's progress informs next year's plan.*

The SDP should be central to the management of the school, involving all teachers. The extent of a resource manager's involvement will be determined by the headteacher and/or finance subcommittee. In practice, resource managers will need to know and understand the content of the SDP. As the management structures of schools change, increased collaboration may lead to a greater involvement in policy-making for resource managers. Hargreaves and Hopkins (1991, p. 4) argue that:

The production of a good plan and its successful implementation depend upon a sound grasp of the processes involved. A wise choice of content for the plan as well as the means of implementing the plan successfully will be made only when the process of development planning is thoroughly understood.

Audit

Resource managers, therefore, need to have an understanding of planning for effective management at operational level. An understanding of the planning process is a necessary prerequisite to the development and implementation of the school development plan. Resource managers need to follow a model of the planning as shown in Figure 5.4.

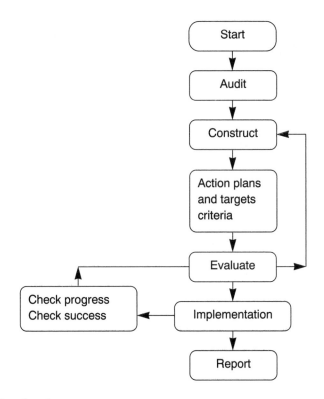

Figure 5.4: The planning process
(*Source:* Blandford, 1997, p. 137)

An audit provides the basis for selecting priorities for development. The context of the audit will be:

- missions, aims and values of the school
- policies and initiatives
- inspections and reviews
- staff appraisals
- views of all stakeholders: staff, governors, parents, pupils and community.

A full audit is time-consuming; a programme of specific small-scale audits may be more practical and achievable within the school setting. A resource manager may be allocated responsibility for financial audits. A comprehensive audit will include:

- interviews with colleagues
- lesson observation – where appropriate
- review of documentation
- writing up findings.

The outcomes of an audit should reveal strengths and weaknesses in order to provide a basis for action planning. The audit also identifies priorities for development. Having completed the audit, the next stage is to construct a plan which is manageable, coherent and achievable. The DES (1989, p. 10) suggests that the plan should include:

- the aims of the school
- the proposed priorities and their timescale
- the justification of the priorities in the context of the school
- how the plan draws together different aspects of planning
- the methods of reporting outcomes
- the broad financial implications of the plan.

Resource managers should recognise that the urgent and unavoidable linking of priorities will lead to increased collaboration between staff and other stakeholders.

Action Plans

Once the SDP has been completed, detailed action plans can be drawn up. This involves managers and staff deciding on the way forward to implement the SDP. Action plans are a means of operationalising the strategy and contain;

- the agreed **priority** area
- the **targets** – specific objectives for the priority area

- **success criteria** against which progress and achievement can be judged
- the **tasks** to be undertaken
- allocation of **responsibility** for tasks and targets – with *timescales*
- **resources** required.

Action plans prepare the way forward for the implementation of the SDP. How this will work will depend on several factors. Hargreaves and Hopkins (1991, p. 65) identify the activities required to make the plan work:

- *sustaining commitment during implementation*
- *checking the progress of implementation*
- *overcoming any problems encountered*
- *checking the success of implementation*
- *taking stock*
- *reporting progress*
- *constructing the next development plan.*

People management is the key to successful implementation of the SDP. Resource managers have a critical role in this process.

Department Development Plan

Oldroyd and Hall (1990, p. 29) quote HMI (1984):

Whether a pupil achieves or underachieves is largely dependent on the quality of planning, execution and evaluation that takes place within departments.

A department development plan (DDP) is similar to the school development plan. The DDP should reflect the aims of the SDP and provide an operational framework for implementing the action plans emanating from the SDP. If it is to be effective, the DDP should be placed in the context of the school, LEA and national planning (Blandford, 1997). Figure 5.5 illustrates the position of the DDP within the school structure. In brief, a DDP should contain the following:

- a summary of the department's aims and objectives
- the method of achieving the aims and objectives
- monitoring and evaluation.

The DDP should enable staff to work 'together' towards a common goal. As such the plan should have a sense of direction and purpose, the central aim being to improve the quality of teaching and learning within each area of responsibility. Points for consideration are:

- aims and values
- schemes of work

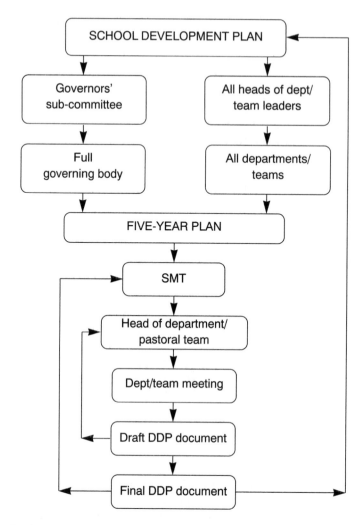

Figure 5.5: Position of DDP in SDP
(*Source:* adapted from Blandford, 1997, p. 141)

- policy documents
- teaching and learning
- assessment and reporting.

A department/team development plan should also include statements on:

- special educational needs
- equal opportunities

- differentiation
- resources.

The process by which the DDP is constructed will reflect the style of management. Consulting colleagues may be time-consuming; however, failure to do so may also be time-consuming. If a plan is to be effective it will need to be developed collaboratively. As Caldwell and Spinks (1988, p. 37) indicate in their model for the collaborative school management cycle (*see* Figure 4.8), staff as team members should participate in:

- goal-setting and need-identification
- policy-making
- planning of programmes
- preparation and approval of programme budgets
- implementing
- evaluating.

An example of good practice is given in Table 5.2.

Weaknesses in development planning

Gray (1991, p. 39) comments:

Most schools and colleges are now required [. . .] to produce formal plans. The planning process has become an important component of the management tasks of headteachers, [. . .] and other managers in the education service.

However, planning may not always be effective, as explained by Hargreaves (1995, pp. 222–4):

- **Getting started** – if staff are not fully behind the idea, their level of involvement will be limited and difficult to monitor and evaluate.
- **Audit** – when this stage is missed because of pressures to produce a plan quickly, problems may remain undetected. In addition, staff will not have a baseline from which to assess progress.
- **Plan and priorities** – a common weakness is to adopt too many priorities, which prevents plans from being monitored and evaluated in depth.
- **Action Plans** – are often vague and unspecific, without associated success criteria. This is related to limited guidance on: what evidence to collect, success criteria and how to judge the quality of implementation.
- **Implementation and evaluation** – development plans need evaluating. If progress checks are not built into the plan, monitoring disappears and with it any possibility of corrective action.

Table 5.2: Department development plan (two years)

AREA	1995 *Autumn term*	1996 *Spring term*	1996 *Summer term*
Curriculum	New Key Stage 3 syllabus introduced, incorporating post-Dearing changes. Timetable blocked with Years 8 and 9 (exception 8.1/2) 5 week blocks. New GCSE course introduced. Heavily revised Year 11 course in operation. A-level course commences in Year 12.	First term of revised Key Stage 3 course evaluated. First coursework folio completed by Year 10. First term of Key Stage 4 evaluated. Completion of presentation Year 12 scheme of work.	Full evaluation of Key Stage 3 course. Second coursework folio completed by Year 10. Adapt Year 8 programme in the light of changes in sub-programme.
Resources	Key Stage 3 – all core texts increased to 30 per set. GCSE – Key Geography 1 textbook included within scheme of work. A-level core text purchased/library set up. Resource area refurbished/stock catalogued. Premises: refurbishment of Geog. Res. Area/Staff Office. Improve environment of HU 4/5 and corridors.	Key Stage 3 – final phase of scheme of work initial development. Introduction of further differentiated materials. Inclusion of two units of 'geography-related' material as part of IT training. Enter bid for screens/ new furniture HU 5/ carpet for resource area/staff area. Blackout for HU 3/ blinds for staff office.	Increase number of books in Pupil Lending Library. Increased use of reprographics. New chairs/staff office. Continued production of differentiated materials. Bid for personal computers for department.
Management	Assessment: introduction of 'title-page recording' of pupil work. New department marking policy introduced. Centralised recording system introduced. 'Cause for concern' pro forma introduced.	Evaluate 'cause for concern' pro forma.	Recruit increased numbers for GCSE course 1996/98. Review Year 10 course.
Other	Year 11 Seven Sisters visit. Year 8 farm visits. Head of department commences MA.	Year 12 Earth Surface Pro. Ctr. Year 8 Manufacturing Industry Year 9 environ. visit.	Year 8 rivers/Year 10 Seven Sisters. Year 11+12 res. fieldwork. Year 11/12 Channel Tunnel.

Table 5.2: contd

AREA	1996 Autumn term	1997 Spring term	1997 Summer term
Curriculum	Year 11 coursework: folio 3. Year 11 geographical enquiry. Timetable fully blocked (Years 8 and 9).	Evaluate GCSE coursework. Revision sheet for new courses.	First 'decision-making exercise'. First MEG 3 examination. Adapt Year 9 programme in the light of changes to sub-programme.
Resources	Purchase of fieldwork equipment.	Ensure efficiency of filing system – review.	Identify textbook condition and bid for future purchase.
Management	Full computerisation of assessment. Department policy evaluation.	Full knowledge for pupils as to how assessed. Market new 'assessment culture'. Second in department to take greater role in unit revision and at A-level. Senior in department to lead field trips.	Evaluate KS 3 and GCSE course and report.
Other	Year 8 farm visits (inc. dairy). Full fieldwork programme.	Year 12 Earth SPP. Year 8 man. industry. Year 9 Geo. Museum.	Fieldwork as 1996. Senior in dept will lead as part of continuing professional development.

(*Source:* Blandford, 1997, Table 7.2, pp. 148–9)

Hargreaves (1995, p. 224) concludes:

The unequivocal duty of the [...] senior management team is to assume oversight of the school's monitoring [...] systems.

This will be discussed in Chapter 10.

Resource process

In the context of resource management, planning is the systematic determination of future resource allocation (Guthrie *et al.*, 1988):

[...] a financial plan translates intentions into resource allocation that reflects the school's priorities.

CIPFA (1988, pp. 27–45) provides a summary of the key factors influencing resource management planning:

- **Demography** – pupil numbers, changes in population levels.
- **Neighbouring schools** – pupils' and parents' choice – the relationship between schools may be co-operative or competitive. There are benefits to be gained from collaboration.
- **Pupil destinations** – statistics on where pupils go when leaving school: school, college or employment.
- **External policies and guidelines** – central government, LEA and, for Voluntary Aided schools, the Diocesan (clergy), and with GM schools the Funding Agency for Schools (FAS) – schools need to be clear whether guidelines are mandatory or advisory.
- **Other major changes** – resource managers should consider whether there are other factors involved.

Figure 5.6 represents the resource allocation model designed by the American National Policy Board for Educational Administration (NPBEA). As the figure indicates, the planning process does not happen in a vacuum. It is important to consider external and internal factors. The NPBEA model illustrates the position of resource management in the planning process. The first step in the resource allocation process involves governors, headteachers and senior managers (resource managers) to determine procedures and means to meet predetermined needs and goals for a specified time period. The process is described as follows:

Procurement

Resource managers need to identify what specific resources are needed and how the fiscal, personal and material resources can be obtained. The amount, type and quality of resources will vary according to the management's skill in identifying and obtaining the resources.

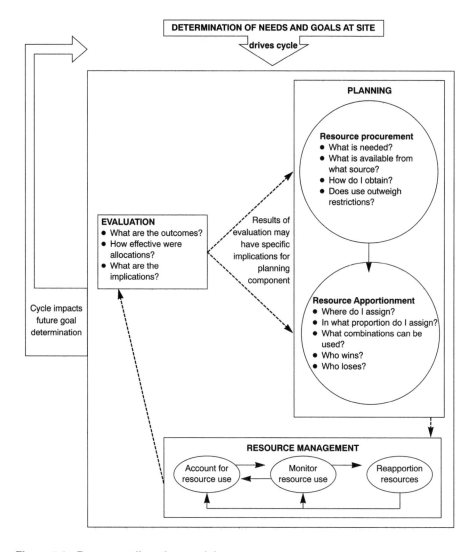

Figure 5.6: Resource allocation model
(*Source:* NPBEA, 1993, p. 13–7; reproduced by permission of the publisher, National Policy Board for Educational Administration, Virginia, USA)

Apportionment

According to Guthrie *et al.* (1988, p. 216):

> *Budgets are the financial crystallisation of an organisation's intentions. It is through budgeting that decisions are made about how to allocate resources to achieve goals.*

At this stage, resource managers need to work with the finance subcommittee and budget holders in order to determine and assign resources to the appropriate areas. Questions will need to be answered such as:

- How much?
- What combinations are optional?
- Who gains?
- Who loses?

Management

During this phase, resource managers need to:

- account for procured and apportioned resources
- monitor resource arrival, resource use, resource storage and retrieval
- reapportion unused or under-used resources during the school year.

In addition, appointments should be reflected in budget documents. All aspects of resource management will require supplementary documents, schedules and procedures.

Linking plans to budgets

Knight (1993, pp. 35–7) states:

Producing a plan for the school is one thing. Actually linking it to the budget is another. This linkage is technically quite difficult for various reasons.

These include timescales, integration of different elements, constraints and development. As Knight (1993, p. 36) explains: 'SDPs need a long time horizon [...] a budget only covers twelve months.' The non-coincidence of academic and financial years can be problematic, as shown in Figure 5.7.

Knight's (1993, p. 35) solution to this non-coincidence of academic and financial years is to think of a plan comprising:

- *a long-term strategy, say 4–5 years*
- *a medium-term strategy, say 1–3 years*
- *operational planning for the current school year and the start of the next one, i.e. 0–1 year.*

Knight suggests that only operational planning needs to be linked to the budget. Resource managers need to be aware of potential difficulties arising from the non-coincidence of academic and financial years. It is critical that

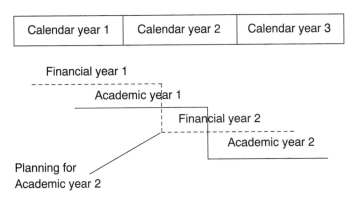

| Calendar year 1 | Calendar year 2 | Calendar year 3 |

Financial year 1

Academic year 1

Financial year 2

Academic year 2

Planning for
Academic year 2

Figure 5.7: Non-coincidence of academic and financial years
(*Source:* Knight, 1993, p. 36; reproduced by permission of the publisher, Heinemann Educational Publishers)

resource managers work with school managers, governors, funding agencies, the LEA and the local community to resolve such problems.

Administration

Resource managers need to plan their own work. In practice, resource managers need to understand administrative processes if they are to operate effectively as managers and teachers in a school. The suggestions shown in Table 5.3 will help resource managers plan their response to the daily flow of paper placed in their 'in-trays'.

The following suggestions will also help:

1 **Diary.** Keep an up-to-date diary in which you identify busy periods during the term; aim to prioritise.
2 **Filing cabinet.** Always file away information. Check through files regularly discarding any out-of-date or irrelevant information. You may need to obtain a filing cabinet for your classroom/office.
3 **Computer.** Use and develop your computer skills. Preparing responses/reports in advance saves time. Keep a catalogue of programs and files for easy reference.
4 **Folder – current.** A useful 'litmus test' for each document is to create a 'current' folder which you will refer to several times throughout the day. If a document is not relevant it can be filed away.
5 **Things to do.** Add documentation to your daily 'things to do' list; where possible complete all responses in advance of the date requested.

6 **Team – delegation.** There may be a specific area of work in which a team member has an interest. Develop his/her skills in this area and delegate some of your paperwork.

7 **Reading.** When reading documentation, highlight key words and points of action. This avoids unnecessary reading and could provide the framework for your written response.

8 **Response.** When responding to a document ensure that your points are relevant and relate to specific areas of the document (*see* section on 'Communication' in Chapter 4 for further advice).

9 **Keep a copy!** Always keep a copy of responses, filed with related documentation.

Resource managers will need to keep all aspects of their work well documented.

Table 5.3: Documentation action plan

Category	Responses	Paper	Consultation (List who to contact)	Action
A	Within 24 hrs	Resource/budget matters requiring immediate response	Headteacher, staff, external agencies	Read and write
B	Within 48 hrs	External agencies, governors, senior management papers	Senior management team, staff	Meetings: read and write
C	Within 1 week	Meetings/agendas/reports – dept/school/LEA	LEA/governor/ senior management team	Meetings: read and write
D	Within 2 weeks	Report	Government/ SMT	Read and write
E	Within 1 month	Documentation not requiring a response, but could be useful at a later date		Read only/ research

Summary

If schools are to be effective, resource management has to be planned. Knowledge and understanding of the planning process is therefore central to resource management. Planning is a messy, repetitive and confusing aspect of a manager's life (Blandford, 1997). In resource management the critical element, finance, is not static. In addition, human resources and material resources are factors in the framework for resource management planning that change on a daily basis. Therefore the parameters for resource management, in practice, are identifiable but changing.

Consistency in resource management can be determined through strategic planning and operational planning. A strategy is a broad statement which relates to the overall approach and direction of the school towards the achievement of its mission. Developing and maintaining a strategy involves establishing a framework within which an operational plan can take place (Blandford, 1997).

Vision and mission statements are critical to the effectiveness of strategic and operational plans. A vision moves an organisation forward from where it is now to where it would like to be. A precise goal is more credible than a vague dream. If a school is to be successful, it has to be effective. A measure of a school's effectiveness is the ability of the staff to work towards achieving the school's vision, i.e. working towards a shared set of values and beliefs. The vision statement should be succinct and should contain, within a few words, the philosophy underlying the professional practice within the school. A genuinely *good* school with characteristics of openness and trust, shared values and beliefs, will be an effective school.

Strategic planning in all schools will occur annually through the school development plan. The value of a school development plan (SDP) as an operational tool will rest with the senior management team. Within the content of the SDP, vision, mission and aims can be achieved. Having determined the school development plan managers need to consider how the plan will be put into operation. Operational planning is about tables and targets: who does what, when and how. Operational planning is detailed. It aims to achieve a particular set of objectives within a given time.

An SDP encompasses national, LEA and school initiatives, providing schools with a framework for strategic planning. The SDP will identify existing achievements and needs for development. Each school's aims – vision and mission – will be stated and reflected at every stage of the plan. The SDP enables schools to manage themselves in an effective, coherent manner within both local and national contexts.

The main purpose of an SDP should be to improve the quality of learning for pupils. In practice, all management activities should relate to the SDP if they are to have a central role in school life. Once the SDP has been completed, detailed action plans can be drawn up. This involves managers and staff deciding on the way forward to implement the SDP. Action plans are a means of operationalising the strategy.

A department development plan is similar to the school development plan. The DDP should reflect the aims of the SDP and provide an operational framework for implementing the action plans emanating from the SDP. If it is to be effective, the department development plan should be placed in the context of the school, LEA and national planning (Blandford, 1997).

Resource managers need to plan their own work. In practice, resource managers need to understand administrative processes if they are to operate effectively as managers and teachers in a school.

6

■ ■ ■

Priorities

Introduction

Determining priorities is central to resource management. Resource managers, as members of the senior management team and as advisors to the governing body finance subcommittee, need to consider the impact of their management decisions on classroom practitioners and pupil learning. Resource management in schools affects the learning process and this chapter focuses on the priorities that influence that resource management. Government reforms reflected clear priorities for education which aimed to raise standards in schools.

Key principles included:

1 Each school should take responsibility for achieving high standards, and should account for its performance to parents and the local community against the standards set by the National Curriculum. It should set targets for improvement and review its performance against them annually.

2 Within that framework, schools should have as much freedom as possible to make their own decisions, spend their own budgets, and plan their own futures.

3 Schools should use this freedom to build on their distinctive strengths, responding to the needs and wishes of local parents to provide more choice and diversity.

4 That will give a better match between what schools offer and what parents want – which is a good education suited to their child's individual abilities, interests, needs and ambitions.

In practice, headteachers aim to raise standards as appropriate to their pupils' needs. As shown in the previous chapter, school development plans are designed to ensure that resources are available for schools to function according to the needs and wishes of the pupils, parents and local community.

Many headteachers and their management teams are limited by a lack of funding.

Headteachers, governors and resource managers need to prioritise within the budget, allocated according to central and local government policies. This suggests that plans for school budgets should be (LMS Initiative, 1990, p. 31):

primarily a 'bottom-up' process [. . .]. Those responsible for the various activities are likely to have ideas and suggestions as to how they could be improved and/or extended. What is required from the 'top down' is guidance to provide the framework within which proposals can be developed. This needs to cover at least seven elements:

- *Objectives;*
- *Background information;*
- *Analysis of strengths and weaknesses;*
- *Plan development plans;*
- *Parameters for plans;*
- *Likely level of resources;*
- *Priorities.*

In practice, school income expenditure is not static; there are few items on the budget which are totally fixed. Budget priorities will fall into one of two categories: revenue or capital costs. Revenue costs encompass staff, materials and administration. Capital costs encompass premises-related expenditure. Knight *et al.* (1993, pp. 56–7) define fixed costs as those which are not triggered by pupil numbers. These include:

- deputy heads' salaries
- discretionary (bonus)
- support staff salaries
- building repairs and maintenance
- cleaning
- grounds maintenance
- furniture and fittings.

Variable costs, determined by changing factors and triggered by pupil numbers, include:

- basic teacher salaries
- teacher support salaries
- advertising and other establishment expenses, and INSET
- water, if metered

110

- books, stationery and materials
- insurance and other services with charges relating to pupil numbers.

As shown, the budgetary process is the responsibility of the finance sub-committee, a subcommittee of the governing body and the headteacher. The LEA allocates funds (school budget) to the school; the finance subcommittee then decides on the distribution of those funds. The process of distribution is often based on previous expenditure under headings prescribed by each LEA scheme for the allocation of funds within each school:

1 employees
2 capitation
3 premises
4 contingency
5 transport expenses
6 client receipts
7 supply and services.

Within this process the finance subcommittees, headteachers and resource managers will have to determine priorities for their schools. As the LMS Initiative (1990, pp. 34–5) comments, school budgets can be defined in the context of available time and space. Under the ERA, governors have greater discretion over the length and timing of school sessions and can consider flexibility and new approaches in the plans. However, irrespective of available finances, members of staff can only work a certain number of hours per week. Equally there is only so much that can happen in a school day. All activities require space, therefore plans should include an indication of the space required in order to avoid double booking of rooms and other facilities. Priorities should be known. Resource managers need to indicate to budget holders the criteria against which proposals requiring additional funding will be judged.

Staff

The headteacher, governing body and resource manager each have a significant role in all employment matters. The most important aspect of a school's spending is its teaching costs, typically 65–90 per cent of the total school budget. Staff-related costs include the management, administration and employment of:

1 teaching staff
2 non-teaching staff
3 transport-related expenditure

4   agency (contracted) services

5   central administration.

Savings may arise from actual or expected vacancies but any vacancy should be considered against supply cover costs. Staff turnover may lead either to a saving or to higher expenditure. In addition, part-time and overtime costs will be difficult to estimate. Whatever the budget for full-time, part-time, supply cover or vacancies, this should be closely monitored. LEAs may include peripatetic and advisory teachers in the delegated budget. Governors need to prioritise according to the needs of pupils and staff. Estimated costs should be included in the school budget.

A Guide to the Law for Governors (DFE, 1993) clearly states the need for an open whole-school pay policy which has been written in full consultation with staff. Knight *et al.* (1993, p. 86) explain that relevant bodies can:

- *decide at which point within the range to pay head and deputies or to pay above the range if they wish*

- *decide how many, or if any, teachers shall be paid at deputy head salary*

- *decide how many teachers they will employ*

- *decide what level and length of experience outside teaching is to be counted as qualifying for points*

- *decide whether [. . .] a teacher shall be awarded a point for each year of service to the school and whether to withhold points for unsatisfactory service*

- *decide the number of points to award for responsibility*

- *award up to three points for excellence in the classroom, subject to annual review*

- *award up to two points to holders of posts difficult to fill or in order to retain the post holder (but this situation must be reviewed every two years)*

- *award an extra point for qualifications in SEN and can also reward other expertise in the teaching of SEN pupils.*

As Knight *et al.* (1993, pp. 86–7) conclude, there is under-use of pay discretions by relevant bodies. However, the most serious constraint on the use of salary discretion is the size of the school budget share. Further, Knight *et al.* (p. 87) comment:

Employment law and redundancy procedures are an important consideration and over the past few years many schools have solved budget problems by adjusting the number of teachers employed.

Resource managers need to be aware of the above and that each member of the teaching staff must be provided with an individual salary assessment together with a job description. Maychell (1994, pp. 11–34) identified some of the main considerations that influence staffing decisions, as discussed below.

Pupil–teacher ratios

The NFER study (NFER, 1994) found that in primary schools pupil–teacher ratios (PTRs) increased both before and after the ERA. The same pattern existed in secondary schools. Existing data for primary and secondary schools does not suggest a link between increasing PTRs and LMS. The study commented that headteachers felt that having a delegated budget gave them only the potential to adjust PTRs. Critically, Fletcher-Campbell (NFER, 1994) found that secondary school headteachers were adjusting class sizes in some subject areas, e.g. maths, science and English. It is axiomatic that as the financial situation has become more constrained, pupil–teacher ratios have increased. This is illustrated in Table 6.1. Levačić (1995, pp. 140–1) concludes:

> In 1994–5, LEA education budgets were further squeezed by failure to raise Standing Spending Assessments in line with teacher pay awards [. . .]. The net impact of changes in the level of funding on schools' real resources and the resulting decisions has been rising pupil–teacher ratios and average class sizes.

Table 6.1: Changes in pupil–teacher ratios and average class size since introduction of local management

	Pupil–teacher ratios		Average class size		Primary classes with 31–35 pupils (%)
	Primary	Secondary	Primary	Secondary	
1989	22.0	15.3	26.1	20.6	16.8
1990	22.0	15.3	26.4	20.7	17.5
1991	22.2	15.5	26.8	21.0	18.9
1992	22.2	15.8	26.7	21.2	18.7
1993	22.4	16.1	27.0	21.4	19.9

(*Source:* DFE, 1994; Crown copyright)

Davies and Braund (1989, p. 40) state that this highlights the debate concerning efficiency and effectiveness within schools:

> In seeking efficiency schools may become concerned with delivering the same education at less expense, while effectiveness would seek to achieve a high quality of education provision.

One headteacher's response to her own staffing crisis is to work for nothing, maintaining low PTRs by paying her deputy headteacher half salary and herself no salary (Spencer, 1996, p. 3). Alternatively budget deficits can be met by increasing pupil numbers while reducing staff costs. Dean (1996c, p. 2) describes:

> A grant-maintained grammar school for girls [. . .] has gone £100,000 into the red. The high school will admit extra pupils from September while three of its 52-strong staff take early retirement in an attempt to alleviate the shortfall.

This may not be feasible for the majority of schools, as 100 headteachers responding to a TES survey (TES Survey, 1996, p. 6) reported teachers were regularly taking classes of more than 35 children. Increased PTRs do not enhance the effectiveness of teaching and learning in schools. The paradox of the ERA is that while LMS provides headteachers with the opportunity to offer a wide range of choices in relation to staffing costs, they have to meet the National Curriculum requirements.

Staff mix

In most cases, school budget formulae are calculated by *average* rather than *actual* staff costs. Small schools are an exception; budgets are calculated according to the number of staff required to deliver the National Curriculum. Schools with a majority of staff at or near the top of the pay scale therefore have difficulties as staff costs exceed their budget. As Maychell (1990, p. 17) found:

> The Audit Commission [1993, p. 7] reported that there had been an increase in the proportion of teachers at the top of the pay scale, from 50 percent of the teaching force in 1990, to over 70 percent in 1992.

A more recent concern – *wage drift* – has been identified by Elliott and Duffus (1996, pp. 51–85). In brief, wage drift is the difference between the percentage increase awarded each year by the Teachers' Pay Review Body and the actual salary increase received. Governors, who now have a large share of the responsibility for determining teachers' pay, should ensure that what teachers are paid over and above the amount determined by the Teachers' Pay Review Body is properly accounted for and managed. Elliott and Duffus (p. 3) advise:

> If money does not come from the Government or local education authorities, it is not unreasonable to forecast that the outcome will be better paid but fewer teachers responsible for larger classes.

The cost of teachers' incentive payments

Beyond provision, headteachers will also face similar difficulties with incentive allowances, extra payments given to teachers who:

- have extra responsibilities
- are outstanding classroom teachers
- teach a subject where there is a shortage of teachers
- work in a post which is difficult to fill.

The governing body has discretionary powers on how incentive allowances are to be used within a school. However, the governing body should stay within the parameters set by the DFE in *A Guide to the Law for Governors* (DFE, 1993). In practice, the overriding problem is that there is a budget constraint which makes it difficult for governing bodies to award incentive allowances.

Non-contact time

Resource managers need to be aware of alternative methods of creating additional funding. As an example, Knight (1993, p. 162) found that staff deployment can be changed:

> [...] a school with ten classes will need the following number of teachers:
>
> 10.0 working at 100 per cent contact time
>
> 11.1 working at 90 per cent contact time
>
> 11.8 working at 85 per cent contact time
>
> 12.5 working at 80 per cent contact time
>
> 13.3 working at 75 per cent contact time
>
> 14.3 working at 70 per cent contact time.

Maychell (1994, pp. 19–34) found that if teacher non-contact time is increased, senior managers have their non-contact time reduced or the school needs to employ extra teachers. However, this has to be managed carefully as non-contact time is a highly valued commodity in all schools.

Supply cover

The cost of the teaching staff budget is also affected by arrangements schools make for supply cover (Maychell, 1994, pp. 20–1). Nightingale (1990) indicated that this aspect of the staff budget is problematic.

LEAs have discretionary powers over supply cover. Resource managers need to be aware of the key pitfall, i.e. paying for the same post twice. In large schools (Davies and Braund, 1989, p. 42) it may be possible to cover absences internally. LEAs' advice and practice varies.

The LMS Initiative (1990, p. 55) indicates the possibility of planning for absences, e.g. INSET, and for the unexpected, e.g., sickness. Schools and the LEA should list suitable supply teachers and their availability. Schools should budget for the possibility of long-term absences, e.g. staff may wish to be seconded in order to develop their careers. Resource managers should consider the possibility of budgeting for short- and long-term staff absences for this purpose.

Governors will also determine whether teachers who have public duties can have leave of absence. Schools should be careful about setting precedents. A more cautious route would be to adopt existing LEA practice. LEAs should provide adequate insurance for such situations.

Part-time staff and temporary contracts

On-costs for part-time staff may exceed the full-time equivalent. Resource managers need to consider the position of part-time staff within the budget.

Part-time staff also need to be informed of their conditions of employment. The NFER study (NFER, 1994) found that the number of staff on temporary contracts had increased since LMS. Maychell (1994, p. 24) commented:

> *By employing some teachers on temporary contracts, schools can save money and also give themselves more flexibility, allowing a quicker response to a change in circumstances, such as a fall in pupil numbers or a cut in the budget.*

Non-teaching Staff

Appointments for non-teaching staff are very similar to teaching staff. Appointments of non-teaching staff are made by governors; when a new post has been created it is up to the governing body to decide the level or grade for the new position.

Support Staff

There has been an increase in support staff since LMS. Maychell (1994, p. 26) found that this was because of the increasing demands on teachers' time and the perceived benefit to pupils in having an extra adult in the classroom to provide help and support.

Administrative Staff

Davies and Braund (1989, p. 43) advised that LMS would allow budget holders in schools to increase administrative support for their area. Maychell (1994, pp. 36–9) found that there was a significant increase in the number of office staff since LMS. The increase in office administrative staff hours corresponds to the size of the school.

Caretaker and Maintenance Staff

The position of the caretaker may be problematic. Under the 1988 Local Government Act, caretakers who are engaged for more than 50 per cent of their time on a defined activity, e.g. school cleaning, are required to be part of competitive tendering arrangements. This position still applies if the LEA wins the contract or if schools use their own staff.

In addition, caretakers and manual workers (maintenance and cleaning) can be paid bonuses depending upon productivity agreements. Caretakers may also receive overtime payments when required to open/close the school in the evening or at weekends when non-school activities take place. Resource managers have to make an assessment of the likely bonuses (and overtime) when drawing up their budget, as the LMS Initiative (1990, p. 57) comments:

> *For budgeting purposes, the preparation of a budget for cleaners and grounds maintenance staff will only be necessary if the school provides the services 'in-house'. Otherwise a budget would be required within the premises expenditure category and, if provision has been delegated, the cost would be the contract price.*

Resource managers have responsibility for ensuring value for money and should, therefore, consider competitive tenders for non-teaching work in schools.

School Meals Staff

The question of school meals provision is difficult as LEAs have discretionary powers of whether to delegate responsibility. If schools decide to provide a school meals service at the same or lower cost as the LEA, the responsibility must be delegated. Resource managers will then need to budget for the provision including preparation of staffing budgets.

Circular 7/88 (DES, 1988b) indicates that LEAs are bound to delegate the budget for lunchtime supervision as a separate element of the school meals service. A possible means of increasing effectiveness of the service is to decrease the length of lunchtime breaks. The cost of free meals to teaching staff who volunteer for lunchtime supervision also falls within the delegated budget.

Supplies and Services

Supplies and services currently within the Potential Schools Budget are:

1 books
2 stationery
3 apparatus and equipment
4 postage
5 office expenses
6 telephones
7 examination fees
8 hired and contracted services
9 clothing and footwear
10 board and lodging
11 maintenance allowances
12 insurance (central provision under LEA)
13 administrative costs of governing bodies.

The above is similar to capitation, although resource managers need to prepare their own budgets. Resource managers need to assess the priorities for this area of the budget against other resource claims and National Curriculum requirements. This may prove problematic as there is increasing pressure on funding for all supplies and services.

Research by the Book Trust charity, reported in the TES (21 June 1996, p. 7), suggests that primary schools in England, Wales and Scotland are spending less than a third of the amount necessary for adequate coverage of the National Curriculum. Secondary schools are spending less than half the amount the Book Trust believes is needed to ensure an adequate supply of books. The Book Trust recommends that primary governors budget for £45 per pupil. They conclude:

There are clearly schools with inadequate expectations as to their book needs [. . .] such schools must place a higher priority on books as a vital and cost effective resource for learning.

Premises

Under LMS, the LEA remains the owner of the premises of maintained schools. Many LEAs have therefore decided not to delegate responsibility for structural repairs and maintenance. Two factors influence the school budget:

1   whether responsibility for structural repairs and maintenance has been delegated under the LEA scheme
2   contract arrangements (LEA) for school cleaning and grounds maintenance.

Resource managers should prepare two budgets – one for routine small-scale maintenance and one for decoration. The LEA will be able to provide advice for major works, as will private firms of architects and surveyors. An important link between the school and LEA will be the clerk to the governors, paid to service the governing body. Governors should select their own clerk and budget accordingly. Resource managers need to manage the following premises-related expenses, currently within the Potential Schools Budget:

1   repairs, alterations and maintenance of buildings, plant, fixed equipment
2   maintenance of grounds
3   school cleaning
4   energy costs
5   rents
6   rates
7   water services
8   fixtures and fittings
9   cleaning and domestic supplies
10   premises insurance.

Insurance

In brief, all LEAs are required within their LMS schemes to make central provision for the insurance of governors in all schools against potential liability incurred in the exercise of their responsibilities.

Generally, LEAs will provide advice about insurance for schools through a buildings advisory service. As landlord, the LEA may also wish to undertake inspections for its own purposes, as it has a duty to ensure that the school has sustainable plans for carrying out its tenant responsibilities. This is an area of concern for LEAs, governors and resource managers. It is necessary to determine who is responsible for:

- premises (fire and damage)
- contents (including hired equipment)
- building work on site
- public liability including:
    - illness caused to pupils
    - pupils on school visits
    - any goods produced by the school and sold to raise funds (check tax position too)
    - employer's liability
    - legal expenses
- fraud
- work experience
- loss of income from lettings
- pupil injury (including sports activities)
- personal effects (including cars used by the staff in the course of their duties or necessarily parked on school premises).

Resource managers are responsible for all aspects of insurance – public liability, performances, buildings and staff. Insurance policies should be checked and expert advice sought from LEA officers as appropriate.

Compulsory Competitive Tendering

LMS brought real benefits to teachers and pupils by improving the working environment through (Moisan, 1990, p. 57):

- *rapid and cost-effective minor repairs*
- *the implementation of effective energy-saving procedures*

- *targeting development funds on school-based priorities*
- *the engagement of supply teachers by schools direct.*

Having determined a school's priorities, resource managers must take the lowest bid for service contracts; where small schools only employ three or fewer full-time staff, compulsory competitive tendering (CCT) does not apply. As Knight *et al.* (1993, p. 97) explain:

> *CCT was introduced in order to allow private companies to bid for work which was traditionally carried out by employees of the local authority and to allow schools with delegated budgets the freedom to draw up their own specifications for certain work in order to obtain value for money.*

> *School cleaning, meals, grounds maintenance, vehicle repair and servicing are all defined activities under the terms of s. 2 of the Local Government Act 1988, and as such are subject to competitive tendering legislation.*

As LMS/GMS were introduced, contracts for specific activities were placed by the LEA, which then decides which would be available for renewal. At the point when contracts are due to be renewed several options are available to the school (Knight *et al.*, 1993, pp. 97–8):

1   *It can continue to participate in the next LEA contract which is subject to CCT legislation.*

2   *It can organise its own contract, which can be done in one of three ways:*

(a) *by setting up its own 'in-house' direct service organisation (DSO) (schools should ensure that the client role is kept totally separate from that of a contractor)*

(b) *by inviting tenders from various contractors, including the DSO of the LEA*

(c) *by dealing directly with private contractors.*

Cost and quality are important considerations when making decisions about services. Time is also a primary consideration. How much time is available to the resource manager for premises maintenance and repair? Maychell (1994, p. 49) lists further considerations:

- *How much can the school afford to pay?*
- *What were the relative costs of different service options in relation to the benefits of the options?*
- *Could savings be made if the school changed its existing service arrangements?*
- *Could the school afford to take a risk, i.e. did it have a contingency fund to draw on if the new arrangements proved unsatisfactory?*
- *Were there any services that the school could do without?*
- *Could any of the services be met from its existing staff resources?*

Resource managers should note that the school (Knight *et al.*, 1993, pp. 98–9):

- *must comply with the LEA regulations and standing orders on tendering*
- *must manage the contract during its duration*
- *must accept the financial outcomes*
- *cannot then ask the LEA to do the work (if things go wrong) until the LEA contract comes up for renewal.*

Figure 6.1 gives a step-by-step guide to compulsory competitive tendering for maintained schools (LMS).

Administration

Schools may be given responsibility for some areas of central administration. The service agreement between schools and LEAs will indicate the level of support available from local authority solicitors, accountants or other offices. Equally schools may wish to consider the use of private providers. Some LEAs will retain funds, thereby restricting competition as these are technically discretionary items. In addition, transfer payments may be delegated to schools at the discretion of the LEA, including pupil support, i.e. board and lodgings, clothing and footwear, and maintenance allowances. The need for this provision will vary from school to school. The issue of pupil support is a complex area and schools may seek advice from their LEA on this matter.

Additional factors

LEAs use contingencies and reserves to cover pay and price increases. Schools will need to apportion sufficient resources to cover unforeseen happenings, e.g. replacing broken equipment or unplanned repairs to premises.

Inflation should also be considered, although this is included in the LEA's General Schools Budget (GSB). Finally, as described in Chapter 12, schools are able to add to their income through:

- charges for services to pupils
- lettings
- fund-raising.

Summary

Determining priorities is central to resource management. Resource managers, as members of the senior management team and as advisors to the governing

1 School decides to stay with LEA contract (CCT applies)	
School	**LEA**
• Accepts or modifies draft specification. • Decides whom to include in list of contractors. • Checks list of contractors. • Decides which personnel will work at the school.	• Consults school on level of service, i.e. draft specification. • Draws up specification and contract. • Draws up list of contractors. • Invites tenders and awards contract. • Monitors and administers the contract.

2(a) School decides to set up its own DSO (CCT applies) In this case the school has a dual role.	
School	**DSO**
• Sets up DSO. • Prepares specification and contract (expert advice may be needed). • Draws up list of contractors from approved list. • Invites tenders and awards contracts. • Monitors and administers the contract. NB: Problems could arise if, in future years, the school DSO fails to win the contract.	• Prepares tender. • Operates contract if awarded.

2(b) School invites tenders from contractors, including the LEA and DSO (DSO bound by LEA tendering regulations and standing orders.)
School
• Prepares specification and contract (expert advice may be needed). • Draws up list of contractors. • Invites tenders and awards contract. • Monitors and administers the contract.

2(c) School decides on private contractor (CCT does not apply.)

Figure 6.1: Step-by-step guide to CCT for maintained schools
(*Source:* Knight *et al.*, 1993, pp. 99–100)

body finance subcommittee, need to consider the impact of their management decisions on classroom practitioners and pupil learning. Resource management in schools affects the learning process. In practice, headteachers aim to raise standards as appropriate to their pupils' needs.

In practice, school income expenditure is not static; there are few items on the budget which are totally fixed. Budget priorities will fall into one of two categories: revenue or capital costs. Revenue costs encompass staff, materials and administration. Capital costs encompass premises-related expenditure.

As shown, the budgetary process is the responsibility of the finance sub-committee, a subcommittee of the governing body and the headteacher. The LEA allocates funds (school budget) to the school; the finance subcommittee then decides on their distribution. Within this process the finance sub-committees, headteachers and resource managers will have to determine priorities for their schools. Resource managers need to indicate to budget holders the criteria against which proposals requiring additional funding will be judged.

The headteacher, governing body and resource manager each have a significant role in all employment matters. The most important aspect of a school's spending is its teaching costs, typically 65–90 per cent of the total school budget. Governors need to prioritise according to the needs of pupils and staff. Estimated costs should be included in the school budget. Resource managers need to be aware of the above and that each member of the teaching staff must be provided with an individual salary assessment together with a job description.

Budget deficits can be met by increasing pupil numbers while reducing staff costs. The paradox of the ERA is that while LMS provides headteachers with the opportunity to offer a wide range of choices in relation to staffing costs, they have to consider the National Curriculum requirements and educational requirements of their pupils.

Under LMS, the LEA remains the owner of the premises of maintained schools. Many LEAs have therefore decided not to delegate responsibility for structural repairs and maintenance. Resource managers should prepare two budgets – one for routine small-scale maintenance and one for decoration. Resource managers are responsible for all aspects of insurance – public liability, performances, buildings and staff. Insurance policies should be checked and expert advice sought from LEA officers as appropriate.

Having determined a school's priorities, resource managers must take the lowest bid for service contracts; where small schools only employ three or fewer full-time staff, CCT does not apply. Cost and quality are important considerations when making decisions about services. Time is also a primary consideration.

Schools may be given responsibility for some areas of central administration. The service agreement between schools and LEAs will indicate the level of support available from local authority solicitors, accountants or other offices. Equally schools may wish to consider the use of private providers.

The need for resource managers to prioritise is evident. However, in practice governors and senior management teams have limited resources and conflicting priorities. The paradox of the ERA is that while school leaders have been given the opportunity to manage funds the National Curriculum determines how the funds are allocated. This is in direct contrast to school leadership prior to the ERA when there was no prescribed curriculum and no local management of funds. While the priority of central government is to raise standards school managers remain restricted by prescriptive policies and the need to meet performance targets. If schools are to improve education managers should have greater freedom to allocate resources according to local needs.

7
■ ■ ■

Understanding budgets

The purpose of budgets

The purpose of a budget is to plan ahead in order to achieve objectives and targets. Once a budget is set, a resource manager, budget holder and class teacher can monitor progress towards these objectives and targets. A budget is (Parkinson, 1994, p. 6):

- *a plan for the future*
- *a statement of resources matched to intentions*
- *a practical agenda for action.*

A budget, related to a period of time, is important because:

- *it sets out the targets to be achieved*
- *it defines the activities that are necessary to achieve these targets*
- *it sets out estimates of the required resources*
- *it links our actions to the organisation's longer-term objectives.*

Management is central to budget design. Resource managers define the transformation of resources (material and human) into departmental or school outputs. The financial representation of the operation includes different accounting statements – budgets, projections, cash accounts, operating statements and balance sheets.

This chapter examines several budget design models which may contribute to the effectiveness of school resource management. Planning models are borrowed from business management. As Knight *et al.* (1993, pp. 19–20) explain, *a budget is a multi-purpose management tool adaptable for different purposes.* In detail:

A budget is one of those items which is taken for granted because of its familiarity – it is often seen simply as a statement of planned expenditure against which actual expenditure can be matched. A much wider range of functions have, however, been identified and include the following:

- *planning*
- *forecasting*
- *matching expenditure to income*
- *establishing priorities*
- *comparing the value of alternatives*
- *implementing plans*
- *co-ordinating school activities*
- *allocating resources*
- *authorising expenditure and activities*
- *communicating objectives to personnel*
- *motivating personnel by delegation*
- *controlling expenditure*
- *strengthening accountability*
- *obtaining value for money, economising*
- *matching inputs against outcomes.*

All managers must know and understand the process of designing a budget. Individuals should have an understanding of the financial management of their school. Wider understanding enables class teachers and budget holders to place the operation and resource management of their classrooms and departments in the context of the school as a whole.

It is important for governors, senior managers and resource managers to define the financial values for the school. Managers should then decide on the appropriate place for the financial values of the school. These can only be meaningful when teachers and budget holders understand the vision, mission and aims of the school. Without such understanding it will be difficult for resource managers to determine whether resources are being used effectively or efficiently.

It should always be remembered that it is the aims and priorities of the school which drive the budget. The budget is a translation of these aims and priorities into resources. But aims and priorities cannot be considered in isolation from resources. The budget should be part of a single plan for the school which outlines (LMS Initiative, 1990, p. 24):

- *the aims and values of the school;*
- *what the school is seeking to achieve (its objectives);*
- *activities it intends to pursue in order to achieve these objectives;*
- *the resources and the management and delivery arrangements it intends to use to implement its intentions; and*
- *the monitoring it proposes to use to establish how well it has done.*

In the past, many schools have calculated their capitation budget using an incremental approach. This means that they used the previous year's capitation distribution as a base budget and just altered one or two items (or added a certain percentage). This tended to be a very conservative and cautious approach. Under LMS, when schools have much bigger budgets to control, resource managers need to develop a broader understanding of budget design.

Programme budgeting

Programme budgeting is known in practice as the Planning Programming Budgeting System (PPBS). As Knight *et al.* (1993, p. 23) explain:

It is a very logical approach to budgeting, based upon a trenchant critique of the conventional budgetary system, whereby budgets are built upon a 'line-item' basis, category by category, without any specific linkage to objectives or to an assessment of the extent to which the objectives have been achieved.

Jones and Pendlebury (1996, p. 77) comment:

The advantages [of PPBS] can be summarised as follows:

1 *It provides information on the objectives of the organisation.*

2 *It cuts across conventional lines of responsibility and departmental structures by drawing together the activities that are directed towards a particular objective.*

3 *It exposes programmes that are overlapping or contradictory in terms of achieving objectives.*

4 *It concentrates on long-term effects.*

5 *It provides information on the impact that existing and alternative programmes will have on objectives, and the associated programme costs.*

6 *It enables resource allocation choices to be made on the basis of benefit/cost relationships.*

A facet of the PPBS adopted by schools is programme planning. This involves budgeting by programme:

1 development of an educational plan
2 collection and appraisal of data
3 preliminary expenditure plan
4 preliminary review plan
5 formal budget document
6 adoption of budget
7 administration of budget
8 review and audit.

Resource managers need to begin with the objectives of the organisation in order to create the overall programme structure. The programme structure has to be such that the programmes serving the same objective are grouped together into programme categories. Programme categories are then broken down into specific activities known as programme elements. These costs and benefits are then aggregated to provide a basis for decision-making. A choice can then be made between alternative programmes. A possible PPBS for a school is shown in Figure 7.1.

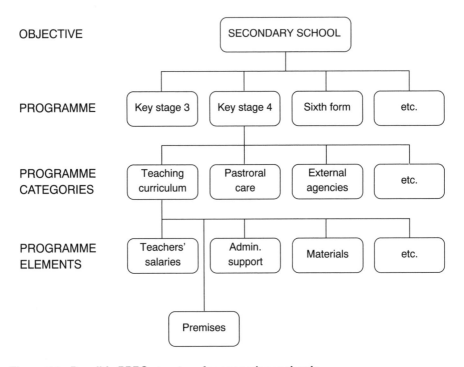

Figure 7.1: Possible PPBS structure for secondary schools

The expenses of each programme element will be presented as a total amount or classified as salaries, materials, services, etc. The budget of each programme category is the sum of the budgets of its programme elements. The programme structure approach to budgeting is therefore a system which relates the expenditure at each stage of the budget to the purpose of the expenditure.

It is possible to subsume all of the above into the SDP. Resource managers need to measure the effect of the budgetary process as determined by the model used for its design and operation. Brockmann (1972) recommends the adoption of PPBS for several reasons:

1   *Programme [planning] reflects an educational plan [. . .].*

2   *Programme planning is holistic rather than incremental.*

3   *Programme planning focuses on the programmes that are new as differentiated from programmes that are continuing [. . .].*

4   *All programmes affect all other programmes in the unit [. . .].*

5   *Incremental budgeting is eliminated [. . .].*

6   *Contingency funds will not be available next year.*

While each of the above is valid in the broader educational context, a change to PPBS may be too radical for some schools. As Knight *et al.* (1993, p. 23) comment:

> *The logic for programme budgeting is very strong and for a time PPBS had a very high profile in the USA. In education it was used extensively by school boards, although not much in schools themselves. However, it had two serious disadvantages:*
>
> - *it was much more time-consuming than the traditional method, with extensive documentation;*
> - *it still needed to be converted into a line-item budget for effective expenditure monitoring and control.*

In practice, public sector resource managers have not applied the PPBS model. A more appropriate method of determining the budgetary process may begin with Brockmann's (1972) basic planning questions:

- *What are we trying to do?*
- *Are there different ways to do it?*
- *How much will it cost to do it?*
- *How can we tell when we have done it?*

Incremental budgeting

In essence, incremental budgeting means basing any year's budget on the previous year's actual or budgeted figures, together with an allowance for inflation and possibly a deduction to encourage cost reductions (Parkinson, 1994, pp. 25–26). Incremental budgeting has the advantage of being relatively simple to implement. It may be appropriate for schools where activity and resourcing levels change little from year to year. A more negative aspect of incremental budgeting is that the previous year's inefficiencies and imperfections will be carried forward. A possible problem is the adding on of a percentage rather than thinking through the process in a creative way. In business, incremental budgeting is known for lending itself to 'budget games' and the 'hockey stick' effect as described by Parkinson (1994, p. 25):

Playing budget games: If managers know that, particularly in hard times, budget proposals are likely to be cut – say by 10% – then it is not a complete surprise to find that they artificially inflate their budgets for planning and control purposes. [. . .] Some managers identify with budgets on a personal level because a larger budget involving more people and more resources means – at least in their minds – that they will become more important and powerful. This further inflationary factor will destroy the realism of budgets.

Playing hockey: As the end of the financial year approaches, a budget holder [. . .] may find that there is spare money left in the budget and is tempted to spend it without sufficient reason or control. This waste of money can spoil the otherwise good record of the budget holder. This is sometimes termed the 'hockey-stick' effect [. . .;] the curve on the hockey stick may well go either way. You can imagine a budget holder who has to curtail expenditure towards the end of the year. It may be that resources have been used wisely, but circumstances have changed. This can have serious harmful effects upon the activities under the control of the budget holder.

The problems of incremental budgeting can be avoided in the approaches to the management of budgeting systems.

Zero-based budgeting

An alternative to the above is zero-based budgeting (ZBB). As Hartley (1979) states:

> [. . .] the primary purpose of ZBB is to exert a greater control over budgets, requiring justification of every proposed expenditure, beginning theoretically from a base of zero.

Parkinson (1994, p. 26) states:

> Zero-based budgeting starts from the relationship between targets, activities and inputs. Budget holders must ignore their previous budget and concentrate on next year's targets, establishing from first principles the level of resourcing they require. Budget holders should prepare budgets for several different levels of activity, starting at a minimal level, then detailing the extra resourcing required for increases. Resource managers can then determine the appropriate mix of activities that reflect the available resources and their prioritised targets.

All budgeting procedures involve an identification of organisational objectives. In the context of these objectives, zero-based budgeting involves three basic stages as described below.

Identification of decision units

A decision unit should have the following characteristics:

1 *a specific manager should be clearly responsible for the operation of the programme*

2 *it must have well defined and measurable impacts*

3 *it must have well defined and measurable objectives.*

In education the decision unit could be at any of the levels given in Figure 7.2.

Having identified appropriate decision units, the next step is to define the objectives of each.

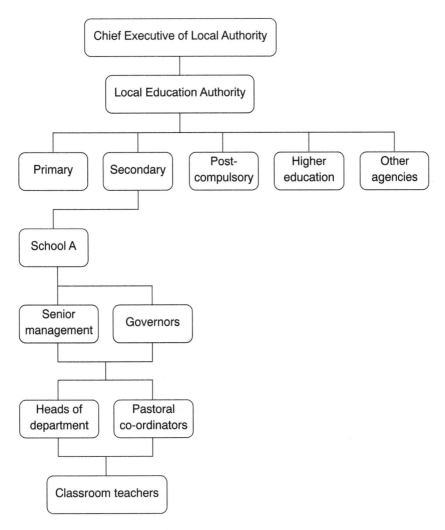

Figure 7.2: Decision units (education)

Development of decision packages

These are intended to identify alternative ways of performing the functions of a decision unit and to determine the effect of different levels of effort on each alternative. This will show that the decision unit manager has considered different ways of undertaking the function, and is in a position, with management, to review the alternatives.

Review and ranking of decision packages

Decision packages are then ranked according to the priorities identified in the school development plan. In the context of formula funding and local management of schools, zero-based budgeting is a device that could help individual schools to determine how best to make use of the cash limited amounts they have been allocated. ZBB is appropriate for schools undergoing rapid change. However, the approach is very time-consuming and, therefore very expensive, as Knight (1993, p. 26) states:

> It is even more time-consuming than PPBS because of its extensive paperwork, and it is also extremely threatening to budget holders. Nowhere do schools currently operate it in its pure form.

The concept of ZBB could be useful if applied to the developmental aspects of the budget. Knight advises that ZBB could also be used very effectively as part of a whole-school review. Zero-based budgeting is also used as an approach to budgeting, a way of thinking of starting from zero which tends not to happen in the incremental budgeting process.

Rolling budgets

Parkinson (1994, p. 26) considers that flexibility should be built into any budgeting system:

> Rolling budgets have emerged from the idea that in day-to-day management there is a relatively short amount of time for decision-making. The situation is the same in the majority of schools at this level, therefore budget holders should not be concerned with the full year ahead. A rolling budget operates within a system whereby the 12-month budget of targets and resources is divided into quarterly periods. This rolling budget approach is referred to in business as budget phasing or profiling.

The advantage of a rolling budget is the degree of flexibility. Resource managers are in a position to divert resources from one part of the school to another without the typical problems of ownership and demotivation found with other budgeting systems. This can be achieved with creative accounting methods – the virement of funds from one heading to another as appropriate. However, high levels of administration are required. Resource managers would have to consider whether the benefits outweigh the costs.

Fixed and flexible budgeting

Fixed and flexible budgeting helps to take account of changes and is particularly useful in measuring performance and in establishing what needs to be done. Business managers talk about fixed and flexible budgets, as Parkinson (1994, pp. 26–7) states:

Fixed budgets: A budget that is designed to remain unchanged, regardless of the level of activity. Fixed budgets are almost useless for assessing performance if the level of activity does change.

Flexible budgets: Flexible budgets (or variable budgets) are designed to show how budgeted figures change with levels of activity. The budget allowance under each heading is revised in the light of the actual level of activity attained. This provides a meaningful comparison for the purposes of cost control between the actual cost and a budget allowance based on the same level of activity.

An example of the application of fixed and variable budgeting is described by Davies and Braund (1989, pp. 29–30) whereby school costs are divided into:

- **Fixed costs** – those that the school has to pay irrespective of the number of pupils on roll, e.g. building maintenance and heating.
- **Variable costs** – those that will increase or decrease according to the number of pupils on roll, e.g. teachers, text and exercise books.

In practice some expenditure would have both fixed and variable elements, e.g. a school caretaker is a fixed cost, overtime is a variable cost. Davies and Braund estimate that, in schools operating at or near their pupil capacity, 70 per cent of expenditure is variable and 30 per cent is fixed, as Figure 7.3 illustrates. Resource managers need to understand which of the school's costs are fixed or variable as this is a useful planning tool. This process would highlight high fixed costs and areas where improvement is necessary. Resource managers need to identify and co-ordinate these factors.

As discussed later (Chapter 11) open enrolments, where parents can choose to which school their children go, and the movement of pupils between schools have a big effect on budgets because pupil numbers determine a school's income.

Cost centres

Knight (1993, p. 15) places variable and fixed costs in the school context. In contrast to Davies and Braund, Knight considers, *in one sense no costs are totally 'fixed'*, as it is not clear who controls costs in schools – central government, governors, headteachers, other agencies. Knight (1993, pp. 1–18) develops the idea of schools as cost centres. In brief:

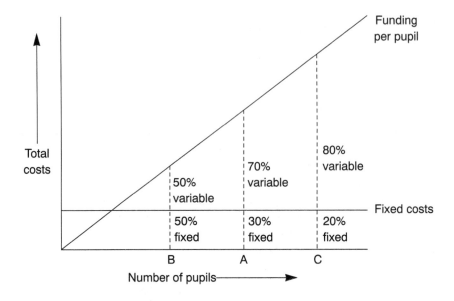

Figure 7.3: Fixed and variable costs
(*Source:* Davies and Braund, 1989, p. 30; reproduced by permission of the publisher, Northcote House Publishers Ltd)

A working definition for 'costs' is:

resources foregone to acquire other human or physical resources to achieve an objective. [. . .] The resources foregone need not be financial.

As Knight explains, resources could be the time, morale, motivation or energy of the members of the school community. However, the inclusion of both financial and non-financial elements within cost centres creates problems. According to John Fielden (1986, p. 3):

Costing is the art of measuring the consumption of resources in financial terms. Contrary to most perceptions there can be a large element of subjectivity in costing exercises. There are often no easy ways of measuring resource use or of converting it in monetary terms, and the person carrying out the costing will therefore have to make assumptions or value judgements.

Full cost accounting refers to the theory that costs are measured at the point where they are consumed. That is, the final amount in full cost accounting takes into account all expenditure from purchase to use. As an example, premises and administrative costs would be included in the amount of funds allocated for the teaching of pupils. This process can be complex, as Knight (1993, p. 11) cautions:

Full cost accounting can lead to wildly fictitious allocations. And recharging is not always appropriate – it can undermine the resourcing of valuable services (e.g. if schools choose not to 'buy' the school library service).

A facet of cost-based budgeting is opportunity cost, where a sum of money is offered to purchase a designated resource and the resource manager uses that amount for a more needy item. As Knight (1993, p. 12) explains:

If the opportunity foregone appears of greater value than the opportunity accepted, then the expenditure is misconceived.

The process of cost-based budgeting centres on cost information. Knight (1993, p. 13) classifies these into *prime* and *subsidiary costs*. Prime costs are those that are required for teachers to teach and pupils to learn. Subsidiary costs are additional to that which is required but are generally part of the school's budget, although in practice the distinction is not clear, as shown in Figure 7.4.

Fundamental to full cost accounting is the process of identifying unit costs; applied to schools, this would be the amount required to educate each pupil (unit):

$$\text{Unit costs} = \frac{\text{Total costs}}{\text{Number of units}}$$

The process involves grouping together units according to areas of income and expenditure. Each area can be audited and comparisons can be made between departments and schools. In addition, costs can be reapportioned as appropriate. In practice the process involves dividing the school into responsibility centres, e.g. subject areas or year groups, for budgeting purposes. Knight (1983, p. 134) states:

In management accounting, responsibility centres have a high place. Under this approach a large organisation divides up its areas of responsibility and traces all costs and revenues to the individual managers responsible.

However, as unit costs represent a static total divided by a static number of units, this may be an inappropriate budgeting method for some schools.

Planning units

The principles of cost centres are transferable to planning units. This approach breaks down the functioning of the school into activities. As a framework for budgets, planning units appear to encompass elements from good business practice. Schools can be divided according to subject departments, year groups or classes. The breakdown should include all school activities, including support services such as maintenance and cleaning.

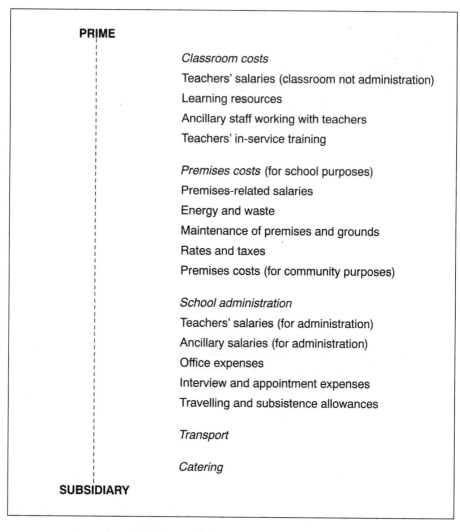

PRIME

Classroom costs

Teachers' salaries (classroom not administration)

Learning resources

Ancillary staff working with teachers

Teachers' in-service training

Premises costs (for school purposes)

Premises-related salaries

Energy and waste

Maintenance of premises and grounds

Rates and taxes

Premises costs (for community purposes)

School administration

Teachers' salaries (for administration)

Ancillary salaries (for administration)

Office expenses

Interview and appointment expenses

Travelling and subsistence allowances

Transport

Catering

SUBSIDIARY

Figure 7.4: Prime and subsidiary costs
(*Source:* Knight, 1993, p. 13; reproduced by permission of the publisher, Heinemann Educational Publishers)

Virement

One advantage of the increased control that schools now have over budgeting is the ability to vire from one budget heading to another. Virement is a term derived from a French word meaning the authorised transfer of surpluses under one heading to make good deficiencies under another. Jones (1995, p. 43) advises:

The key points to note are two-fold.

1   *The overall budget is adhered to: it is a surplus which is being used to make up for a deficiency elsewhere.*

2   *The transfer is authorised [. . .].*

The authorisation to vire may be built into the budget by the government, funding agency, LEA or governing body. In the current climate of devolved budgets virement may be the responsibility of a resource manager. However, as Jones (1995, p. 44) comments:

Observation suggests that this freedom is more preached than practised and that strong central control remains a prominent feature of local government.

At the most senior levels, virement is a political matter. If education is overspending and requires the transfer of funds from other departments, authorisation is needed. The withdrawal of budgetary authority through the reduction of funds from departments is a matter of policy to be settled at Cabinet level. Once authorised, this is virement. Jones and Pendlebury (1996, p. 38) comment:

It is clear from the Treasury manual on government accounting that virement is welcomed. [. . .]. Even so, the Treasury may decide to refuse virement if it feels that the expenditure would:

1   *be on a new service of which Parliament should be aware;*

2   *be novel or contentious;*

3   *arise from a major change of policy;*

4   *be large in relation to the original provision [. . .];*

5   *[. . .] be likely to involve heavy liabilities in later years; or*

6   *involve expenditure on running costs in excess of the department's running cost limit.*

These factors should also be considered at LEA and school level. Resource managers who wish to benefit from the flexibility of virement must seek the authority to do so. No manager should spend outside his/her powers without authorisation. Unauthorised transfers are not virement; these are liable to detection in the auditing process and will probably lead to disciplinary action.

Which budget design?

A budget format should be suited to the organisation's purpose. Resource managers should produce a format which leads budget holders to describe, in detail, what is needed and what is wanted. Different information will be required for different stages of the budget process, as Knight *et al.* (1993, pp. 29–30) state:

[. . .] for the analysis stage you need information about your objectives and your SDP [. . .]; about the alternatives available to you [. . .]; and provisional data on funding, enrolment and other budget factors.

For construction, control and monitoring you need a budget set out in the traditional line-item format. For monitoring and control you need regular progress reports to match actual expenditure against projected expenditure.

The main functions that have been suggested for the annual budget include (Jones and Pendlebury, 1996, p. 53):

1 *determining income and expenditure;*

2 *assisting in policy making and planning;*

3 *authorising future expenditure;*

4 *providing the basis for controlling income and expenditure;*

5 *setting a standard for evaluating performance;*

6 *motivating managers and employees;*

7 *co-ordinating the activities of multi-purpose organisations.*

The above applies to LEAs, schools and departments. Many of the functions are closely related. A budget is important and, for resource managers, it is the most important financial exercise that they undertake.

Planning

Planning is central to the budgeting process, and includes the procurement and apportionment of resources to meet the goals and needs established for the time cycle. Planning models borrowed from business management – PPBS, Programme Evaluation and Review Technique (PERT), zero-based budgeting (ZBB), multi-year costing techniques, forecasting and projection techniques, cost-benefit and cost-effectiveness – may enhance the resource manager's ability to plan for the procurement and apportionment of resources. Hoyle *et al.* (1990) found that successful adaptations of some of these models have resulted in simplified reporting procedures and easy-to-understand budget documents.

As a starting point, a business plan may be appropriate. This is a concept borrowed by the public sector from the private sector. It is a document that is required by a bank from potential borrowers (Jones, 1995, pp. 60–2). There are two points to consider when preparing a business plan:

1 It must be credible – the forecasts must be based on reasonable interpretations of past performance.

2 A new culture is assured for the freedom of its managers.

The business plan in a local government environment is more limited than in the private sector, providing the parameters for both resourcing and delivery of services within which the school or department must operate. The Local Government Management Board (LGMB) (1995) defines a business plan as the *methodology for identifying and matching supply and demand for service*. The LGMB suggests that there are nine stages in the process of developing and implementing a business plan:

1 *Identification of current activities*

2 *Identification of current clients/customers*

3 *Assessment of services currently offered*

4 *Discussion of services to be provided*

5 *Determining the best way of providing services, including a (possibly radical) reappraisal of structures*

6 *Setting objectives*

7 *Monitoring progress*

8 *Marketing*

9 *Taking other considerations into account.*

In practice, the business plan is a financially based document that recognises competition and managerial freedom. In schools, a business plan is also a service-based document with an emphasis on delivery and the overall responsibilities of the whole organisation.

A business plan can continue an old culture, not releasing managers from past pressures to develop future strategies. Resource managers must be able to develop a budget that reflects present and future staffing and premises requirements. Resource managers must also acknowledge government legislation, LEA policy and school policies. Resource managers should also have the skills to assess staff and community needs and to develop marketing and public relations programmes. In addition, resource managers need to be able to access computer support systems. Critically, resource managers need to develop strategies for enhancing interpersonal relationships.

In America, the National Policy Board for Educational Administration (NPBEA, 1993, pp. 13–9 to 13–10) summarises the effective measures to be taken by resource managers when preparing a budget. These include surveying historical, current and future demographic data for the school site, incorporating needs assessments into project planning, establishing a system for prioritising competing claims for resources and using project planning charts.

In sum, resource managers should develop marketing strategies and create a planning cycle for the purchase and replacement of materials and equipment. Resource managers should consider internal and external sources of funding, personnel and material acquisition. They should also follow LEA procedures relative to building improvements when developing building and staffing plans.

Summary

The purpose of a budget is to plan ahead in order to achieve objectives and targets. Once a budget is set, a resource manager, budget holder and class teacher can monitor progress towards these objectives and targets.

Management is central to budget design. Resource managers define the transformation of resources (material and human) into departmental or school outputs. The financial representation of the operation includes different accounting statements – budgets, projections, cash accounts, operating statements and balance sheets.

All managers must know and understand the process of designing a budget. Individuals should have an understanding of the financial management of their school. Wider understanding enables class teachers and budget holders to place the operation and resource management of their classrooms and departments in the context of the school as a whole.

It should always be remembered that it is the aims and priorities of the school which drive the budget. The budget is a translation of these aims and priorities into resources. But aims and priorities cannot be considered in isolation from resources.

Programme budgeting is known in practice as the Planning Programming Budgeting System (PPBS). A facet of the PPBS adopted by schools is programme planning. Resource managers need to begin with the objectives of the organisation in order to create the overall programme structure. The programme structure has to be such that the programmes serving the same objective are grouped together into programme categories.

It is possible to subsume all of the above into the school development plan (SDP). Resource managers need to measure the effect of the budgetary process as determined by the model used for its design and operation. In practice, public sector resource managers have not applied the PPBS model. A more appropriate method of determining the budgetary process may begin with Brockmann's (1972) basic planning questions:

- *What are we trying to do?*
- *Are there different ways to do it?*
- *How much will it cost to do it?*
- *How can we tell when we have done it?*

In essence, incremental budgeting means basing any year's budget on the previous year's actual or budgeted figures together with an allowance for inflation and possibly a deduction to encourage cost reductions. The problems of incremental budgeting can be avoided in the approaches to the management of budgeting systems.

Parkinson (1994, p. 26) states:

> *Zero-based budgeting (ZBB) starts from the relationship between targets, activities and inputs. Budget holders must ignore their previous budget and concentrate on next year's targets, establishing from first principles the level of resourcing they require. Budget holders should prepare budgets for several different levels of activity, starting at a minimal level, then detailing the extra resourcing required for increases. Resource managers can then determine the appropriate mix of activities that reflect the available resources and their prioritised targets. Zero-based budgeting is also used as an approach to budgeting, a way of thinking, of starting from zero which tends not to happen in the incremental budgeting process.*

Parkinson (1994, p. 26) considers that flexibility should be built into any budgeting system. Rolling budgets have emerged from the idea that in day-to-day management there is a relatively short amount of time for decision-making. The situation is the same in the majority of schools at this level, therefore budget holders should not be concerned with the full year ahead. A rolling budget operates within a system whereby the 12-month budget of targets and resources is divided into quarterly periods. This rolling budget approach is referred to in business as budget phasing or profiling.

Fixed and flexible budgeting helps to take account of changes and is particularly useful in measuring performance and in establishing what needs to be done. In practice some expenditure would have both fixed and variable elements, e.g. a school caretaker is a fixed cost, overtime is a variable cost. Resource managers need to understand which of the school's costs are fixed or variable as this is a useful planning tool.

Full cost accounting refers to the theory that costs are measured at the point where they are consumed. That is, the final amount in full cost accounting takes into account all expenditure from purchase to use. As an example, premises and administrative costs would be included in the amount of funds allocated for the teaching of pupils.

The principles of cost centres are transferable to planning units. This approach breaks down the functioning of the school into activities. As a framework for budgets, planning units appear to encompass elements from good business practice. Schools can be divided according to subject departments, year groups or classes. The breakdown should include all school activities, including support services such as maintenance and cleaning.

A budget format should be suited to the organisation's purpose. Resource managers should produce a format which leads budget holders to describe, in detail, what is needed and what is wanted. Planning is central to the budgeting process, and includes the procurement and apportionment of resources to meet the goals and needs established for the time cycle. As a starting point, a business plan may be appropriate. This is a concept borrowed by the public sector from the private sector. The business plan in a local government environment is more limited than in the private sector, providing the parameters for both resourcing and delivery of services within which the school or department must operate.

Resource managers should consider internal and external sources of funding, personnel and material acquisition. They should also follow LEA procedures relative to building improvements when developing building staffing plans.

8
■ ■ ■

Building and managing
a budget

Introduction

Financial delegation has moved the allocation and management of resources away from LEAs to schools. If resources are to be managed effectively in schools, school managers need to understand the budgetary process (Davies, 1994, p. 327). This is not merely about spending money; budgeting involves management. Davies (1994, p. 328) describes the position of budgeting within a cycle of educational management activity as shown in Figure 8.1.

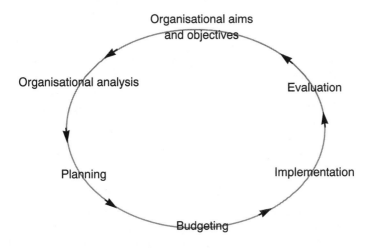

Figure 8.1: The educational management cycle
(*Source:* Davies, 1994, p. 328)

The budget is a key document in management and has two aspects, as Jones (1995, p. 63) explains:

1 *It is a key operational planning document, derived from higher-level considerations such as are expressed in strategy documents and business plans.*

2 *It is a key financial control document, which can be used for keeping within spending limits and ensuring that income is as planned.*

The management of budgets is a process of planning, monitoring and control. The UK Chartered Institute of Management Accountants (CIMA, 1994) suggests the following definition of budgets:

A plan quantified in monetary terms, prepared and approved prior to a defined period of time, usually showing planned income to be generated and/or expenditure to be incurred during that period and the capital to be employed to attain a given objective.

Thus resources, quantified in financial terms, are made available to managers with a view to enabling targets to be achieved. In practice, outline budgets for long-term plans are prepared by governors, senior managers, budget holders and resource managers followed by more detailed plans for the short-term (immediate) that are consistent with the school's vision (aims). Parkinson (1994, pp. 6–7) explains:

*The budgeting process is made up of three elements: first, the **objectives** of the organisation are defined: secondly, these objectives are translated into **plans** which are consistent with the policies and guidelines laid down by management; and thirdly, performance is **monitored** and **controlled** against these plans once they have been expressed in monetary terms.*

At each stage, managers need to ask: 'What are we trying to do?'

The majority of schools have a number of purposes. These may be described in organisational terms as a pyramid of purposes. Organisations need to know what their purpose is and where they are going. It is important for resource managers to understand the mission and values of their organisations to ensure that the right objectives are being set. There needs to be an effective control to monitor and evaluate the budget process. The budget can be viewed as an important guideline for school/department plans and activities. The budget can be one measure of the effectiveness of governors, senior managers, resource managers and budget holders. If budgets are realistic then individual managers will be convinced of the attainability of their targets even if the individual has to work hard to reach them.

Effective resource management places an emphasis on the interrelationship between financial and resource management and the wider planning context – school and staff development plans and marketing, which impact on teaching and learning. Davies and Ellison (1992, pp. 19–20) explain that, *as with the overall school development plan, the budgetary process is a continuous cycle of activity*

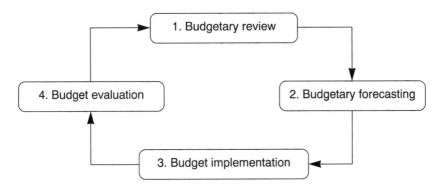

Figure 8.2: The budgetary cycle
(*Source:* Davies and Ellison, 1992)

– it sets the educational priorities into a financial context and can be seen to comprise four stages, as shown in Figure 8.2.

Resource managers need to follow each stage, as follows:

- **Budgetary review.** Assessment of the current financial position and the causal factors. Key categories are income and expenditure.
- **Budgetary forecasting.** Assess the impact of future financial trends, and what will be required to resource the school.
- **Budget implementation.** Place current decisions in the context of the review and future projections. A useful staged implementation process could be:
  - Set out headings and sub-headings of the budget.
  - Allocate fixed costs to headings.
  - Allocate recurrent costs.
  - Bring forward items from the review and forecast; establish priorities.
  - Decide between alternative projects and courses of action.
  - Put budget forward for approval by the institution's governors.
  - Set check points during the year for possible virement opportunities.
- **Budget evaluation.** It is important that institutions do not ignore this vital part of the budgetary cycle. Evaluation is the key to the production of an effective budget.

In sum, the budgeting process should allow each school *to plan, co-ordinate, control and evaluate its activities* (Davies, 1994, p. 329).

Planning

Many schools' senior and resource managers recognise the significance and importance of the planning process for all concerned. Planning for the next financial year may take place many months in advance and should be managed by an experienced resource manager.

The school development plan, as shown in Figure 8.3, should provide the framework for the budget.

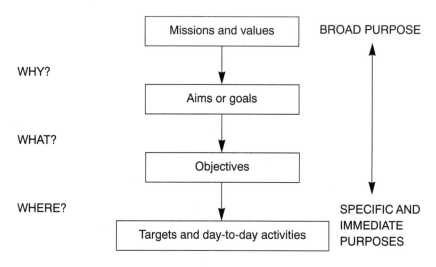

Figure 8.3: School development plan

Each school has long-term aims and goals which should be translated into shorter-term objectives and then into targets for budget holders. There are also key limiting factors that need to be taken into account before planning can start. In schools, these will be the cash limits set by central and local government. If a school does not have a sufficient number of staff with the right skills, or the right equipment, then it will be limited in what it can do. Once the budget constraints have been identified, the budget process can commence (Parkinson, 1994, p. 18).

Budget construction

There is little written about budget construction. Resource managers should start the process within the framework of the function of schools:

- pupils to learn
- teachers to teach.

The focus of budget construction is the pupil. Pupils require space and time to learn; they also require teachers. Teachers need materials to assist the learning process. Traditionally schools have divided pupils' experience into curriculum areas. Resource managers allocate the task of identifying curriculum needs to middle managers, who are responsible for curriculum delivery and pastoral support.

The preparation and implementation of the budget will be carried out within certain constraints. These are a consequence of government legislation, local education authority policies and/or school policies. Therefore decisions made at the macro or micro level will influence school budgets.

Prior to completing its budget, the LEA should indicate to schools the overall level it is proposing. This will reflect LEA pupil numbers, on which the resource allocation formula will be based. The budget will also reflect the government's intentions for funding local government services and Standard Spending Assessments (SSAs).

From this information, schools should be able to formulate a more accurate estimate of the income generated by their pupil numbers. Schools should also add projected income from lettings and other sources (*see* Chapter 12 on Opportunities). This total will, in essence, be the 'cash limit' for the school. In anticipation of unforeseen expenditure, schools and LEAs should include a contingency.

An example of information presented by local education authorities to schools concerning their school budget share is shown in Table 8.1.

As Table 8.1 illustrates, issues and decisions related to items of expenditure are determined by government legislation, LEA policy, the school development plan and school policies. Elements of expenditure are detailed in the LMS Initiative classification of expenditure (1990, pp. 50–68). These include:

- *Employees*
- *Premises*
- *Transport*
- *Supplies and services*
- *Transfer payments*
- *Central administration charges*
- *Contingencies and resources.*

Other areas for consideration in budget construction are the relationship between academic and financial years, inflation and income. Finally resource managers will have to consider:

Table 8.1: School budget share – for a primary school with 140 pupils, none of whom are in special units

1. NUMBERS ON ROLL:									
Year groups	Infants	Juniors	Yr 7	Yr 8	Yr 9	Yr 10	Yr 11	Yr 12	Yr 13
Jan '96 Actuals	58	82	0	0	0	0	0	0	0
Pry/mid. pupils in spec. units	0	0	0	0					
SBR5s	6								
(April 95 actuals ×1/3)	2.00								
Nursery pupils	0								
SENA pupils (sec. only)			0	0	0	0	0		
Special unit	MLD KS1	MLD KS2	Nursery	SPLD	Hearing	Lan-guages	Phys-ical	Autism	
Places	0	0	0	0	0	0	0	0	

2. ALLOWANCES:	£
2.1 Basic flat rate	33 162
2.2 Special unit rate	0
2.3 Special unit places	0
2.4 Age weighted pupil units	160 164
2.5 Split site/federated schools	0
2.6 Service school factor %	0
2.7 Social needs factors	0
% free meals 3.71	
2.8 Small school salary protection	5 612
2.9 Small school curriculum protection	0
2.10 New schools allowance	0
2.11 New schools new year group allowance	0
(infants × 7/12) 0.00 (junior × 7/12) 0.00	
2.12 Service school budget protection	0
2.13 SENAs (secondary only)	0
Total formula budget 1996–97	**198 938**

3. ADD RENTS AND RATES:	5 791
School budget share 1996–97	**204 729**

4. OTHER NON-FORMULA ADJUSTMENTS:	£	£
Recharge to meals (energy)	124	
Recharge to meals (rates)	74	
Recharge to meals (admin)	391	
Safeguarding/protection – teachers	0	
Safeguarding/protection – non-teaching	0	
Total non-formula adjustments		**589**

138

- monitoring and control:
  - operational information
  - financial information
  - information on performance
- budgetary control reports:
  - actual expenditure to date
  - expected or budgeted expenditure
  - differences or 'variances' between them
  - forecasts of likely actual expenditure for the year (specific to each school)
- financial control
- management structure.

Having received their school budget share resource managers are then in a position to draft the school budget. Table 8.2 provides a model of the template for a primary school budget.

Staff

School governors (and senior mangers) are responsible for determining the number and grading of employees. The total costs associated with staff will account for between 60 and 90 per cent of the school's total expenditure. Schools should plan accordingly. Small changes in this area of the budget will equate to large changes elsewhere. Governors may consult the LEA to ensure that they are aware of guidelines for non-teaching staff. It is important to note that non-teaching staff are a valuable resource. Administrative and non-educational tasks may be performed in a cost-effective way. Time gained will allow teaching staff to concentrate on teaching and preparation.

The LEA should assist governors and the resource manager with the process of preparing budgets for staffing. This should include:

- the total budget available
- staff numbers
- salaries, wages and allowances (incentive allowances and London weighting)
- overtime/bonus payments and part-time claims
- national insurance
- superannuation
- vacancies
- absence levels
- supply cover
- increments

Table 8.2: Primary school budget template

SCHOOL:			CAPITATION NO:	
	GROSS ALLOCATION A	NON-FORM ADJUSTS B	ROLLOVER 1995/96 C	TOTAL ALLOCATION (A – B + C)
EMPLOYEES:				
Full/part-time teachers	92 691			
Heads and deputies	58 174			
Supply teachers	1 000			
Supply insurance premium	1 264			
County supply premium	1 608			
Education support assistants	14 605			
Caretaker/handyperson (payroll)	4 320			
Admin. & clerical	5 761	−391		
Clerk to the governors	285			
Mdsas salaries	3 303			
Interview expenses				
Staff duty meals	700			
Car allowances/travel	800			
Recruitment (advertising)				
SUB-TOTAL EMPLOYEES	184 511	−391		
PREMISES:				
Caretaking & cleaning	400			
Contract cleaning	165			
Repairs & maintenance				
Rep & maint DPS pool (aided schools)				
Rates & rents	5 865	−74		5 791
Other fuels				
Electricity	1 400	1 124		
Gas	1 400			
Oil				
Water services	800			
Grounds & maintenance & rent	1 600			
Cleaning & domestic supplies				
SUB-TOTAL PREMISES	11 630	−198		
SUPPLIES & SERVICES:				
BSM, FAE, Admin, etc.	7 575		141	7 716
Non cheque book				
SUB-TOTAL CONTINGENCY				
INCOME:				
Lettings				
	205 318	−589	6 088	210 817
SIGNED (HEADTEACHER):			DATE:	

- training requirements
- pay awards.

Headteachers, deputy headteachers and teachers are paid in accordance with the 1987 *School Teachers' Pay and Conditions Document* (DES, 1987). Administrative, professional, technical and clerical staff (APT&C) are graded as are manual workers, depending on occupation. Caretakers are paid weekly rates determined by floor areas, as are cleaners. Pay awards are dated as follows:

- Teachers   1 April
- APT&C   1 July
- Manual workers 1 September.

In community schools, staff are sometimes part-funded from community budgets. Budgets should be drawn up on the basis of actual salaries and wages.

Teachers and APT&C staff may also be awarded increments:

- Teachers   1 September
- APT&C staff   1 April.

Increments will affect the total budget, as they are added to the school's costs during a budgeting year. Resource managers should estimate the number of teaching staff entitled to increments on 1 September based on 5/12ths (April–August) of the annual cost at the existing level and 7/12ths (September–March) at the higher level.

National Insurance (NI) and superannuation will need to be calculated and added to the basic salary budget. National Insurance rates are based on bands of pay levels and will therefore vary from time to time. Superannuation rates are set at a fixed percentage of an employee's pay. Although, in most LEAs, payroll administration will remain with the LEA, employer's NI and superannuation should be estimated for each employee.

Resource managers need to estimate pay awards. The LEA will have made an allowance for its forecast of cost increases and will inform schools of that forecast. Managers should include this estimate in their budget and also consider the effect this will have on superannuation payments and NI bands.

Draft budget

The draft school budget should be presented to several groups from within the school community for discussion. Teaching staff should be shown the budget. The governing body finance subcommittee, as the official representative of the full governing body, is able to change the allocation of funds in the budget if necessary. The full governing body then has to approve the budget before it is returned to each LEA finance committee. Once set under the budget headings, there is scope for the virement of funds.

Table 8.3 is an example of a draft primary school budget.

Implementing the budget

The process of determining the final budget operates on a timescale of approximately three months. This process may be complicated by a change in the Aggregated School Budget (ASB) during this period. It is the duty of the headteacher to inform the finance subcommittee of any changes as they occur. The headteacher is also responsible for adjusting the amounts allocated under each heading within the budget, should the school's allocation be reduced. Once estimates (which should exceed the total cash limit) have been established for resources, schools should adjust the estimates to the cash limit. Any reductions to the budget should be realistic.

A school's budget is recorded both centrally and locally. The headteacher is sent a computer printout by the LEA; this is coded according to the preset headings. This document includes all payments made to the school or by the school. This will be overseen by senior management, as appropriate. Should the figures not agree with those on the school's Schools Information Management System (SIMS), the headteacher will then contact the LEA finance department. All staff, teaching and non-teaching, are paid direct from the LEA and these payments are recorded in the document. In addition, the school has a cheque book to be used for local payments.

Having planned the budget and received approval from the LEA, resource managers then operate the budget. Resource managers must know and understand government legislation and LEA policies that govern the assignment and use of resources. Resource managers also need to understand the rationale for building contingency funds, have knowledge of costing concepts, and have the interpersonal skills to involve senior and middle managers and their teams in the decision-making process. Resource managers also need to have the skills and ability required to attract new clients – parents and pupils.

Resource managers should have the ability to work with senior managers and governors to match the strengths of teachers with the needs of students. Senior and middle management teams are involved in the management of specific areas, for example:

- **material resources and systems** – e.g. SIMS computing system within the school dealing with income from the LEA
- **buildings and maintenance** – the allocation of tasks to the LEA, school and contracted specialists for the maintenance and servicing of the school environment

Table 8.3: Draft primary school budget

	INCOME	£	EXPENDITURE	£
1	Formula	205 318	Teaching staff	156 354
2	LEA initiative	2 847	Secretary	5 761
3	GEST	4 710	MDSA	3 303
4	Local approach	3 000	ESA	23 405
5	Rollover	2 696	Cleaning	5 320
6	Swim	870	Clerk	285
7	5% trigger	4 914	Travel	800
8	Interest	300	Lunches	700
9	Letting income		Teacher insurance	2 974
10			Supply	2 000
11			Swimming	550
12			Governor training	636
13			**Sub-total**	**202 088**
14			Water	800
15			Electricity	1 400
16			Gas	1 400
17			Grounds	1 300
18			Repairs/cleaning	165
19			Telephone	400
20			Postage	200
21			Photocopier	650
22			Equipment insurance	140
23			Minibus	300
24			Cleaning materials	400
25			Rent of grounds	300
26			BSM	6 000
27			**Sub-total**	**13 455**
28			Rent & rates	5 791
29			Recharges	589
30			Reserve funds	1 500
31			Unallocated funds	1 232
32			**Sub-total**	**9 112**
33				
34	**TOTAL**	**224 655**	**TOTAL**	**224 655**
35	**New building**			
36	Start-up funds			

- **INSET** – teacher training, funded directly by the LEA
- **GEST** – central government funded professional development.

Resource managers will need to assign materials and equipment according to established criteria, link essential materials to SDP and DDP goals and establish a contingency fund. This applies to curricular and extra-curricular programmes. Resource managers may also suggest and encourage management and staff to retrieve and move out of use stored materials and equipment. They will need to develop guidelines and time frames for grant expenditures and initiate a volunteer programme to assist classroom teachers.

Resource managers and budget holders need to monitor the implementation of the budget throughout the year as shown in Table 8.4.

Table 8.4: Budget activity and action

Budget activity	Activity
Planning	A budget is drawn up for a period of time; this is what ought to happen.
Reality	Events take place in that time period; this is what actually happens.
Comparison	The planned and actual activities are compared: differences may be revealed and measurements of progress and performance made.
Validation	Explanations for the differences are sought.
Action	Action is taken where appropriate.

A further consideration in the implementation of the budget is the increased involvement of a wide range of people in the funding process. Knight (1993, p. 149) comments:

With the growth of school self-management there is more risk of abuse of school funds.

David Goodman in *School Governor* (quoted in Knight, 1993, pp. 149–50) states:

Under local management of schools, people will be no more or less honest than hitherto, but the risks will increase:

- *The drive for lean overheads will lead to reduced controls.*
- *Decentralisation makes separation of duties more difficult to achieve.*
- *Local processing destroys the fear of detection by the centre.*

Knight (1993, pp. 150–1) suggests some guiding principles that can be established as shown in Table 8.5.

Table 8.5: Guiding principles

Principles	Responsibilities
Separation of powers	Different people should be responsible for different functions.
Responsibilities	These need to be well defined and understood by all.
Personnel	Need for careful selection and training.
Income	All cash should be paid into the school account, and receipts issued with a recording and reconciliation system.
Banking, deposits, investments and loans	Policies should be established.
Orders	Budget holder and finance clerk.
Contracts	Include rigorous definition of service standards and specification, tender documentation, advertising procedures, receiving, evaluating and awarding tenders and monitoring performance.
Payments	Made to invoices with delivery notes for goods received, authorised by a senior manager. Cheques should require two signatories. Petty cash payments should be firmly controlled.
Records	Include orders, invoices, delivery notes, statements, receipts, vouchers and other records, as specified.
Inventories	Policy and requirements known by all staff.
Security	Safes for cash; security and supervision of premises and insurance.
In-department audit	Periodic review by external managers and auditors.
Unofficial school funds	Firm guidelines are required incorporating much of the above.

(*Source:* Knight, 1993, pp. 150–1; reproduced by permission of the publisher, Heinemann Educational Publishers)

Accountability

The resource manager's responsibilities also include accountability for materials, equipment, and personnel assignments and performance. Resource managers need to know and understand government and LEA regulations governing LMS/GM accounting. They must be familiar with the LEA's accounting system and language and its reporting, auditing and inventory procedures. This involves maintaining accurate records of the resources purchased, received, expended, stored and wasted during a given time period. Resource managers must also be able to provide written reports to external funding agencies and to account for money received. Periodic accounting is

145

required by law. Resource managers will need to produce accounts to governors, senior managers, staff, parents and the LEA.

Effective work schedules and time plans can serve as accountability measures for employing staff. Appraisal documentation provides accountability for staff performance, job descriptions and the identification of specific roles in relation to the SDP. The NPBEA (1993, pp. 13–14) describes the responsibilities of resource managers in accounting procedures as specifying records that must be maintained to account for expenditures, in addition to retaining multi-year inventories of materials and equipment. Resource managers should keep files of premises and school meal service schedules and maintain internal accounts for activity funds. They should also maintain daily records of cash received at the site and ensure that there are regular deposits. It is essential that resource managers submit the required reports to the LEA, governors, senior managers, budget holders and staff. These will include monthly and yearly financial statements for the school and involve the examination of reports by appropriate staff or departments.

Within the budgeting process, resource managers need to identify building level budget codes according to the LEA system. It is also important to develop guidelines for grant expenditures in order to meet grant agency submission and reporting deadlines. This process is similar to preparing bids and reports for LEAs.

All meetings, requests, commendations, warnings and correspondence concerning inter-agency collaboration efforts should be documented and copied.

Budget holders

As stated, the SDP should provide the framework for the budget. The SDP may include several different plans with financial implications – department (curriculum) plans, premises and ground improvement, and so forth. Budget holders have responsibility for determining and managing their department/team's budget. The budget should be included in the department development plan (DDP). Budget holders need to know and understand the budgetary processes involved in the financial management of the whole school. The following provides a framework that enables budget holders to participate in budget construction:

- **Preparation.** This first stage should involve all budget holders. Heads of department, year heads and resource managers should consider their targets and associated resourcing requirements for the next year. The targets must relate to the headteacher's vision and mission for the school as described in the SDP.

- **Collation.** Once all budget holders have completed the first stage as outlined above, there is a need for a process of collation and checking to ensure that the aggregate of each budget submission is consistent with the school's aims and objectives. In practice, there is rarely agreement at early budget meetings. The claims of individual budget holders will, inevitably, add up to more than the total resources available to the school. Many middle managers will be guilty of bidding for more resources than they require, and this may be endemic throughout the school. Senior and resource management may not have realistic information to challenge the inflated budget estimates effectively.

- **Authorisation.** Given that proposed budgets at the collation stage may lead to conflict, some negotiation will need to take place between senior managers and individual budget holders. Resource managers will have to ensure that budget holder targets match the SDP and that the resourcing is appropriate. If not managed properly by senior and resource managers this stage is often seen by budget holders as a rejection of their proposed budget, without reason. If an approach which combines 'top-down' with 'bottom-up' is adopted and an emphasis placed on communication, the middle managers are likely to be more understanding.

- **Implementation.** Implementation needs great care. Targets need to be set and a reporting system to be in place. The reporting system should provide managers with the information they need to monitor progress and make decisions about what to do next.

In contrast to the above, current practice may involve a bidding system, whereby budget holders decide on the amount required to fund the running of their department/subject/pastoral area for the next financial year. A useful method of preparing a bid is to compare financial statements from the previous year with those of similar departments/teams, looking for areas where money could be saved and identifying the areas which need additional funding. Budget holders should begin with basic needs and move to additional operational expenditure. In this process, budget managers should aim to spend all the capitation (the amount allocated from the school funds to each area for teaching materials), cost each item, then attempt to justify the cost. Finally, budget holders should make a copy of each list and circulate it to colleagues for comment.

When completing financial documentation to be forwarded to senior management, budget holders should ensure that they follow the 'house style'. Headings shown in Table 8.6 may be appropriate.

This process leads budget holders to prioritise expenditure within the budget. Once this is done, the management of resources will involve:

- a stocktake of each room's resources
- detailed accounts of each year's losses/gains

Table 8.6: Department/team annual capitation

Department/ team	Item	Cost	Purpose	Staff/room	Essential/ optional

- estimated use of stock according to:
  - number of pupils in each room
  - curriculum activity, e.g. art will involve more consumables than drama
- identification of new materials/equipment related to specific activities.

Table 8.7 illustrates a typical proforma that could be used to audit stock.

Table 8.7: Department/team stock audit

Room	Staff/ subject	Class	Materials/ equipment required	In stock	To order	cost
		1				
		2				
		3				
		4				
		5				
		6				
		7				

A useful method of preparing financial statements is to record materials used throughout the year. This avoids the additional administrative pressure of the annual 'stocktake'. Another possibility is the delegation of the stock-keeping to a member of the department/team. An example of current good practice is given in Figure 8.4.

Essentially Figure 8.4 and Table 8.8 show evidence of budget reviewing, budget forecasting and budget implementation. Budget holders may also consider prioritising items in the bid and indicating the purpose of each purchase.

Table 8.9 (p. 151) indicates capital expenditure allocated to departments in a secondary school. In this example all capital is 'drip fed' to subject co-ordinators at regular intervals during the academic year. This would appear to allow senior managers to retain control of all spending. It would be more manageable if capital funding was allocated to subject co-ordinators at the start

---

Capital Bid
Geography Department – June 1995

There follows a prioritised listing of capital items which the Geography Department wants to purchase in the financial year April 1995 to April 1996.

However, purchases would be made on the understanding that they would also cover the financial year 1996–7 and will make the Geography Department self-sustaining for some considerable time in the future.

I believe, however, that the resources of the Department need upgrading now so as to provide pupils with a sound long-term base of excellent materials.

Introduction

In the following paper 'Proposed Future Plans for Geography at School A', I have set out in detail how I wish to see the Department develop over the next three years. I am particularly keen to expand upon the resource base in Year 9 where there are presently very few resources – 17 *Interactions* textbooks used by six tutor groups are the only fairly recent textbooks available in school. Similarly at GCSE, despite recent purchases, we only have 22 copies of *Wider World* and 12 copies of *Key Geography 2*. These are the only modern resources available for teaching three groups of 22 pupils in Year 10 and two groups (of 22 and 26) in Year 11.

I am pleased to report that no books have gone astray since September – four damaged Key Stage 3 books have been charged to the pupils found to be responsible.

Figure 8.4: Capital bid

of the financial year. Given the changes to school management, the need to allocate funds and the increase in responsibilities at all levels of the school structure, this degree of control would appear to be inappropriate.

Budget holders may have the need or opportunity to bid for extra funds during the course of the academic year. Figure 8.5 (p. 152) is an additional bid which relates to the original bid (Table 8.8) for the Geography Department and is clear and concise.

Having completed the process of bidding for resources, records of purchase need to be retained.

Consumables and reprographics must be included in all school budgets. Photocopying is expensive; all copies need to be recorded. An example of good practice is given in Figure 8.6 (p. 153).

Table 8.8: Department capital spending (Bid A)

1. Textbooks to facilitate teaching at GCSE and to support new MEG syllabus 3 GCSE course in keeping with new syllabus development (similar changes would have been required even if we had kept with same board).		
14 copies of *Key Stage Geography 2*	@ £6.99 =	£97.86
30 copies of *Key Stage Geography 1*	@ £6.99 =	£209.70
1 copy *Resource Pack KG 2*	@ £41.50 =	£41.50
1 copy *Resource Pack KG 1*	@ £41.50 =	£41.50
3 copies of *Wider World*	@ £8.75 =	£26.25
30 copies of *British Isles*	@ £3.50 =	£105.00
2. Textbooks to add urgently to main stock at Key Stage 3		
8 copies of *Foundations*	@ £7.25 =	£58.00
5 copies of *Connections*	@ £7.25 =	£36.25
20 copies of *Interactions*	@ £7.25 =	£145.00
New material		
35 copies of *Places*	@ £7.25 =	£253.75
1 *Teacher's Resources Guide*	@ £41.50 =	£41.50
Geography Eye Satellite Resource Pack	@ £22.20 =	£22.20
3. TV/video equipment (joint bid with History) – Granada (22–24 June)		
24″ remote control TV and video	@ £250.00 =	£125.00
4. Fieldwork equipment		
1 thermometer	@ £16.95 =	£16.95
1 anemometer	@ £17.95 =	£17.95
5. Teaching equipment		
1 world globe	@ £15.45 =	£15.45
Total capital bid	=	**£1253.86**
With discounts that I have discussed with all three possible suppliers, this figure will drop to £1000–1050. This would amount to a bid of £500 per year over two years.		

Management

A direct consequence of LMS is the change in relationship between teaching staff and management. Examples of the dysfunctional elements of LMS are manifested in terms of distrust of managers by staff through a tendency to resist management decisions which may give rise to internal conflict. These characteristics have been identified by Marconi and Seigal (1989) within the

Table 8.9: School capital allocation

Department	Maximum allocation	Allocation July	Allocation November
English	1 626	1 076	
Music	52	52	
Technology	351	0	
Geography	337	337	212
History	376	267	
Soc. Ed.	143	0	
Mod. Langs	1 545	1 545	
Maths	1 094	674	460
Art	54	0	150
Bus. Ed.	27	0	
Science	1 105	780	325
Library	1 027	633	294
Medical	696	0	
HOY/Pastoral	18	0	
SEN	812	124	535
S.11	10	0	
Drama	270	TBA	140
RE	24	0	
PE	92		
IT	40	0	
Total	9 699	5 488	2 116

context of behavioural accounting in response to the budgeting process. They also explain the benefits of participation as discussed in Chapter 4. Resource managers should consider:

- the development of an open-management style: Thomas *et al.* (1989) cite examples of the changed role of staff under LMS, which begins with the role of the headteacher
- the introduction of a structure which incorporates a collaborative decision-making process (Spinks, 1990)
- the embodiment of the principles of programme planning within the budgetary process – it is possible to incorporate some of the important principles of the PPBS cohort once a full LMS scheme is in place (Spicer, 1990)
- the assessment of the success of the budgetary process in terms of what the institution can do for people (House, 1973).

A-level Capital Bid (revised) – Geography 13/10/95

The amount allocated so far is £101.00.

Further to our recent conversation and bearing in mind this is a new course, the Department would like to bid for the following:

4 copies *Geography – An Integrated Approach*, D. Waugh	£88.00
2 copies *Population Geography*, H. Barrett	£27.00
4 copies *The Geography Settlement*, P. Daniel/M. Hopkinson	£54.00
1 copy *Process and Landform*, A. Clowes/P. Comfort	£13.50
Reprographics though could be as rearranged if 'capital'	£30.00
Total	**£212.50**

This represents a shortfall on the existing budget of some £110.50.

This is a realistic proposal of the minimum expenditure required to set up the course. All extra materials – videos, reproducible masters, journals, past papers, staff copies of texts – to be provided privately.

Figure 8.5: Revised department capital spending bid

In practice the links between accounting decision-making and human behaviour will bring out the implications of operating an overall budget process. Resource managers who are responsible for personnel, fiscal and material resources rely on a variety of knowledge and skills (NPBEA, 1993, p. 13–11). These include: knowledge of traditional and non-traditional funding sources and LEA discretionary funding policies; knowledge and skills in purchasing and requisition procedures; grant seeking and writing; knowledge of support agencies (outside agencies, LEA support) and marketing skills that may increase resource support at the school site; and skills in staff recruitment related to LEA policies and practices, including staff interview and selection procedures.

At a fundamental level, resource managers have responsibility for material resources, which involves using inventories to justify purchases, completing purchase requests for the replacement of materials and equipment, submitting an annual list of needed materials and equipment and establishing criteria for selecting materials and equipment.

Reprographics Department

Invoice for services purchased – date(s) :   *December '95*

Department/organisation: *Geography*

Teacher in charge/invoice to: *Head of Department*

1. **Photocopying services:**

    (a) Reprographics Department service   @ ..... pence/copy = £......

    (b) Reprographics Key services   @ 5   pence/copy = *£1.95*

    Number of copies recorded   *39 copies*

    Total photocopying charges   *= £1.95*

2. **Duplicating services:**

    Total paper/card duplicating charges as price list   *= £24.60*

3. **Other services as detailed:**

    Total for other services   = £

    For period stated, total charges owing/debited

    to departmental capitation account named: *= £26.55*

    Date of this invoice:

    Please direct enquiries connected with this invoice to department head.

Figure 8.6: Record of consumables/reprographics

Summary

If resources are to be managed effectively in schools, school managers need to understand the budgetary process. This is not merely about spending money; budgeting involves management. The management of budgets is a process of planning, monitoring and control. In practice, outline budgets for long-term plans are prepared by governors, senior managers, budget holders and resource managers, followed by more detailed plans for the short-term (immediate) that are consistent with the school's vision (aims).

Effective resource management places an emphasis on the interrelationship between financial and resource management and the wider planning context, school and staff development plans and marketing, which impact on teaching and learning. Many schools' senior and resource managers recognise the significance and importance of the planning process for all concerned. Each school has long-term aims and goals which should be translated into shorter-term objectives and then into targets for budget holders.

There is little written about budget construction. Resource managers should start the process within the framework of the function of schools:

- pupils to learn
- teachers to teach.

The focus of budget construction is the pupil. Pupils require space and time to learn; they also require teachers. Teachers need materials to assist the learning process.

The draft school budget should be presented to several groups from within the school community for discussion. Teaching staff should be shown the budget. The process of determining the final budget operates on a timescale of approximately three months. A school's budget is recorded both centrally and locally.

Having planned the budget and received approval from the LEA, resource managers then operate the budget. Resource managers must know and understand government legislation and LEA policies that govern the assignment and use of resources.

Resource managers will need to assign materials and equipment according to established criteria, link essential materials to SDP and DDP goals and establish a contingency fund.

Resource managers and budget holders need to monitor the implementation of the budget throughout the year. The resource manager's responsibilities also include accountability for materials, equipment, and personnel assignments and performance. Resource managers need to know and understand government and LEA regulations governing LMS accounting.

A direct consequence of LMS is the change in relationship between teaching staff and management. Examples of the dysfunctional elements of LMS are manifested in terms of distrust of managers by staff through a tendency to resist management decisions which may give rise to internal conflict. In practice the links between accounting decision-making and human behaviour will bring out the implications of operating an overall budget process.

At a fundamental level, resource managers have responsibility for material resources, which involves using inventories to justify purchases, completing purchase requests for the replacement of materials and equipment, submitting an annual list of needed materials and equipment and establishing criteria for selecting materials and equipment.

9

■　■　■

Information technology

Introduction

Critical to the effectiveness of resource management in schools is the ease with which schools can control and monitor relevant administrative procedures. As the LMS Initiative (1990, p. 17) identified, there are certain types of school-based administrative arrangements which have increased the administrative burden and the number of tasks required for control. This chapter considers the use of information technology (IT). In addition, school governors and senior managers need to assess the need to appoint additional administrative staff for the purpose of resource management. Lancaster (1989, pp. 174–5) comments:

> *In attempting to manage information as a resource, many organisations are turning to formal management information systems [. . .] a network designed to provide the right information to the right person at the right time at minimum cost.*

Computer systems

The majority of schools and LEAs have introduced financial and management information systems to provide the necessary information for schools to control their finances and, for LEAs, to monitor and evaluate the schools' performance. The LMS Initiative (1990, p. 17) advised that systems are likely to be required for:

- *pupil records and profiling;*
- *staff and personnel records;*
- *examination administration;*
- *admissions;*
- *curriculum management and timetabling;*
- *careers advice;*

- *training needs;*
- *financial administration, covering payroll, expenditure, central purchasing, maintenance of buildings and grounds, income, central accounting and budgeting, local accounting and budgeting and [. . .] grant claims.*

In the maintained sector, school and LEA computer systems need to be compatible or networked. Detailed advice should be available from central government and LEAs. Once systems have been implemented, training in their use will be necessary. This is easier if staff have been involved during the system implementation phase.

Service level agreements between the LEA and the schools will need to be drawn up concerning computer systems. This includes maintaining and running existing systems and developing new systems.

Financial spreadsheets

This section returns to the issue of implementing, controlling and managing the school budget. Essentially, it concerns ways to harness the power and flexibility of PC spreadsheets to manage financial information. Knight (1993, p. 104) explains:

> *A spreadsheet is a computerised combination of a very large piece of paper and a multi-function calculator. Its format is a grid of rows and columns. The point at which a row and a column intersect is known as a cell. Each cell is uniquely indexed and information is stored in cells either as text, numbers or formulae.*

A typical spreadsheet would look like Figure 9.1.

Well-known spreadsheet packages are Lotus 1-2-3 and Microsoft Excel. An example of the use of spreadsheets follows.

	A	B	C	D	E
1					
2	Teaching staff	£200 000			
3	APT&C staff	£25 000			
4	Hourly-paid	£20 000			
5	TOTAL	£245 000			
6					Cell
7					

Figure 9.1: Example of a spreadsheet

Models and spreadsheet modelling

In business, until recently, accountants designed and controlled financial information systems in the UK (Parkinson, 1994, pp. 51–73). Managers tended to rely on accountants for guidance in financial management. The arrival of the PC changed this pattern. Managers are now in a position to use and design their own small-scale information and decision-support systems. The spreadsheet has provided a 'user-friendly programming environment' for financial modelling.

Spreadsheets provide a problem-solving environment. The problem is not automatically solved; the spreadsheet merely enables us to see the results of changing any of the assumptions built into a model using statistical functions, or any of the data inputs. In addition, the charting capability helps to produce graphical forms of presenting numerical data that can be included in reports to governors, senior managers, staff and the LEA. As spreadsheets are now part of an integrated package, extracts and spreadsheet outputs can readily be incorporated into management reports. Kendall and Stuart (1979) provide a definition of a model:

> [...] a specification of the interrelationships of the part of a system in verbal or mathematical terms, sufficiently explicit to enable us to study its behaviour under a variety of circumstances and, in particular, to control it and predict its future.

In practice, a model may be defined as a 'representation of reality' which in this context includes a means of simulating the financial affairs of a school. Once the underlying structure of the financial problem has been established, a model may be built and manipulated in order to suggest possible outcomes. The model must be a reasonable reflection of reality. Models may be manipulated and analysed more easily than any real system, and invaluable insights may be gained from 'what if?' analysis (Parkinson, 1994). Such examination will enable a resource manager to see the effects of deviations from base conditions, and also to asses the validity of different models.

Identifying and defining the problem

This should be defined as clearly and completely as possible so that the most significant factors are not overlooked. The problem may relate to the financial ramifications of the SDP, DDP or individual projects. Unless the problem is expressed in detail, a realistic model will not be possible.

The model may include far more complex relationships, e.g. number of staff employed set against the number of pupils on roll, beginning with a description of the problem then leading to causal relationships. When analysing the problem, the statement of the problem should identify:

- the nature of the decision to be made
- the output information required (e.g. management report)
- the input information required to produce the outputs

- the processing needed to convert inputs to outputs, that is to say the sequence of arithmetic, logical or other operations needed to process the inputs into the outputs.

As Parkinson explains:

> *Testing the model is an iterative process. It involves trial and error with simple data inputs, finding and correcting errors of logic and procedure within the spreadsheet. There is always the very real danger of errors being left in spreadsheets even though they are considered to be complete – a consequence of inadequate testing.*

> *'What if?' analysis is a technique of sensitivity analysis that involves building a model based on assumptions that typify the most likely case. Then the value of each input is changed in turn, usually by small increments, and the effects on the output variables noted. The effect of changes to combinations of inputs should also be considered. In this way a wide range of causes and effects are simulated from which a resource manager can try to deduce valid guides to improve decision-making at all levels.*

> *When one value on a spreadsheet is altered, all its dependent values are changed automatically. The identification of causal relationships is therefore enhanced. All spreadsheets now have a 'goal-seeking' facility where it is possible to start with a desired output and the spreadsheet software will identify the required inputs. The model may have to be reassessed, and if necessary the structure changed, so that the model is improved in an iterative way.*

> *It is essential to document the definition, analysis, specification, reason, programming and testing of spreadsheet models. In practice, however, the need to tackle a problem quickly will often mean that its documentation is postponed until after it has been used, or even postponed indefinitely. If a report is to be produced, then the documentation process is incomplete unless a full report specification is also included. Such a specification must include:*

> - *titles*
> - *descriptive labels*
> - *page numbers and text*
> - *spreadsheet settings*
> - *column widths and formats*
> - *calculations and protection modes.*

> *A directory showing these details should be a feature of the manager's specification when commissioning modelling work. It is also helpful to include information that is necessary to customise a spreadsheet, e.g. any special commands, special equations, input data and the other key factors required to produce the report. Other relevant information, such as management concepts, is also likely to help prospective users. It is particularly helpful to include a section that explains the inherent logic of the model.*

Model construction should be part of a continuous process. The model should be reviewed and kept up to date, as models that do not reflect actual conditions sufficiently closely can lead to wrong management decisions.

Advantages and disadvantages of spreadsheet modelling

A financial model will consist of facts and assumptions which are related in an explicit and systematic way. When the model is implemented as a spreadsheet, the input data (unassembled information) is accurately and speedily manipulated into useful management output. A budget is a good example of a financial model that seeks to represent the real activities of the organisation and to predict the impact of the future upon the organisation. Some budgets are managed manually, others via a mainframe computer, or, more usually, via the resource manager's own spreadsheet software on a PC.

Business experience (Parkinson, 1994, p. 53) has established that spreadsheet models offer managers some significant advantages within the workplace. These include:

- the provision of a framework for problem-solving
- a better understanding of a particular problem through the process of designing and building a model to help manage the problem
- the facility to test a wide range of possible scenarios exploring 'what if?' situations
- savings in time and money.

Spreadsheet models enable resource managers to manage and plan with the benefit of superior financial information. Resource managers can test out the implications of their plans well before action needs to be taken. This approach allows managers to establish the likely impact of their plans on assets and liabilities, cash flow, budgets, break-even points and so on. This process also enables resource managers to learn more about their organisations, reassess their targets (SDPs), explore problems, search for new options and manage financial information on a day-to-day basis. A real bonus is that the tedious mathematical calculations are removed, allowing time for more productive activities. Modelling can be a learning process in which the current model represents a limited understanding and knowledge of the situation. Through model building, with its repeated testing and improvement, resource managers can seek to increase their knowledge and understanding.

Pressure from other activities may reduce the time available for planning. In contrast, the process of building financial models for planning and decision-making requires a large initial investment of time. However, recalculations for changed 'what if?' assumptions require only seconds.

Critically, a model can only predict and behave within its design constraints, therefore the output from a financial model must be placed in the context of school life. Learning about modelling should enable the resource manager to increase his/her knowledge and understanding of the school environment and external influences. Once this happens, models can be used in the workplace to help manage financial information. Whether looking backwards or forwards, the resource manager must be aware of the strengths and weaknesses of the financial information he or she is dealing with. Other points to consider are (Parkinson, 1994, pp. 53–4):

- there is a danger of over-simplification – crucial factors may be omitted at the design stage
- not every important relationship can necessarily be expressed explicitly in terms of built-in spreadsheet functions
- the design of the spreadsheet model may be too rigid to cope with future changes
- users may forget that spreadsheet models produce predictions based on the programmed logic which may be flawed
- managers may have a tendency to manipulate spreadsheet models to produce their desired outcomes (not bad if directed to SDP aims)
- some managers may fail to recognise their own limitations and produce badly implemented spreadsheets, while other managers may fail to recognise the limitations of the spreadsheet software and try to build over-elaborate spreadsheets on too large a scale.

In order to maximise the advantages and minimise the disadvantages, it is important to adopt a systematic approach to the design of a spreadsheet model that first considers the context of modelling and then the specific details of the model in question.

Spreadsheets for flexible budgeting and breakeven analysis

Schools produce a series of budgets for different levels of activity: maintenance, curriculum, visits, etc. Each budget should take account of likely variations as they may provide the only practicable means for retaining control. An effective alternative is to have a fixed budget for a high level of activity. The low and high budgets will then bracket the expected range of activity. Alternatively, some intermediate level of activity may be derived from the low and high budgets if the extra costs are assumed to vary directly with the extra level of activity; this process is a flexed budget.

The following business example could be transcribed to school. In Table 9.1 the first budget assumes that 8 000 hours will be worked, which corresponds to the lowest level of activity. The second budget assumes 12 000 hours of working and this corresponds to the highest level of activity. The flexed budget of 10 000 hours is the mid-point of the low and high budgets.

Table 9.1: Fixed budgets for low and high levels of activity

	Low	High	Flexed
Hours of work	**8 000**	**12 000**	**10 000**
Costs	£	£	£
Supervision	10 000	17 200	13 600
Depreciation	16 000	22 500	19 250
Consumables	9 600	14 400	12 000
Heat and light	1 800	2 200	2 000
Power	12 000	18 000	15 000
Cleaning	1 200	1 600	1 400
Repairs	4 000	7 000	5 500
Indirect wages	16 000	24 000	20 000
Rent and rates	7 200	7 200	7 200
Total	77 800	114 100	95 950

(*Source:* Parkinson, 1994; reproduced by permission of the publisher, The Open University)

If it can be assumed that the increase in costs between these levels of activity is solely due to variable cost, then the variable cost per hour will be the difference between the high and low budgeted costs divided by the extra 4 000 hours workload. The flexed budget for working hours anywhere in the range of 8 000 to 12 000 can be calculated by applying the variable costs in each cost category to the hours worked in excess of 8 000 hours, plus the budgeted costs for 8 000 hours of work.

Cash and balance sheet planning

Resource managers also need to understand the principles of cash planning and balance sheet planning. Many businesses fail because of cash flow problems. While this cannot happen to schools, a cash flow model could indicate the possible need for extra funds and can help in any funding decision – such as whether to use credit facilities or whether to apply for larger grants. The output includes both capital and revenue items. Resource managers need to understand the difference between income received and payments made. Cash planning includes:

- pre-paid expenses
- unpaid expenses
- capital expenditure
- projected costs.

Balance sheet planning

A forecast balance sheet is a summary statement covering the past five years' expenditure, and the next five. A balance sheet considers the sources of finance and the balance between long-term loans and LEA funds. Its purpose is to provide an overall plan for the business (or school), a statement of intent, and to present to those concerned a blueprint for future strategy.

Checks and controls

If properly designed, implemented and operated, a financial model should save time, effort and money in the future. These savings will be lost if the checks and controls built into the model are inadequate or inappropriate.

Internal audit and control are the methods and measures established by management to safeguard assets and to ensure the reliability of records. These also promote operational efficiency.

An internal audit will require staff to check upon the adequacy of office systems and procedures. Internal control ensures staff conform to standard procedures. An external audit is conducted by the LEA or an independent firm of auditors. Any auditor will be concerned to ensure that an efficient system of internal control exists. Audit procedures are often based on predetermined tests designed to satisfy the external auditors that the internal control system is properly operated and effective.

Problem-solving

If problems occur with PC software these may be due to:

- **Completeness of input.** In large systems, the control techniques include one-to-one checks for data. There are often no such controls on PC-based systems.
- **Accuracy of input.** Pre-lists and batch totals may also confirm the accuracy and validity of the input data. Sometimes 'hash totals' are used in large systems as a safeguard against data being lost or corrupted.
- **Authorisation of input.** Password protection usually ensures that only authorised users have the power to input data; this could lead to vulnerability in the system. Internet connections are also a big security risk.
- **Updating controls.** Where control accounts are maintained there is a check in the validity of transaction processing. In the absence of such control accounts, the only control is independent validation.
- **Maintenance controls.** Usually only authorised persons may update software since unauthorised amendments can create spurious information. It is essential that standing data and programs are correctly maintained.

Management

Resource managers producing spreadsheets for their own use may not need the above controls, but audit and control issues should be considered if additional staff are involved and as a way of improving systems. Knight *et al.* (1993, p. 105) summarise the main use of spreadsheets as :

- *worksheets* to perform calculations
- *databases* to store, sort, extract and analyse data quickly
- *charts and graphics* to present information in an easily understood way

As shown, worksheets can be used for calculations which range from simple arithmetic and statistics to multi-linked financial models. These are best used for large or complex calculations where manual recalculation would be time-consuming, or for modelling. Modelling deals with multi-variables and 'what if?' situations.

A database will store interrelated data in list form. The selected data can then be extracted to provide the user with information. Schools often hold information on database programs, which are more powerful than spreadsheets. Data can be transferred from these programs to spreadsheets in order to perform calculations.

Spreadsheets are also a useful mechanism for preparing charts and graphics for the enhancement of report writing. Different graphics will provide pictorial representations of data. The overall quality and potential impact of the report will, as a consequence, be much improved.

The use of information technology in schools has developed beyond that of an administrative tool. Management information systems (MIS) are an aid to communication and financial management. As a consequence, management and staff require training in order to use the system as appropriate. Lancaster (1989, p. 181) comments:

> It is generally accepted that computers can be used either to restrict information by removing the need for information processing and analysis to be delegated, or can be used to facilitate the dissemination and communication of information.

Headteachers and senior managers will need to assess the dissemination of information within their institutions. Similarly, headteachers need to ensure that they use information and financial systems to assist them in the effective management of teaching and learning. If information technology is to be of use, the packages need to:

1 **be flexible:** so as to accommodate curriculum, financial and administrative needs
2 **follow good accountancy procedures:** all financial elements must satisfy this important principle, including an audit trail that can accommodate LMS and GM models

3 **be secure:** as a system which has such a variety of activities will need a wealth of security passwords – pupils, via the Internet, are known to be accessing confidential files and manipulating them

4 **be easy to use:** with support manuals containing clear instructions. In addition, instructions on each working screen will help the process

5 **have user appeal:** many school teaching and support staff will not be expert in the use of computers – systems will need to be created that accommodate the needs of those with limited computer skills

6 **be comprehensive:** to satisfy school, LEA and college demands. All systems should be usable within any one authority.

Summary

Critical to the effectiveness of resource management in schools is the ease with which schools can control and monitor relevant administrative procedures. School governors and senior managers need to assess the need to appoint additional administrative staff for the purpose of resource management.

The majority of schools and LEAs have introduced financial and management information systems to provide the necessary information for schools to control their finances and, for LEAs, to monitor and evaluate the schools' performance. In the maintained sector, school and LEA computer systems need to be compatible or networked. Service level agreements between the LEA and the schools will need to be drawn up concerning computer systems.

Managers are now in a position to use and design their own small-scale information and decision-support systems. The spreadsheet has provided a 'user-friendly programming environment' for financial modelling. In practice, a model may be defined as a 'representation of reality', which in this context includes a means of simulating the financial affairs of a school.

A financial model will consist of facts and assumptions which are related in an explicit and systematic way. When the model is implemented as a spreadsheet, the input data (unassembled information) is accurately and speedily manipulated into useful management output. Spreadsheet models enable resource managers to manage and plan with the benefit of superior financial information. Resource managers can test out the implications of their plans well before action needs to be taken.

Critically, a model can only predict and behave within its design constraints, therefore the output from a financial model must be placed in the context of school life. In order to maximise the advantages and minimise the disadvantages, it is important to adopt a systematic approach to the design of a spreadsheet model that first considers the context of modelling and then the specific details of the model in question.

164

10
■ ■ ■

Measuring performance

Introduction

Since 1979, the aim of the government has been to improve the quality of provision in education while obtaining better value for the money spent. Given that schools must improve quality and provide value for money, measuring performance, monitoring and evaluating practice have become integral elements in the management of schools. Management is central to the efficiency and effectiveness of the monitoring and evaluation process. Holt (1990, p. 99) states:

> The monitoring and evaluation process should not only inform us about the quality of what is being offered in schools, it should actually promote a raising of standards.

Measuring performance raises many issues, and the notion of equity of educational provision is central to resource management. This chapter encompasses three themes: measuring performance, monitoring and evaluation, and equity.

Measuring performance

As a consequence of the ERA, LEAs are expected to monitor and evaluate more systematically than hitherto the work of schools, colleges and other educational services (Audit Commission, 1989). Circular 7/88 directs LEAs to develop 'performance management of governing bodies'. The impact of performance indicators can have a marked effect on school practice (Brighouse, 1990). School managers are to measure performance in their schools according to performance indicators, as Young (1989, p. 205) explains:

> It will be the task of all concerned with the education service to design a system of performance indicators in collaboration with each other that reflect the educational outcomes which schools in particular see as important and aim to help in

understanding how to attain those educational outcomes. The approach should be collaborative, formative, aimed at interpretation not judgement [. . .].

Measuring performance in schools extends beyond finances/resources. Parents judge schools on the basis of location, leadership, National Curriculum standard assessment test results, examination results and socio-economic factors. Teachers often feel that they have a wider view of what constitutes good education than many parents, who are stereotyped as being over-concerned with 'uniform, discipline and exam results'. John Elliot (1981) researched the attitudes of parents in a high technology area towards an 11–18 comprehensive; parents selected the school on the basis of a balanced education including personal and social development. These parents placed a greater emphasis on their children being happy and enjoying lessons than they did on examination results.

In practice managers need to be aware that departments must be helped to develop the skills of self-evaluation in order to give teachers ownership of any changes which are required. Teachers need feedback from colleagues, parents and pupils as to the effectiveness and efficiency of their work. As discussed in Chapter 4 INSET is a useful means of teams working together towards effective and efficient practice. Teachers work in relative isolation within their class-rooms. However, teamwork towards common objectives can lead to improvements in practice. Teachers will form impressions of colleagues' work from minor 'happenings': noise in the corridor, lack of material when absent and standards of reporting are a few important examples. Examination results and attendance figures will also influence a teacher's view of a school, as do suspensions and formal sanctions for indiscipline.

The focus on management performance has created dilemmas for senior management teams. Efficiency or 'value for money' is steeped in controversy which relates directly to resource management. The Audit Commission has contributed towards this aspect of education, highlighting the 'cost per pupil' and outcomes. Coopers & Lybrand (1988) further complicated matters by regarding contact ratio and PTRs as 'process indicators' together with teacher turnover, reward/sanction systems and homework policy. In contrast, Holt (1990, p. 106) found that teachers considered performance indicators negatively:

- *any numerical measures need a good deal of explanation and background information if they are not to be misleading.*
- *you cannot assess performance unless you are clear about what you are trying to do.*

Performance indicators, as with all other aspects of school management, are inextricably linked to SDPs. Measuring efficiency, effectiveness and productivity is the most difficult aspect of resource management (Knight, 1983, p. 96). Schools are in the position of measuring the cost of teaching and learning. This is not new, as Knight (1983, p. 97) states:

Parents who opt out of the state system actually place a cash value on their chosen school and its likely output in terms of their particular child.

However, measuring actual costs against outputs is very difficult, as educationalists have found. Examination results and musical achievement can be measured. In contrast, moral education, artistic ability and personal motivation cannot be measured. Socio-economic facts are critical to the issue of measurement. While two schools may have similar costs (size of building, number of pupils/teachers, etc.), their output will be dependent on wider social and economic factors, in addition to the motivation and aspirations of parents and pupils. Performance-related assessment is possible. However, in practice comparisons between schools are very difficult to quantify. Glatter (1996, p. 4) comments:

Has education focused sufficiently on results and outputs? [. . .] Many would argue that Education has been excessively preoccupied with inputs and unnecessarily wary of any attempt to focus on results. [. . .] Performance tables have a role to play, [. . .] more schools are involved in benchmarking their performance against other institutions.

How to measure performance can be problematic. Michael Rutter (1979) used five measures of outcome:

1   Attendance
2   Academic attainment in public examinations
3   Pupil behaviour
4   Delinquency
5   Employment.

While 1, 2 and 5 are measurable, 3 and 4 are judgement-based and therefore very difficult to quantify. Qualitative approaches to measurement may help with these issues; this research paradigm is time-consuming and criticised by some educationalists and social scientists.

School indicators and performance review

The LMS Initiative (1990, p. 102) defines the fundamental questions for performance review:

Where do we want to go?

How do we get there?

How are we going to get on?

The performance review should emerge from the SDP and provide the structure within which these questions can be answered. It should be designed by each school to meet its own needs. However, it will not be possible for a school to review all activities each year. This should be limited to a number of priority areas that relate to the key aims and objectives of the school. Areas of concern that arise during the academic year should also be examined.

As shown, measuring performance in education is not straightforward. Although aims and objectives can be defined, it is difficult to establish how the achievement of aims can be measured in practice (LMS Initiative, 1990, pp. 102–3). This has led to the development of performance indicators, which are not exact measures of performance. The LMS Initiative (1990, pp. 102–3) explains that performance indicators:

> [. . .] are measures which are thought to have a relationship (and therefore be 'indicative' of) the aspect of performance in question: they can only be approximations or proxy indicators.

Further, the LMS Initiative (p. 103) warns that performance indicators can be open to misinterpretation and are rarely conclusive. However:

> they are a powerful [. . .] tool for internal school management. [. . .] [Performance indicators] can identify the strengths and weaknesses of the performance of a [. . . school] and its efficiency and effectiveness.

Indicators

In practice, managers should compare where the school is to where it should be. There is a spectrum of indicators, quantitative and qualitative, that are likely to demonstrate aspects of performance including (LMS Initiative, 1990, p. 103):

- economy (i.e. measure the cost of resources used, having regard to their quality)
- efficiency (i.e. the relationship between the output of the service and the input of resources used to produce it)
- effectiveness (i.e. the relationship between the output of the service and the desired outcome for it).

The most developed set of indicators focus on the resource consumption (or input) aspects of performance, whereby the school is a consumer of resources and indicators are concerned with the economic and efficient use of inputs. Most attention has been given to quantitative indicators based on costs which are used in the drive for increased value for money. While quantifiable, this area is narrow and does not reflect the overall efficiency and effectiveness of a school. The LMS Initiative (1990, p. 104) summarises the three aspects of performance central to efficiency and effectiveness:

- inputs (i.e. the resources consumed in running the school)
- processes (i.e. the way resources are organised to provide the quality of provision of the 'educational experience')
- outputs (i.e. the achievements of the school).

The above are based on management theory used to analyse industrial and commercial organisations. They can be applied to educational organisations as the LMS Initiative (1990, p. 105) explains. The discussion is summarised in brief below.

Inputs (resources)

These are generally quantitative and include teaching and non-teaching staff, premises, facilities and equipment. Used in isolation, these have limited use and can be misleading. Measures include (LMS Initiative, 1990, p. 105):

- *pupil-staff ratios (for teaching and non-teaching staff)*
- *total unit costs (e.g. cost per pupil).*

Quality of provision (process)

This relates to the education process experienced by pupils including (LMS Initiative, 1990, p. 105):

- *the learning process in terms of the style of teaching, level of interaction with pupils and teacher expectations*
- *the curriculum offered in terms of its relevance, balance and breadth, and the range of options possible*
- *extra-curricular activities offered*
- *the ambience of the school in terms of its physical appearance, atmosphere and the attitudes of staff – teaching and non-teaching.*

All of the above are difficult to define. What constitutes a 'good' school is, inevitably, open to interpretation. The LMS Initiative (1990, p. 106) advises that qualitative judgements are important in assessing the quality of provision through:

- *self-assessment by staff and pupils*
- *internal review by senior teaching staff (e.g. head of department observing the performance of her/his staff – also this might form part of a staff development and appraisal process)*
- *external review by experts (e.g. LEA inspectors, HMI) or peer groups in other schools (although any observation process runs the risk of changing the behaviour of those being observed).*

Achievements (outputs)

This is the most important dimension requiring assessment. Critically, it will also be the basis on which the school is able to market itself to potential parents and pupils. For pupils, achievements are likely to include (LMS Initiative, 1990, p. 106):

- *success in terms of children's learning and development ([. . .] success can be viewed as 'value added' to the pupils [. . .])*
- *success in other activities (e.g. achievements)*
- *positive attitudes (e.g. initiative, confidence, enthusiasm to learn, sensitivity to others)*
- *standards of behaviour (e.g. punctuality, levels of truancy, care of school property)*
- *post-school destinations (e.g. into employment, further and higher education or training and the views of those destinations of the ex-pupils they receive/recruit).*

All of the above are complex to define and measure. Governors and staff should decide which aspects of achievement are important, based on the school's aims and objectives (SDPs). The school will also have to set performance in the context of external factors and the need to balance success in one area of development/achievement against failure in another.

Combining measures

Any measure of a single aspect of performance is of limited value and can be misleading. Achievements should be placed in the context of quality of provision, which is dependent on resources. The LMS Initiative (1990, p. 107) suggests that schools operate from a baseline in terms of:

> *[. . .] the resources they command [. . .] also the achievements of pupils and the nature of the community each school serves.*

Further (p. 108):

> *A record of relevant indicators kept over several years can help a school assess whether it is moving in the right direction – and with speed.*

Performance indicators, as a system of evaluating past performance, are only of value if the process influences future planning. The development and use of indicators should be guided by a number of factors (LMS Initiative, 1990, p. 110) including:

- *the importance to the school of the objective or activity to which the indicator relates*
- *the perceived usefulness of the indicator as an effective signal of performance (this will determine the credibility in the school)*
- *the ease and cost of collection of the relevant information*
- *the likely validity of the indicator over time*
- *the comparability with indicators used by other schools locally or nationally*
- *the existence of LEA or [DFEE] requirements or recommendations.*

It is axiomatic that the indicators chosen should reflect the objectives of the school.

Sources of information

These will include (LMS Initiative, pp. 110–11):

- *inspection reports [internal and external] [. . .]*
- *appraisal results*
- *surveys of views of pupils, parents and external bodies [. . .].*

In sum, indicators help the school to judge how well it is doing compared with what it seeks to do. Indicators also help to identify areas of the school's activities that require closer examination. Critically, indicators can affect behaviour as well as measure it. Essentially, performance indicators are a valuable tool in the process of school planning, and as a means of monitoring and evaluating school practice. The purpose of evaluation is to collect highly objective data that will identify achievement and indicate change in specified areas. Resource managers need to know how to develop surveys that accurately assess attitude changes among pupils, staff and parents.

Monitoring

Monitoring is an ongoing process, integral to teaching and learning. In the process of planning education Hargreaves (1995, pp. 220–1) suggests that the two questions a school leader needs to ask are:

- *Who is monitoring what, in which ways and with what effectiveness?*
- *Who is responsible for adjusting what, in which ways, when and with what effectiveness?*

As Figure 10.1 illustrates, having implemented a plan (SDP, DDP or lesson plan), managers and class teachers need to monitor its progress. If plans are not monitored, it will not be possible to determine whether their objectives have been achieved. Monitoring also enables managers and teachers to obtain the best results from the available resources and lead their team towards agreed objectives. Monitoring is made easier if objectives are:

- clear and practical
- agreed by all members of the team.

Once objectives have been agreed the department/team can move forward with confidence. From clear objectives comes a sense of purpose. It may be difficult to obtain co-operation and agreement when deciding on departmental objectives. However, it is important to reach agreement within your team if your plan is to work effectively.

Monitoring also provides the basis for evaluating practice. Teams/departments are able to measure and compare their performance against agreed criteria. Monitoring may also assist middle managers in the planning of staff

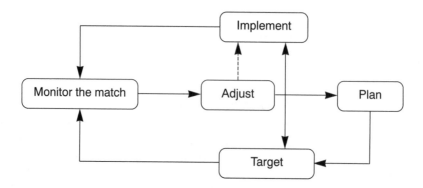

Figure 10.1: Development planning feedback loop
(*Source:* Hargreaves, 1995, p. 221; reproduced by permission of the publisher, Journals Oxford Ltd)

development by providing an insight into the strengths and weaknesses in their departments/teams. Most significantly, monitoring will provide a framework in which staff can reflect on their own practice, an outcome of which is enhanced job satisfaction.

Monitoring is an ongoing activity and requires regular progress reports – it should not be left to the end of the year. Monitoring information is needed to enable schools to follow the school development plan. As the LMS Initiative (1990, p. 72) explains, this will include:

- *operational information*
- *financial information*
- *information on performance.*

Other aspects of monitoring are defined by Hargreaves (1995, pp. 224–5), who distinguishes between internal monitoring and external monitoring. Internal monitoring involves headteachers and senior managers gathering feedback on the critical aspects of the life and work of the school. Managers may under-estimate the capacity of staff and students to hide things from them. Equally staff and students may be good at identifying required adjustments.

External monitoring (p. 226) involves headteachers and the senior manage-ment team acting as 'gate-keepers' of external demands. In doing so, the SMT will need to filter the school's values and vision in order to avoid any external imposition so it does not destroy its good features. Adjustments will need to be made to accommodate changes and to create development structures to respond to new challenges. External agencies may also provide supportive networks that will strengthen staff/student commitment.

In sum, monitoring should confirm allocation of funds, guard against ineffective allocation and intervene with appropriate resources when faced with unexpected challenges. In order to carry out monitoring resource managers must have knowledge and skills in information collection and time management.

Monitoring resources

Monitoring aims and objectives in action is a constant and consistent activity in schools (Davies and Ellison, 1992, p. 24). Key questions are:

- *Who monitors the school in action?*
- *How is the monitoring carried out?*
- *How are the governors [and parents] kept informed [. . .]?*
- *How is the evaluation carried out?*
- *Who prepares the financial report?*

The NPBEA (1993, p. 13–15) defines the monitoring of resources as:

- *demonstrating current knowledge of the curriculum and pupil progress (assessment)*
- *use of spreadsheets to track changes and patterns in resource use*
- *[monitoring] school–business partnerships*
- *overseeing [LEA and grant agency] cash collection and reporting procedures*
- *tracking [staff needs, full-time and part-time]*
- *revising job descriptions on a [regular] basis*
- *maintaining data on [staff cover and] employee absenteeism*
- *logging grievance issues and grievance frequencies*
- *determining and documenting levels of staff performance*
- *conducting [staff appraisals]*
- *encouraging staff to use periodic [staff] assessments*
- *monitoring [pupil numbers]*
- *monitoring [extra-curricular costs]*
- *monitoring the expected life span of equipment*
- *noting overuse and underuse of the school building*
- *regulating the building maintenance plan.*

For operational and financial information, resource managers need to monitor actual expenditure and operations regularly and to take corrective action. Monitoring of actual spending against budgets is likely to reveal projected over- or underspending. The LMS Initiative (1990, p. 73) advises that if there is a projected overspend of the total budget, schools should ask:

- *Is it likely to correct itself? Is it just an advance of expenditure?*
- *What action can be taken to bring expenditure back to budget? Is this desirable?*

173

- *If corrective action is not desirable, should any of the provision for contingencies be used?*
- *If no contingency funds are available, how can future expenditure be brought back into line?*

Alternatively, if there is a projected underspend schools should consider:

- *Is it just a timing difference and the amount will be spent in a later period?*
- *Should it be committed for another purpose this year or carried forward to next?*

Maychell (1994, pp. 106–7) found that there were different approaches among NFER case study schools in monitoring their budgets. For some, monitoring was optional while for others it was critical to the budgeting process. Headteachers found the time involved in producing budget statements for each area of the curriculum proved difficult. Some headteachers kept a record of spending but did not produce budget statements during the course of the year.

Financial regulations should specify the action to be taken when variations from the controlled budget reach particular levels. Schools should establish their own rules; a set of questions similar to the above will need to be asked if any individual budget heading looks as if it might be over- or underspent.

Evaluation

Whereas monitoring is an ongoing process, a means of checking progress, evaluation is an overall check on whether objectives are achieved within the planned timetable. Evaluation should be a collaborative process. The desire to achieve success is motivating; evaluation should focus on success in addition to identifying areas which require improvement. In practice, external and internal accountability are central to educational and management practice in schools. The appraisal of teachers is a key factor in the evaluation process. The introduction of job descriptions and school curriculum policies has given teachers a greater role definition by which they can evaluate their position in the school.

In addition, governing bodies are required to manage the implementation and evaluation of their own policies. Senior and middle managers are required to provide evidence to support the efficiency and effectiveness of teaching and management. Evaluation is a component of development planning and an essential prerequisite to preparing any subsequent plan. The DES (1989, p. 17; Crown copyright) stated that the purpose of evaluating SDPs is to:

- *examine the success of the implementation of the plan*
- *assess the extent to which the school's aims have been furthered*

- *assess the impact of the plan on pupils' learning and achievement*
- *decide on how to disseminate successful new practices throughout the school*
- *make the process of reporting easier.*

The process of evaluating the impact of a plan on practice is critical to the successful implementation of the plan. Evaluation is a collaborative exercise involving (Oldroyd and Hall, 1990, p. 34):

- asking **questions**
- gathering **information**
- forming **conclusions**

in order to:

- make **recommendations**.

In contrast to monitoring, evaluation encompasses reviewing the status of a plan's objectives. Through the evaluation process, managers will determine the need to change objectives, priorities and/or practice.

Hargreaves and Hopkins (1991) stress the importance of evaluation in enhancing the professional judgement of teachers. Evaluation can lead to a change in teachers' perceptions of their practice. For middle managers, the evaluation of department plans can provide the basis for action. Oldroyd and Hall (1990, p. 41) offer a checklist for planning and evaluation, as shown in Figure 10.2.

Budget evaluation

As stated, the evaluation process is the most difficult for schools. Maychell (1994) found that not all schools made the time to evaluate the effectiveness of their budgets. In contrast, some spent more time evaluating than developing the budget. Knight (1993, p. 151) describes three aspects of budget evaluation:

1 *Financial efficiency – comparing the out-turn budget with the start-of-year estimate.*

2 *Resource efficiency – looking at what the money was spent on.*

3 *Effectiveness – assessing whether the expenditure has achieved the outcomes hoped for.*

Knight (1993, p. 152) also gives practical advice on how to evaluate the budget:

*A solution is to see budgetary evaluation in two stages: **functional** evaluation of financial and resource efficiency, carried out annually, and **strategic** evaluation, occurring as part of the school's normal evaluation process, whenever it occurs.*

In brief, **functional budget evaluation** should be carried out at the end of the financial year. The process should be both reflective and practical involving governors, resource managers and budget holders.

---

1. **Purposes, broad guidelines, aims** or **objectives** for the subject under scrutiny which are:

   - clear

   - indicators of desired performance or outcomes.

2. **Questions** which are:

   - unambiguous

   - penetrating

   - useful.

3. **Information** which is:

   - accessible

   - related to questions

   - not too voluminous to handle.

4. **Conclusions** which consider:

   - conditions

   - effects

   - assumptions

   - alternatives.

5. **Reports** which are:

   - concise

   - focused on audience's need

   - likely to inform decision-making.

6. **A good evaluation brief:**

   - specifying much of the above.

Figure 10.2: Checklist for planning and evaluation
(*Source:* Oldroyd and Hall, 1990, p. 41; reproduced by permission of the publisher, National Development Centre for Educational Management and Policy)

Strategic budget evaluation relates to SDP evaluation and should involve all managers and governors. This evaluation will include non-financial budgets such as the timetable, rooms, PTRs, etc. The evaluation will focus on outcomes, e.g. actual improvements in teaching and learning. In practice, it is important to relate such changes to the resources consumed, i.e. a cost-effectiveness review.

The NPBEA (1993, pp. 13–16 to 13–17) suggests that resource managers and senior management teams are responsible for synthesising and summarising documented information gathered during the school year, in order to define evaluation procedures in the planning stages of the resource allocation cycle. The NPBEA advises that resource managers use cost-effective analysis to quantify evaluations and project consequences of maintaining the present allocation. In sum, resource managers in consultation with the LEA, governors, senior managers, budget holders and staff should be able to (NPBEA, 1993, p. 13–17):

1 *design resource allocation systems*

2 *describe the role of resource allocation in meeting school [aims and objectives]*

3 *identify various non-traditional resources available to schools*

4 *design a strategy to gain resources from [non-LEA] sources*

5 *describe the relationship of resource [funding] to resource appointment*

6 *design a monitoring and [reallocation] system for resource use*

7 *develop an accountability system for resource use*

8 *connect resource allocation to [pupil] outcomes*

9 *develop a system for staff participation in determining goals, [allocating] resources and evaluating the use of resources*

10 *develop and administer a school budget and an activities budget*

11 *define resources as human and material as well as fiscal*

12 *employ technical procedures such as spreadsheets, planning charts, and programme budgeting [. . .]*

13 *design and administer a materials and equipment inventory system.*

Quality of service

Resource managers also need to evaluate the quality of service provision. This is as important as the cost of the service. Maychell (1994, p. 51) lists the questions schools considered when assessing the quality of a service:

1 *How satisfied are we with the quality of the work/provision under existing arrangements, e.g. in terms of general standards of service, response time if there is a problem, management of the service?*

2 *How flexible is the service – does it meet our individual requirements?*

3 *What are the risks if we get involved with a new contractor? (Better the devil you know?)*

4   *How can we be certain new companies meet accepted safety standards? (Schools tended to assume that LEA contractors conformed to required safety standards.)*

5   *Would we have more control if we altered the service arrangements?*

Resource managers should remain focused on the need for schools to provide an environment which raises standards in the provision of education.

Audit Commission

Beyond the school, the Audit Commission has responsibility for monitoring and evaluating public sector spending. The LMS Initiative (1990, pp. 138–9) comments:

> *The members of the Commission, numbering between 13 and 17, are appointed by the Secretary of State after consultation with the local authority associations and other bodies deemed to be appropriate.*

In addition to its audit responsibilities, the Commission is required to undertake or promote (p. 139):

- *comparative and other studies designed to enable it to make recommendations for improving economy, efficiency and effectiveness [. . .]*
- *other studies relating to the provision by such bodies of their services.*

School inspection (OFSTED)

Schools are inspected by a team of professional inspectors appointed by the Office for Standards in Education. The inspection process is determined by government legislation. Within the inspection process inspectors consider how schools manage resources and equate this with value for money (Levačić and Glover, 1996). In the context of public sector accounting, schools have been deemed by OFSTED as giving satisfactory overall value for money, in terms of educational standards achieved and quality of education provided in relation to its context and income (OFSTED Handbook, 1994).

Value for money

In contrast to OFSTED's view Arkin's report (1996, p. 8) suggests that around two schools in five should be making better use of their resources than they are:

> *While schools that make good use of financial resources have clear developmental priorities and target spending on areas of need, those which are judged less efficient tend to lack clear priorities. They often fail to quantify needs and to cost alternatives.*

They take uninformed financial decisions, which result in waste, including underused textbooks and overused photocopiers.

Arkin (p. 8) suggests that the way forward is to link financial and development planning. During the evaluation process resource managers should ask the following key questions:

- *Have we made a clear link between the budget and the school development plan?*
- *Are the governors making enough use of their discretion over teachers' pay?*
- *Have we got the right staffing mix and are people spending their time appropriately?*
- *Do we know why we have a budget surplus or deficit?*
- *Do we shop around for the best deals and negotiate the lowest prices?*
- *Do we waste fuel and water?*
- *Do we know what we are really paying for goods and services?*
- *Do we support our administration with the right technology?*

While the above enables resource managers to evaluate the procurement and allocation of resources within the context of teaching and learning, the questions also raise the issue of equity in education.

Equity

Resource managers need to consider the issue of equity. Simkins (1995, p. 222) comments:

As a starting point, the term 'equity' may be broadly equated with 'fairness' and 'justice' (LaGrand, 1991, Ch. 2) [. . .]. More challenging and complex questions are raised, however, when the issues of distributional equity are addressed [. . .].

In brief, schools are funded from public funds for the benefit of individuals. Resource managers should, therefore, consider whether the school budget is equitable for all students. Thomas (1996, p. 44) comments:

A framework for reporting upon the achievement of national, regional and institutional goals can provide a means for reviewing and reporting upon the efficiency/cost-effectiveness and equity of the school system. It can provide a source of information which, by being more open, brings greater equality in debates which are otherwise heavily skewed in the direction of the professionals.

In schools, within LEAs and at the national level, there is a potential for creating a framework and an information system by which a dialogue of accountability can be encouraged between the range of stakeholders in the system. In practice, do all students receive a fair allocation of the school's resources? Knight (1993, pp. 154–9) provides a checklist for equity, as given in Table 10.1.

Table 10.1: Checklist for equity

Equity for whom?	Gender, ethnicity, social class or intellectual ability.
Comparison with whom?	Inter-school (LEA) or intra-school.
What is to be measured?	
Finance:	Comparisons of costs per student.
Physical and human resources:	PTRs, class size, ancillary staff, library books, etc.
Time allocation:	Fixed or flexible allocation of time according to pupil needs?
School time:	Maximising learning, keeping students 'on task'.
Educational process:	Who does the school favour: gifted or special needs pupils?
Outputs:	When inputs or processes are translated into outputs, are there marked disparities between groups and individuals, e.g. boys in foreign languages?
Outcomes:	Continuation of education, training, employment, occupation and career advancement, delinquency, etc.

(*Source:* Knight, 1993, pp. 154–9; reproduced by permission of the publisher, Heinemann Educational Publishers)

All of the items in Table 10.1 can be measured between schools or internally within a school. Knight (1993, p. 159) concludes that, while efficiency and effectiveness are difficult to measure, equity is more so. As Simkins (1995, p. 224) states:

> *How can [. . .] equity be related to the educational reforms in England and Wales? [. . .] such consequences will arise through the ways in which the reforms influence the allocation of resources among schools and individuals. [. . .]*

> *The formula and local market circumstances [. . .] only determine the degree of equity between schools in the system and hence place constraints on the opportunities which schools can provide for individual pupils. The <u>actual</u> opportunities provided to any pupil within these constraints depend upon a school's internal resource allocation policies, and, in particular, upon how the school chooses to use the freedoms given to it. [. . .]*

An area of education that engages with issues of equity on a daily basis in schools is the provision for pupils with special educational needs.

Special educational needs (SEN)

Levačić (1995, pp. 158–60) highlights sub-groups within schools which require special consideration in the context of equitable provision. With the reduction of LEA services, schools' special educational needs co-ordinators are under significant pressure to provide resources for pupils with learning or behavioural difficulties. Special needs staffing is vulnerable at all levels. Specific areas of need to be considered are:

- travellers
- forces children
- section 11 pupils
- gifted pupils.

Levačić (p. 145) comments:

> The formula guidelines enable LEAs to allocate through the [. . .] additional funding to schools for educationally and socially disadvantaged pupils, provided the LEA can devise 'objective' indicators of these needs.

However, in practice, as Thomas (1996, p. 38) concludes:

> [. . .] those schools with a high proportion of SEN pupils [are] the losers in the change of funding [. . .]. These findings emphasise the need for empirical work to assess the effects of restructuring allocative mechanisms. In this case, the introduction of a pupil-based formula, a key component of the move to a market-based system, has effects which differ between LEAs.

An issue of further concern is, as Levačić (1995, p. 160) suggests, that some schools are deselecting pupils with special needs, thus enrolling pupils with ability and the motivation to succeed:

> The extent that financial and market pressures of local management lead schools to serve pupils with special needs less adequately than previously is dependent on the professional values of teachers, in particular headteachers and deputies, and on the attitudes of governing bodies.

Armstrong of the University of Sheffield (1995) also found integration inequity in the UK. Pupils with special educational needs are particularly vulnerable because some schools are reluctant to accept them, fearing the cost of learning support and the effect on their position in the league tables. In spite of official support for integration and parental involvement in decision-making, as well as a few encouraging examples of fully inclusive policies adopted by a small number of local authorities, full inclusion in ordinary schools remains the exception rather than the rule. In sum, the deselection of special needs pupils is a central issue in the equitable provision of education, as Thomas (1996, p. 42), quoting Doyal and Gough (1991, p. 215), comments:

> Education has a key role in contributing to an individual's need for autonomy of agency and critical autonomy. As a means for leading to autonomy of agency it

implies [...] a core curriculum of subjects, more or less the same for all cultures, including basic numeracy, general social skills, physical and biological processes, general and local history and vocational abilities which are relevant to further employment. Ideally, learning of this kind readies students for active participation in the entire spectrum of practices/choices on which the continuation and, hopefully, the improvement of their well-being depend.

Inequity in practice

Research has also revealed a disparity of funding of inner-city schools (Sheffield City Council, 1992). This reflects the government's financial penalties on LEAs exceeding their spending of SSAs, which is a political not an educational issue. In addition, research (Hardman and Levačić, 1994) has also found that where primary schools have received additional funding since the ERA, secondary schools have experienced a reduction in funding. However, as Levačić (1995, p. 148) states:

The impact of local management or equity is both a contentious and complex subject, since its assessment depends both on how equity is defined and perceived, and on a host of interrelated factors, which are likely to differ in their effects on schools and pupils according to the local context.

Primary and secondary

Bassey (1996, p. 13) reported that:

The Three Wise Men said it in 1992, the House of Commons Select Committee in 1994, the chief inspector and the National Primary Headteachers' Association earlier this year: 'It is wrong that primary school pupils attract much less funding than secondary schools pupils.'

NFER research (1996) also reported substantial variations between local education authorities in the scale of difference between primary and secondary funding. At present, each local education authority decides on the age-weighted pupil unit (AWPU) for each age group of the school population each year. Table 10.2 illustrates the disparity between Key Stages 1/2 and Key Stages 3/4 in seven LEAs.

This issue has also been identified by Thomas (1996, p. 35) who comments:

When the new patterns of resource allocations are examined, however, the basis for deciding the relative requirements of different age groups is not readily apparent. Certainly, there is no consensus on their comparative requirements, so that it is impossible to discern a common view on the resources needed to provide an education, based upon the national curriculum, to pupils of different ages.

The majority of primary and secondary headteachers are concerned by the disparity of provision between Years 6 and 7. Why should the age of a pupil

Table 10.2: AWPUs of seven LEAs in 1995–6

Year	Derbys.	Wirral	Sheffield	Nott'm	Leics.	Bir'ham	Wands.
1	970	991	1 000	1 054	1 166	1 300	1 542
2	970	991	1 000	1 054	1 157	1 160	1 542
3	950	1 000	935	1 005	1 101	1 122	1 285
4	954	1 000	935	1 005	1 101	1 130	1 285
5	954	1 000	935	1 005	1 126	1 158	1 285
6	984	1 008	935	1 005	1 127	1 328	1 542
7	1 452	1 456	1 355	1 433	1 517	1 611	1 542
8	1 452	1 465	1 355	1 433	1 520	1 672	1 542
9	1 452	1 465	1 355	1 433	1 520	1 654	1 542
10	1 676	1 939	1 396	1 778	1 754	1 792	2 442
11	1 805	2 051	1 517	1 778	1 830	1 936	2 442

determine the unit of funding? Bassey examined the difference in the funding of Year 6 and Year 7 children in 91 LEAs in England for 1995–6 in the 'Section 42' returns. He found that the average allocation for a Year 6 child was £1 146 in contrast to £1 553 for a Year 7 child.

Does the nature of pupil learning at a particular stage deserve more teachers? At present it is secondary schools that have these advantages. Bassey argues that primary schools deserve more teachers because of the range of subjects taught by the class teacher in responding to the demands of the National Curriculum.

Bassey concluded that each school-age child, irrespective of whether they are aged 5–10 or 11–16 and irrespective of locality, should attract the same level of unit funding in terms of payments of teachers' salaries. However, as the House of Commons Education Committee (1994; Crown copyright) states:

> [. . .] concentrating on the change in funding between Year 6 and Year 7 can obscure the more important issue: the enormous importance of primary education (which has traditionally not been recognised in the resources it receives) and the continuous nature of the education process. The current funding profile does not recognise this educational continuum [. . .].

The funding of education

Existing research focusing on the funding of education is limited; however, there is a need for governors, senior managers and resource managers to consider this issue when evaluating financial and resource allocations. It is axiomatic that the aims and objectives of the school should reflect governors', managers' and teachers' desires to provide an equitable education for all pupils. However, the *Guardian* leader (2 March 1996, p. 21) implies that a crisis is imminent:

> *The British education system is buckling under the weight of incompatible demands [...] the system suffers from an unprecedented financial squeeze. [...] There is a growing decline in confidence in the basic institution of secondary education – the comprehensive – which is extending to the primary school.*

A comprehensive evaluation of the funding of education has been compiled by Coopers & Lybrand, commissioned by the National Union of Teachers. In brief, Coopers & Lybrand (1996, p. 2) listed the nine criteria to which the NUT believes education funding should conform. Funding should:

- *apply to all schools on an equal basis*
- *ensure that all children and young people have equal educational opportunities*
- *lead to a basic equity of funding between schools*
- *identify and provide for additional educational needs*
- *ensure that Government is accountable for its funding decisions*
- *recognise and distinguish clearly between the responsibilities of local government and central government interests*
- *be as simple as possible*
- *be as transparent as possible*
- *ensure long-term stability in school funding.*

The report found inequalities between and within LEAs in terms of funding, and that there is insufficient justification for these differences in value for money or educational terms (NUT, 1996):

> *The Government falls back on historic spending patterns of local education authorities and caps those whose spending exceeds prescribed limits, without analysing existing needs of authorities.*

Coopers & Lybrand suggest the following proposals for change:

- **Curriculum** – that the government makes some link between the National Curriculum and resources.
- **LEAs and SSAs** – that local authority expenditure control is clearly defined by prescribed categories (primary, secondary and post-16) within the context of SSAs.
- **Formula-based assessment** – that funding should be activity-based, related to provision of the National Curriculum, and determined by a formula-based assessment, incorporating teachers' salaries, class sizes and teacher contact ratios (PTRs).
- **Pupil unit funding** – resources are allocated per pupil unit.
- **LMS management** – LEAs will continue to be responsible for distributing resources to schools.

Further proposals are also made concerning additional educational needs and local responsibilities. Coopers & Lybrand present a new methodology to meet the NUT criteria based on equalisation of need: full details can be found in their report published by the NUT, June 1996.

The way forward?

Inequity in educational provision is a broad issue that needs to be addressed at local and national levels. Gewirtz, Ball and Bowe (1995, p. 179) summarise key factors, uncovered by research into the pressures in schools:

- *increased differentiation and segregation, both within and between schools*
- *a redistribution of resources away from those with greatest learning difficulties, both within and between schools*
- *the commodification of education and the student*
- *the re-orientation, redefinition, and narrowing in scope of schooling*
- *the establishment of methods, structures and values of organisation and management 'borrowed' from industry and commerce.*

The above reflects the need for politicians to relate policies to practice, as Gewirtz *et al.* conclude (1995, pp. 189–90):

> *Typically, advocates of choice in education respond to the English 'market-in-practice' [. . .] the 'market-in-theory' is a utopian vision which is constructed outside of the political and financial realities of modern education systems. It ignores the class interests represented within the state.*

Caldwell (1996, p. 4) has considered the relationship between resourcing in schools and their success in raising educational achievement:

> *[. . .] the extent to which the introduction of the local management of schools has had an impact on learning outcomes has been a matter of contention. [. . .] In a recent report of the National Commission on Education [. . .] such reform is viewed rather modestly in accounting for the impressive performance of some schools that have achieved Success Against the Odds.*

Hutton (1996) suggests building on the good practice that exists in schools:

> *The task is to find a structure which does not endanger the current areas of excellence while turning around the growing crisis in the state sector where it does exist.*

Caldwell (1996, p. 5) proposes that the model developed in Victoria State, Australia – 'Schools of the Future' – may provide guidance for British educators. 'Schools of the Future' encompasses the following principles:

- *encourage the continuing improvement in the quality of educational programmes and practices in Victorian schools to enhance student learning outcomes*

- *actively foster the attributes of good schools in terms of leadership, school ethos, goals, planning and accountability process [...]*
- *within guidelines, enable schools to develop their own programmes to meet the individual needs of students*
- *be accountable to the community for the progress of the school and the achievements of its students.*

This is illustrated in Figure 10.3.

Key features of the model are that it centres on student learning and the relationship between resourcing, accountability, curriculum and people. The model is clear and transferable across cultures, phases and schools. Further investigation is required as to the content of provision and the success of the model in practice.

Critically, educationalists and politicians need to monitor and evaluate the funding of education in relation to pupil needs.

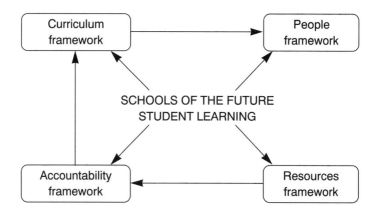

Figure 10.3: 'Schools of the Future' student learning
(*Source:* Caldwell, 1996; reproduced by permission of the author)

Summary

Since 1979, the aim of the government has been to improve the quality of provision in education while obtaining better value for the money spent. Given that schools must improve quality and provide value for money, measuring performance, monitoring and evaluating practice have become integral elements in the management of schools. Management is central to the efficiency and effectiveness of the monitoring and evaluation process.

The focus on management performance has created dilemmas for senior management teams. Efficiency or 'value for money' is steeped in controversy which relates directly to resource management. Performance indicators, as with all other aspects of school management, are inextricably linked to SDPs. Measuring efficiency, effectiveness and productivity is the most difficult aspect of resource management (Knight, 1983, p. 96). The performance review should emerge from the SDP and provide the structure within which these questions can be answered. It should be designed by each school to meet its own needs.

In practice, managers should compare where the school is to where it should be. There is a spectrum of indicators, quantitative and qualitative, that are likely to demonstrate aspects of performance. The most developed set of indicators focus on the resource consumption (or input) aspects of performance, whereby the school is a consumer of resources and indicators are concerned with the economic and efficient use of inputs. What constitutes a 'good' school is, inevitably, open to interpretation.

Performance indicators, as a system for evaluating past performance, are only of value if the process influences future planning. It is axiomatic that the indicators chosen should reflect the objectives of the school. In sum, indicators help the school to judge how well it is doing compared with what it seeks to do.

Monitoring is an ongoing process, integral to teaching and learning. If plans are not monitored, it will not be possible to determine whether their objectives have been achieved. Monitoring also enables managers and teachers to obtain the best results from the available resources and lead their team towards agreed objectives. Monitoring is made easier if objectives are:

- clear and practical
- agreed by all members of the team.

Monitoring also provides the basis for evaluating practice. Teams/departments are able to measure and compare their performance against agreed criteria. Monitoring is an ongoing activity which requires regular progress reports. For operational and financial information, resource managers need to monitor actual expenditure and operations regularly and to take corrective action.

Whereas monitoring is an ongoing process, a means of checking progress, evaluation is an overall check on whether objectives are achieved within the planned timetable. Evaluation should be a collaborative process. The desire to achieve success is motivating; evaluation should focus on success in addition to identifying areas which require improvement. The process of evaluating the impact of a plan on practice is critical to the successful implementation of the plan. In contrast to monitoring, evaluation encompasses reviewing the status of a plan's objectives. Through the evaluation process, managers will determine the need to change objectives, priorities and/or practice.

Beyond the school, the Audit Commission has responsibility for monitoring and evaluating public sector spending. Schools are inspected by a team of professional inspectors appointed by the Office for Standards in Education.

Resource managers need to consider the issue of equity. In practice, do all students receive a fair allocation of the school's resources? An area of education that engages with issues of equity on a daily basis in schools is the provision for pupils with special educational needs. Special needs staffing is vulnerable at all levels. Pupils with special educational needs are particularly vulnerable because some schools are reluctant to accept them, fearing the cost of learning support and the effect on their position in the league tables.

Research has also revealed a disparity of funding of inner-city schools (Sheffield City Council, 1992). This reflects the government's financial penalties on LEAs exceeding their spending of SSAs which is a political not an educational issue. NFER research (1996) also reported substantial variations between local education authorities in the scale of difference between primary and secondary funding.

Existing research focusing on the funding of education is limited; however, there is a need for governors, senior managers and resource managers to consider the issue of equity when evaluating financial and resource allocations. It is axiomatic that the aims and objectives of the school should reflect governors', managers' and teachers' desires to provide an equitable education for all pupils. Inequity in educational provision is a broad issue that needs to be addressed at local and national levels.

In practice, educationalists and politicians need to monitor and evaluate the funding of education in relation to pupil needs.

11
■　■　■
Marketing

Introduction

Resource management extends to virtually every aspect of school management including marketing the school to the community at large. This chapter focuses on the nature and process of marketing. As Davies and Ellison (1991, p. v) comment:

> While it remains the purpose of schools to provide high quality education within a caring environment, simply providing that may not be enough. It is also necessary to be perceived as doing so and communicating that effectively.

In essence, marketing is about managing the relationship between schools and their clients through effective communication. The LMS Initiative (1990, p. 4) comments:

> More recent legislation has been aimed at making schools more responsive to the wishes of parents and the community.

Oldroyd and Hall (1990, p. 14) believe that creating a positive image of the school in the community is important in the climate created by LMS and delegated budgets:

> Existing and potential parents become the clients who ultimately determine the available resource.

Schools receive income directly related to their school numbers. The more children a school is educating, the bigger the budget it receives. Market forces, rather than LEA admission policies, determine recruitment levels. Schools need to recruit in order to generate an income. Resource managers, in consultation with governors, senior managers and staff, need to develop a recruitment policy for their school. As Davies and Braund (1989, pp. 48–9) comment:

> Without fairly buoyant pupil numbers, schools will face the grim prospect of having to cope with a declining budget. The knock-on effect of this would be to restrict the educational opportunities that can be offered. In turn, this could bring about a

downward spiral in pupil recruitment, with fixed costs proving an ever increasing burden. To prevent any such pattern emerging headteachers will need to market their schools vigorously [. . .]. Put another way:

more children = more cash = better quality of education
fewer children = less cash = worsening education.

Parental choice is therefore central to school development. Ironically, however, when schools expand, they suffer a temporary shortfall in cash as budgets are based on the previous year's enrolment figures.

Marketing

Mercer and Mole (1994, p. 39) define marketing as *supply management*. This means:

What you can do to meet the needs and wants of your customers or clients.

This business definition of marketing reflects the prevailing culture in the public sector, including schools. As the financial resources of the school are dependent on the number of pupils (and other issues), schools need to have good communication with local clients, parents and pupils. Open enrolment (allowing parents to select schools within and beyond their traditional 'catchment' area) places further pressure on schools to market themselves.

Schools are marketing to internal and external markets. Internal markets enable one part of an organisation to purchase clearly defined services and goods from another part of the same organisation. Local government operates an internal market for the purchase of goods and services for both internal and external consumption. Internal and external markets include (Davies and Ellison, 1991, p. 11):

Internal markets:

- *Governors*
- *Staff (teaching and non-teaching)*
- *Regular visitors and helpers*
- *Current pupils*
- *Current parents.*

External markets:

- *Prospective parents and pupils*
- *The local community*
- *Prospective staff*
- *Other educational institutions*
- *Commerce and industry*

- *The local education authority*
- *National and local groups and organisations.*

Resource managers need to understand that identifying the market is critical to effective marketing.

Choice and diversity – open enrolment

A major thrust of government policy is choice and diversity. Levačić (1995, p. 6) states this was designed to:

> break the 'provider monopoly' of state education held by local government education authorities, which have administered state schools since 1902.

During the 1970s and early 1980s, when state schools moved from selective education to comprehensive education, all children attended their local school. In practice, apart from the 7 per cent of children who are privately educated, LEAs were able to exert considerable influence over the allocation of pupils to school places. Since the 1988 ERA, open enrolment has been introduced and several new types of state school have emerged, e.g.:

- Grant-maintained
- City Technology Colleges.

Put simply, open enrolment is where parents can choose between schools for their children's education, provided the chosen school has places (Braund and Davies, 1989, pp. 47–9). Following the ERA, schools are able to recruit pupils up to their standard number as determined by the 1980 Education Act; for secondary schools this is set as the number of pupils admitted to each school in September 1979. Primary schools may benefit from further increases due to rising 5s and nursery provision. A child cannot be refused admission to a state school which has spare places. A school reaches capacity when its intake is equal to its standard number. A school can admit more than its standard number or be forced to do so if a parent's appeal is successful. LEAs have protected those schools with falling rolls by limiting the admission of pupils over the standard number in more popular schools. The LEAs may give approval to a request from a school's governing body to increase its standard number. Only the Secretary of State can allow a school's allocated figure to be lowered.

The provisions of the ERA on open enrolment do not remove the original doubts about the achievement of the objective of parental choice. Market forces make it difficult for LEAs to manage pupil numbers economically at a time of continued contraction in the secondary sector (NAHT, 1989, p. 1/4). Senior managers and classroom teachers are now responsible for generating the income required to resource their schools through the recruitment of pupils. In order to market effectively schools must:

- define their marketing aims
- create and build a team
- set marketing objectives and priorities
- choose the promotional approaches
- put plans into action
- monitor and evaluate.

Marketing a school is a client-orientated process which involves (Davies and Ellison, 1991, pp. 71–3):

1 acknowledging the importance of the client
2 responding to clients
3 never letting the client down
4 creating one impression of the school
5 ensuring that the school provides a service as well as a product
6 managing a high quality service approach
7 developing a new philosophy.

Parents

Levačić (1995, p. 7) found that parental influence over schools has increased since the 1980 Education Act which led to the inclusion of parent, teacher and community representatives on governing bodies. Subsequently the 1986 Education Act increased the number of parent-governors, thus ensuring that the LEA could not appoint local councillors as school governors. In addition to increasing parental representation on governing bodies, the government also extended the influence of business on schools, by co-opting members of the local business community onto the governing bodies and by sponsorship of school activities.

The main benefit of recent legislation for parents has been increased choice. The implication for schools is that they have to be more open about the education they are offering. Marketing claims of individual schools are checked against national test results, and other performance indicators (*see* Chapter 10). In return, schools now look to parents for more support, in practice leading to schools in wealthier areas having larger budgets. As experienced in some parts of England and Wales, market forces can result in the closure of those schools unable to prevent the downward spiralling of resources. Davies and Braund (1989, p. 64) comment:

> *Thus under LMS parents will become the final arbiters. Like other consumer services schools will prosper or collapse depending on their ability to interest parents in what they have on offer.*

Parents need to be attracted, and then convinced that the school will offer the best possible education for their child (Oldroyd and Hall, 1990, p. 14):

> *Schools are in competition with each other [. . .]. In some LEAs headteachers have got together to collaborate in marketing their schools, in order to sharpen their public relations, by sharing the costs of a public relations firm to 'sell' their schools more effectively.*

The actual choice exercised by parents is dependent on local conditions. The main admissions criteria of comprehensive schools are proximity of residence or stated order of preference, and sibling connection.

Pupils

Pupils and parents are clients of the school. Greater attention is paid to the concerns of children following the ERA. Parents are influenced by pupils' views, motivation and happiness. Schools are also judged by their results, therefore pupils are under pressure to produce good examination and standard assessment test (SATs) results. Experience has shown that some schools have operated unofficial selection procedures, thus limiting the number of places available for pupils with learning difficulties. A second problem for pupils is the restriction of the curriculum as teachers are guided by attainment targets and assessment tests. More aesthetic areas of the curriculum have been threatened by pressure on the timetable.

Opting out

According to Bush *et al.* (1993), schools opted out of LEA control to avoid reorganisation plans because of opposition to LEA policies, or to reap financial benefits. Levačić (1995, p. 6) explains:

> *The DFEE has been active in promoting GM status by favourable funding, management support services and by making opting out an easier procedure.*

The governing bodies of city technical colleges (CTCs) and GM schools are trusts with responsibility for the schools' assets and are employers of the schools' staff. Levačić (1995, p. 7) states that:

> *A particular feature of school-based management in [England, Northern Ireland and Wales], in contrast to other English-speaking countries except New Zealand, is the decentralisation of decision-making power to a school council. In Canada, the USA and Australia, school councils are advisory.*

Hence governors of grant-maintained schools have a direct responsibility for the recruitment of pupils and, therefore, marketing.

Marketing – education

Foskett (1996, p. 2) comments:

> *Educational marketing has a short history within the wider field of educational research. The academic discourse has focused on theoretical considerations of the market concept within education (e.g. Gray (1991)).*

In practice, as Levačić (1995, p. 24) states:

> *The hypothesis that increased competition between schools will improve efficiency and raise educational standards is a direct application of the market model from the private sector.*

Schools have responded to market-force ideology by adopting a market culture approach which includes:

- the development of a positive view of the role of a marketing perspective
- the development of a system of responsibility and decision-making for marketing
- the use of promotional methods
- ensuring that staff understand the concept of marketing.

Gewirtz, Ball and Bowe (1995, pp. 86–7) comment:

> *It would be difficult to characterise [...] school markets as free markets. [...] As competitive units, attempting to maximise the use of their school-place provision and minimise recoupment costs, they act as corporations rather than small businesses [...]. However, their geographical boundaries are ultimately arbitrary in market terms. [...] schools are situated within a local market with its own particular characteristics. [...] An important part of any local market is the socio-economic and ethnic constitution of the 'consumers' – the parents. Choice and choosing differs between social class and ethnic groups [...].*

This is illustrated in Figure 11.1.

In addition to understanding the influences on the educational market, resource managers need to understand the nature of markets. In the context of markets, there are three types of organisational orientation: product-orientation, service-orientation and sales-orientation, the last of which focuses on promotion and marketing orientation where the customer is central to the philosophy of the organisation. Fundamental to a competitive market structure in education is the notion that markets are customer (or client) focused.

In addition to the competitive structure, a well-functioning market requires consumers to have access to information. Parents tend to receive/hear limited information, second-hand comments and local rumours. Recent legislation has increased the amount of information available, such as league tables of examination results and attendance figures, raw data which does not consider

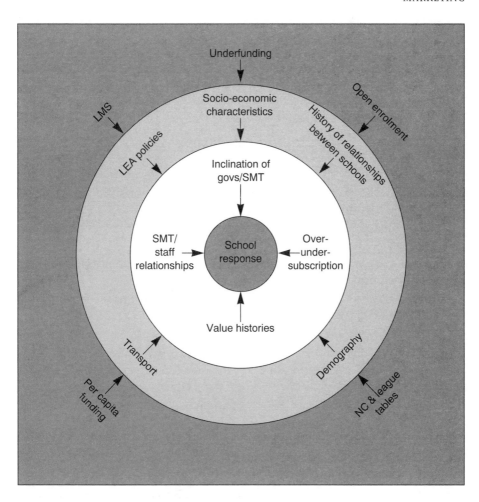

Figure 11.1: Factors influencing school responses to the market
(*Source:* Gewirtz, Ball and Bowe, 1995, p. 88; reproduced by permission of the publisher, Open University Press)
(*Note:* LMS = local management of schools; NC = National Curriculum; SMT = senior management team)

socio-economic issues. OFSTED inspection reports give a more complete picture and are available for purchase. In practice, marketing extends beyond the school. James and Phillips (1995, p. 75) conclude that:

> *much of the literature in the field of educational marketing is characterised by ideas, suggestions, guidance and strategies founded on marketing models taken from non-educational settings.*

Marketing – business

In business, marketing is a philosophy that drives the whole organisation. Effective marketing results from the use of a relatively large number of specific techniques to handle the many individual situations facing managers. There are no general techniques. Mercer and Mole (1994, pp. 39–77) describe marketing techniques appropriate for the promotion of businesses, small and large. Resource managers will find the following applicable to the school context.

Marketing encompasses:

- **Product** – what we offer: our product, service or other offering, and the level of pre-sales or after-sales service.
- **Price** – what we charge: our price, charge or fee, and other costs which a customer may have to pay.
- **Promotion** – how we communicate: building an awareness of, and an interest in, our offering.
- **Place** – how and where we deliver: making our product or service available as and when it is required.

These four elements are interrelated and interdependent. Knowing the levels of product quality, distribution, promotion and price that are acceptable to the customer (client) is, therefore, one key to developing an organisation and enabling it to achieve its objectives.

It is important for resource managers and the senior management team to understand the organisation's objectives in order to select the appropriate marketing strategies. A mission statement acts as the prime reference point, as Table 11.1 indicates (Mercer and Mole, 1994, p. 42; reproduced by permission of the publisher, The Open University).

More effective organisations are those which involve employees at all levels in setting goals by consultation, so that everyone has ownership of the organisation's objectives.

Product or service?

Kotter (1984), a North American marketing guru, defined product as:

> [...] *anything that can be offered to a market for attention, acquisition, use or consumption that might satisfy a want or need. It includes physical objects, services, persons, places, organisations, and ideas.*

It is important to note that organisations which have no tangible products, e.g. solicitors, consultancies or, indeed, schools, still face the same 'selling' challenges as the purveyors of very tangible, physical products. Business literature distinguishes between a *core product*, the *actual product* and an *augmented product*, as illustrated in Figure 11.2 (Mercer and Mole, 1994, p. 43; reproduced by permission of the publisher, The Open University).

Table 11.1 Objectives

Mission statement	The organisation's clearly stated overall purpose: • the reason for its existence.
Organisational objectives	Setting organisational priorities and quantifying these, for example in terms of: • the timescale • the level of growth.
Marketing objectives	Deciding and quantifying: • the number of products or services to be supplied • the types of products or services • the types of customers • in what timescale.
Marketing strategy	Deciding the changes needed to achieve the market objectives in: • product • price • place • promotion.

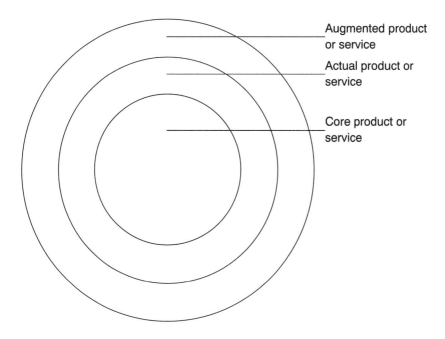

Figure 11.2 Product analysis

Products are defined as (Mercer and Mole, 1994, p. 43):

- *Core product* – *services providing solutions to problems.*
- *Actual product* – *what forms a particular product or service takes. These may include product composition and design, pack sizes, packaging design, a brand name and logo, product information and availability. The product or service description is the basis for establishing precisely how it will meet a need, how it will distinguish itself from competitors' offerings and how these advantages and differences are to be communicated to the potential customer (client).*
- *Augmented product* – *an augmented product includes what is offered to the customer in addition to the actual product.*

Organisation's image

An important, yet intangible, part of the product or service presented to the customer is the image an organisation presents to the outside world. Image is made up of what customers (clients) and the people they listen to know about the organisation, have read or heard, or have themselves experienced. Knowledge and professional staff are key determinants of image. The most sought-after image is a **PERFECT** image:

Professional

Efficient

Reliable

Friendly

Effective

Caring

Trustworthy

Oldroyd and Hall (1990, p. 15) state:

[. . .] *each school will want some ownership of the image it presents to the outside world. Middle managers may be given this responsibility.*

Resource managers need to ensure that their school creates a marketable image.

Designing a service strategy

As stated, marketing objectives should work towards achieving organisational objectives. To begin the design of a product strategy the following need to be examined:

- internal resources (skills, equipment and people available)
- external opportunities and threats (what customers are demanding; what competitors are offering; social, economic, technological and political trends).

Commercial organisations use four main product or service strategy routes to achieve objectives (Mercer and Mole, 1994, p. 44):

- *Market penetration* – *selling more of the same product to the same customer.*
- *Market extension* – *finding different types of customers or different channels for products and services.*
- *Product development* – *developing new or modified products to sell to the current market.*
- *Diversification* – *selling a new product in a new market.*

The customer

It is important to identify what customers' needs are likely to be and to tell them about the benefits that will interest them. Male (1996, p. 2) comments:

The market forces philosophy has been and continues to be the ideological mainstay of legislation and policy [...] which has systematically introduced measures designed to extend the power of the consumer.

A customer does not always come to each buying decision with an open mind. Customers for consumer goods and services may be influenced by a wide range of factors:

- economic factors
- age
- geography
- social class
- culture
- peer pressure
- lifestyle.

A large number of variables impinge upon the customer as he or she makes purchases of goods or services. Understanding customers' needs is not enough. Organisations need to understand exactly who customers are. It is impossible for an organisation to sell to everyone. The first step is to understand which segment of the population the organisation is aiming to serve. Wind and Cardozo (1974) identify a market segment as:

[...] a group of present or potential customers with some common characteristic which is relevant in explaining (and predicting) their response to a supplier's marketing stimuli.

A market segment, then, is simply a group of customers who are likely to have the same needs (Parkinson, 1994). A useful segment has four features:

- **Size** – the segment should be large enough in numbers or purchasing power.

- **Identity** – members of a segment should be identifiable.
- **Relevance** – the basis for the segment selected should be relevant to the important characteristics of the product or service on offer.
- **Access** – the segment, once identified, should be available to be acted on by the organisation.

In brief, customers in the same segment should have a relatively homogeneous set of attributes with respect to their needs, objectives and buying behaviour.

Market research

The data and information collected by market researchers are dependent on the decision-making process. Primary data collected by the researcher in person will answer a specific question. Secondary data from other sources may be less time-consuming and avoid 'reinventing the wheel'. Managers need to decide which data is required.

The research methodology applied to market research, quantitative or qualitative, should be selected according to its relevance to the product or market. These methods need to be studied in detail before embarking on a research programme.

Communication

The major assumption is that all organisations need to communicate, which may not be straightforward. Organisations have both internal and external audiences. The whole communication process is fraught with potential problems, which lead to misunderstandings and failure. For people to accept or believe a message, the target audience needs to have confidence that the message is truthful and relevant to them. The vehicle for the message will also have an effect.

There are many ways of conveying a message to customers, agents and employees. Decisions are required on the most appropriate vehicles to use. The choice of an appropriate communication vehicle is crucial to the success of the communication plan. Table 11.2 lists some of the different types of communication vehicles.

Schools may also communicate through:

- prospectuses, brochures and flyers
- newsletters, invitations
- word of mouth
- media, local press, television
- group promotion.

Table 11.2: Vehicles for communication

Type	Vehicle	Examples
Impersonal	Advertising	Local television
		Press
		Local radio
		Outdoor advertising
	Sales promotion	
	Public relations	Press releases
		Sponsorship
Personal	Personal selling	
	Direct marketing	Direct mail
	Personalised selling	Telemarketing
	Internal media	Memos, letters and reports

No method can be regarded as more successful than the rest. Each channel of communication has its attractions and pitfalls and should be evaluated on what is to be achieved and whom the message is for.

Communication plan

Once an organisation has formed a preliminary idea of its communication needs, it should then prepare a plan for action. This will:

- define the communications problem
- clarify the organisation's objectives
- specify the target audience
- define how the audience is expected to behave
- offer guidance on the creative strategy
- set down the issues regarding media selection and media scheduling.

Communication planning is a continuing task and an ongoing process of evaluation and revision is necessary. This means having a view on how communication channels work and an ability to assess performance.

Advertising

Fisher (1996, p. 13) questions whether advertisers are helpful to children, quoting the National Consumer Council's criticism of sponsored curriculum material for being 'heavy on logos and light on content'. Some believe that children must be protected from commercial values, at school and at home. In practice, advertising works if communicated in the appropriate manner:

- advertising cannot put right what is rotten
- consumers in Western societies are very experienced and expert buyers
- advertisements compete for attention and are only perceived selectively
- much advertising is selective.

This means that:

- it is difficult to know how much to spend on advertising
- it is more difficult to know whether it is really working.

Summary

Resource management extends to virtually every aspect of school management including marketing the school to the community at large. In essence, marketing is about managing the relationship between schools and their clients through effective communication. Schools receive income directly related to their school numbers. The more children a school is educating, the bigger the budget it receives. Market forces, rather than LEA admission policies, determine recruitment levels. Schools need to recruit in order to generate an income.

Schools are marketing to internal and external markets. Internal markets enable one part of an organisation to purchase clearly defined services and goods from another part of the same organisation. Resource managers need to understand that identifying the market is critical to effective marketing.

A major thrust of government policy has been choice and diversity. Put simply, open enrolment is where parents can choose between schools for their children's education, provided the chosen school has places. The provisions of the ERA on open enrolment do not remove the original doubts about the achievement of the objective of parental choice. Senior managers and classroom teachers are now responsible for generating the income required to resource their schools through the recruitment of pupils.

Pupils and parents are clients of the school. Greater attention is paid to the concerns of children following the ERA. Parents are influenced by pupils' views, motivation and happiness. Schools are also judged by their results, therefore pupils are under pressure to produce good examination and standard assessment test (SAT) results.

Schools have responded to market-force ideology by adopting a market culture approach. Critically, resource managers need to understand the nature of markets. In business, marketing is a philosophy that drives the whole organisation. Effective marketing results from the use of a relatively large number of specific techniques to handle the many individual situations facing managers. Resource managers and the senior management team need to understand the organisation's objectives in order to select the appropriate marketing strategies.

An important, yet intangible, part of the product or service presented to the customer is the image an organisation presents to the outside world. Image is made up of what customers (clients) and the people they listen to know about the organisation, have read or heard, or have themselves experienced.

The data and information collected by market researchers are dependent on the decision-making process. The research methodology applied to market research, quantitative or qualitative, should be selected according to its relevance to the product or market.

The major assumption is that all organisations need to communicate, which may not be straightforward. The whole communication process is fraught with potential problems, which lead to misunderstandings and failure. For people to accept or believe a message, the target audience needs to have confidence that the message is truthful and relevant to them. The vehicle for the message will also have an effect. No method can be regarded as more successful than the rest. Each channel of communication has its attractions and pitfalls and should be evaluated on what is to be achieved and whom the message is for. Communication planning is a continuing task and an ongoing process of evaluation and revision is necessary.

12

■　■　■

Opportunities

Introduction

This chapter focuses on the range of fund-raising opportunities available to schools. Glegg (1996, p. 2) comments:

> [State] schools have always been involved in generating additional funds in a small way through parent organisations [...], these efforts have generally been aimed at raising money for specific projects. Things have now progressed to the stage where some schools at least feel it necessary to look for major ongoing funding from sources outside government, [....] in addition to meeting the usual requests for extra money [for specific projects]. It is this aspect which has caused the controversy, and raised questions that go far beyond mere school issues.

The responsibility for determining a school's fund-raising policy rests with the governing body. This applies even when an organisation within the school, e.g. the parent–teacher association, decides its own fund-raising policy. Governing bodies have the power to seek grants and to accept gifts, though they are not obliged to do so if they have grounds for believing acceptance would not be in the best interest of the school. Headteachers or resource managers should not have sole control of the distribution of funds; a collegiate approach will produce the most positive results.

Resource managers need to be able to seek funding from the LEA and external sources and initiate business support for school projects. They should also encourage teachers to apply for classroom teaching grants and seek appropriate and required services from social service agencies. Resource managers should be able to use published databases to draw on sources of resource support, seek appropriate government grants and seek matching grants from the LEA or National Lottery. Resource managers must not overlook guidelines for timelines or fail to develop a strategy for engaging in extra-curricular fund-raising. Pugh (1990, p. 81) suggests:

- *understand the money*
- *realise how to manage the budget*
- *be able to monitor the money and possibly*
- *consider ways of making more money.*

The LMS Initiative (1990) advises that, as a source of income, fund-raising must be genuinely voluntary, in that the receipt of educational provision must not depend on it. Governors and senior managers cannot direct teachers to participate in voluntary fund-raising activities in their spare time. Fund-raising may be considered to be undesirable by those who believe that schools should be funded by government. The LMS Initiative (p. 71) concludes:

> *Schools should consider carefully before including the proceeds from fund-raising as part of the overall budget. Funds raised, or to be raised, by [PTAs] should not be included.*

Drucker in *Managing the Non-Profit Organisation* (1990, p. 71) suggests:

> *The purpose of a strategy for raising money is [...] to enable the non-profit institution to carry out its mission without subordinating that mission to fund raising. This is why non-profit people have now changed the term from 'fund raising' to 'fund development'. Fund raising is going about with a begging bowl, asking for money because the need is great. Fund development is supporting the organisation because it deserves it. It means developing [...] a membership that participates through giving.*

Resource managers need to know and understand an alternative strategy for apportioning revenue according to need – the virement of funds within the school budget.

Virement and virement strategies

Virement means moving around; money can be moved (vired) from one budget area to another. There are opportunities for school governors and resource managers to vire funds. Davies and Braund (1989, p. 36) comment:

> *In a sense, as long as a school is operating within its total budget, the amount it spends on each individual [budget] item is less important. Thus, a deficit of £500 in one budget area can be rectified by viring money from a budget area in surplus.*

If managed, this is of benefit to schools. For example, in mild winters, funds apportioned to heating can be spent in other areas; supply teachers are costly, so if teachers cover for colleagues funds saved can be used to improve/develop materials/premises. Interpreting budgets is important. The resource manager and governors should assess the reliability and importance of the school budget in the context of the school development plan.

In sum, virement is the authorisation to vire expenditure from one budget heading to another. Monthly monitoring of the budget will inform resource managers of variations that are likely to require management. There are computer programs available that will highlight under- and overspending. This facility will greatly assist resource managers.

Policy

Mountfield (1993, p. 14) suggests that there are two approaches to the potentially contentious subject of fund-raising. In brief:

- **The diplomatic low-key approach** – introducing fund-raising projects one at a time, restricting targets to generally acceptable items
- **The democratic approach** – deciding what to do after seeking a mandate to do it. This can be discussed and agreed during open evenings, AGMs or parent–teacher association (PTA) meetings.

Central to the success of a fund-raising strategy, resource managers and fund-raisers need to know:

- What is the money being raised for?
- How much does the item cost?
- Who is likely to contribute?
- How are likely contributors to be informed of the project?
- How are they to be persuaded to contribute?

Resource managers should also consider their motives for fund-raising. Is the fund-raising necessary? Are there alternative methods?

Process

Having decided on the means to create a policy, a strategy needs to be planned. This will consist of the following (Knight 1993, pp. 87–8):

1 *How much did you raise last year – and how does this compare with other similar schools?*

2 *What are your school's strengths in fund raising; e.g. people, ideas, methods, organisation, commitment?*

3 *What are your weaknesses?*

4 *Are any new opportunities for fund raising likely to develop in the near future; e.g. new people, new potential donors, new needs which will appeal to donors?*

5 *Are there any new constraints or difficulties likely to hamper you in the near future; e.g. change in people, other demands, competition!*

Critically, resource managers need to set a realistic target for funding development. Funders will need to know and understand what schools are raising money for and how to plan to raise money. If members of the school community are unhappy about the direction of the funds then do not pursue the idea.

Targets

Knight (1993, p. 88) suggests identifying targets and possible donors:

- *The extended school family – parents, pupils and staff, past, present and future; friends and relations; volunteers at and users of the school; neighbours of the school; suppliers.*

- *The community – individuals, organisations and groups (e.g. civic, political, social, sports, recreational, arts, caring and service, churches, youth or elderly etc.).*

- *Commerce and industry; e.g. a list of businesses, shops, commercial organisations in your area and also in the region. Are there any national firms or organisations which might be interested?*

- *Official bodies – local councils, national bodies and government organisations, the European Community and other international organisations, official bodies for sport, the arts, science, etc.*

- *Charitable bodies; e.g. local and national trusts.*

- *The lottery!*

Management of funds

Once a target has been set, a group of interested individuals will need to form a committee to create a budget. All additional school funds should be treated with the same formality as central funding. Figure 12.1 illustrates the variety of budgeting methods available to resource managers for the management of funds.

Resource managers need to ensure that committee members keep records of all letters sent, phone calls made, income raised and responses. It is important to update the files and to extract files that are no longer needed. A charitable trust may need to be established, as will a network of interested parties. A good funding developer is a talent-spotter, aware of the school's commitment to the project and equal opportunities. Try not to over-extend the project or be over-ambitious.

A SCHOOL FUND FINDING GUIDE

Which of the following does your school possess?

- A School Fund holding money raised from a number of non-statutory sources and for a number of purposes, including donations from individuals, other trusts, and business working in partnership with the school.

- A Governors' Trust Fund holding money raised by, or donated to, governors for use in ways that augment the school's delegated budget. In voluntary-aided schools it is often customary for the term 'Governors' Trust Fund' to be applied to the fund used only to hold the Governors' contribution to maintenance and improvements. Funds of this kind are accepted by the Inland Revenue as having charitable status.

- A Parent–Teacher (PTA), Home–School (HSA), Friends of the School (FSA) or similar Association Fund holding money raised to support the work of the school.

- A Headteacher's Discretionary Fund holding donations made by individuals, or by local grant-making trusts for the welfare of poor or needy pupils and administered by the headteacher.

- One or more Prize Funds producing a small amount of money each year to be spent on awards for pupils of special academic merit, or with other outstanding abilities.

- An Endowment Fund or School Appeal (or Development Trust) Fund holding donations for a particular capital or major resourcing project; only the interest of endowed funds can be used.

- A Community Education/Development Trust Fund holding money raised for the support of one or more educational organisations in the local community, and for poor or needy students, past or present.

- A School Charity Fund holding money raised by pupils and managed by a committee of staff, acting as trustees (N.B. parents, teachers and pupils sometimes also raise and donate money to outside charities, at their request; in such cases they are acting simply as agents of the charities involved).

- A Departmental, Activity or Class Fund holding money raised, often by individual teachers, for a particular subject or group of pupils (for example, money to buy equipment, to pay for music tuition or donations towards a class or departmental visit abroad).

- A School (Trading) Account holding income generated by activities such as premises letting, school uniform shops, book shops, tuck shops, school meals, school journeys, etc. (N.B. As explained elsewhere, this is not strictly a trust fund, nor can it be a charity . . .).

If yours is a school with charitable status, you may also find:

- A Foundation or School Trust holding all major assets including property, investment income, appeal income and fee income.

- An Associated Grant-making Trust such as a city livery company, a church body or a special needs charity that makes regular donations; trusts of this kind may help to maintain the fabric of the school and often fund bursary awards.

- An Endowment Fund to be held 'in perpetuity' with only the annual income (i.e. the interest on the invested capital) available to the school. This may be identical to the main Foundation Trust, or may represent an additional source of income, for example property left to the school under the terms of a will.

Fee-charging charitable independent schools may have:

- Several School Bursary and Scholarship Funds awarded by the school itself from its own trust or fee income.

- Subsidiary Trusts holding Endowing Bursary, Scholarship or Prize Funds given to the school by outside benefactors (the distinction, not always observed in the names schools give their awards, is that scholarships acknowledge talent of some kind; bursaries relieve poverty or need).

Figure 12.1: School funding guide
(*Source:* Mountfield, 1993, pp. 135–6; reproduced by permission of the author)

Income Generation

The school building is a source of income generation, as are pupils, staff and members of the extended community. The school is often the largest resource in the area with premises, land, expertise and time; it is often the most under-utilised. Knight (1993, p. 96) offers a checklist to assist in the generation of income (*see* Table 12.1).

Voluntary Help

Schools may wish to create partnerships with established grant or contract-funded voluntary organisations, or develop their own volunteer scheme.

Central to volunteer help is management. Volunteers need to feel wanted and appreciated, so that the satisfaction they gain is more valuable than the time donated. A source of volunteers is the pupils themselves. Older students can help guide and teach younger students which will be of mutual benefit.

Table 12.1: School income generation

Sales of bought-in products	e.g. stationery or T-shirts sold in a school shop. This category includes percentage commission on second-hand uniform or boot sales, and the inescapable school photographs.
Sales of the school's own products	e.g. plants, trees, food, etc., or printed materials, videos and audio cassettes.
Collection of coupons	from groceries etc.
Sale of services	possibilities include: instructional services – training, coaching, teaching; technical sources – word-processing, translating; caring services – e.g. creche, pre-school; research and development projects for local firms or organisations; consultancy and professional advice.
Sale of advertising	on 'sites', vehicles, in changing rooms or on printed material (but not so as to damage the ethos of the school).
Hire of school facilities	e.g. hall or sports facilities, other rooms, fields, vehicle(s), catering, reprographics, etc. – including space for car boot sales and markets. A few schools have developed conference centres.
Promotion of activities	e.g. holiday schemes, adult classes, entertainments.
Competition entries	including competitions intended for schools and national grocery and similar competitions.
Sales of assets	i.e. unused land or equipment (strictly capital rather than revenue income).

(*Source:* Knight, 1993, p. 96; reproduced by permission of the publisher, Heinemann Educational Publishers)

Sources of voluntary help are listed in the local library and/or community centre.

Further information on trusts, charity status, grants and relevant laws can be obtained from local libraries, the LEA, local authority officers and the community council officer.

School–business partnerships

Should you wish to raise funds from a business, be comfortable with what the donating company represents. As Mountfield (1993, p. 24) comments:

Schools with no experience of business partnerships are often unduly suspicious. Many employers are eager to play their part by investing in the education of the future; they do not see immediate profit as their aim. Companies, like parents, should not be rebuffed when they want to help. It is for those who set the school's policy to seek to involve them in the most appropriate way.

Glegg (1996, p. 6) states:

There are many examples of school–business partnerships which seem to work well. [. . .] Partnership should be of mutual benefit: it is illogical and naive to expect a partnership to benefit only one of the partners.

The British Columbia Teachers' Federation (1996, p. 60) guidelines for the implementation of school–business partnerships are as follows:

- *Partnerships must serve educational not commercial purposes.*
- *Ethical standards and absence of bias must be assured.*
- *Students must not be required to read or listen to advertising.*
- *Corporate logos must be used only for identification and kept to a minimum – they are not to appear on educational materials, school buildings or grounds.*
- *Agreements may only be for a limited time.*
- *Participation must be voluntary, and consent must be obtained from parents, teachers and students.*

Major appeals

Major appeals are rooted in the private sector; in practice many less well-off LEA-maintained schools are now attempting to raise capital appeals for new buildings or to improve play and sports facilities.

Establish a committee to manage the appeal; a separate charitable trust with specific purposes is usually required. Appeals need a target that is carefully planned, with active and able helpers. High-profile support will also be required, and someone effective, of suitable calibre, to run the appeal committee.

Appeals require a budget plan that will include the cost of fund-raising itself. The first task may be to raise the money to manage, promote and make the appeal. Producing publicity material and identifying potential supporters will be critical to the success of the appeal. The appeal needs to be high profile but of short duration. Committee members will need to visit potential contributors in order to generate initial interest. (See Figure 12.2 for a checklist for a major school appeal.)

- What is special, unique, or attractive about us, that will make our appeal stand out from all others likely to be going on at the same time?

- Does anyone know how to write a good appeal letter/brochure?

- How much will the printing and postage cost?

- What do other people think of our school?

- Can the school arrange for letters to go home? [. . .]

- Are there any local charities that fund education?

- Does the local Council for Voluntary Service have a list of names and addresses? [. . .]

Figure 12.2: Checklist for a major school appeal

Organising school fund-raising events

Occasionally school fund-raisers forget the need to make money – some even forget to cover their costs. Others think of nothing but profit. Fund-raising should be fun, not overly time-consuming, and involve as much of the school community as is realistically possible. As Mountfield (1993, p. 29) comments:

> *There are plenty of other important things for parents, teachers and governors to do together to further the work of a school.*

There will be the need for resource managers/fund-raisers to plan their fund-raising strategy. Knight (1993, p. 90) states:

> *Such a 'grand design' has many virtues:*
>
> 1 *It impresses potential donors with the scale of operation.*
> 2 *It gives clear sense of direction and purpose.*
> 3 *It inspires confidence.*
> 4 *It co-ordinates different people and activities.*
> 5 *It links disparate donors so that they feel commitment to something greater than their immediate interests – the whole is greater than the sum of the parts.*

The problem with fund-raising is donor fatigue and limited profit. Pupils engaged in 'mini-enterprises' could be a resource of both fund-raising and ideas. The traditional dictionary of ideas may assist the brainstorming process, as shown in Figure 12.3.

Animal shows, Antique road shows, Art exhibitions

Baby shows, Balloon races, Barbecues, Barn dances, Bonfires

Car washes, Celebrity nights, Come and try it evenings

Demonstrations, Draws and Duck races

Exhibitions: bygones, crafts, flowers, paintings by pupils

Fairs, Family discos, Fashion displays, Fetes, Films, Fireworks

Garden goods, Go-kart races, Gymkhanas

Highland games

It's a knockout

Jam, Jazz and Jumble

Karaoke evening, Kitchen produce

Litter collections, Local business exhibitions

Marathons, Markets, Midsummer balls, Old time Music hall

Name the doll

Odd job offers

Pantomimes, Picnics

Quiz evenings

Races, Rag days, Recitals, Recycling and Rallies

Shows

Talent shows, Tennis tournaments, Treasure hunts, TV quiz

Unwanted and Unused gift sales

Vegetable and Village shows, Vintage car rallies

Whacky races, Wine tasting, What the papers say

Xmas markets

Yoga demonstrations, Your turn next

Zig Zag races, Zoos

Figure 12.3: An ABC of fund-raising

Resource managers need to be aware that planning and the publicity stages of any fund-raising event are vital to success. All events should be organised by a competent and reliable organiser supported by an enthusiastic and reliable committee. Mountfield (1993, p. 31) offers the advice shown in Figure 12.4.

- How long will tickets/programmes/leaflets/posters take to write and design?

- How much will they cost to print?

- How many can we afford to produce? distribute?

- How else can we let people know what's happening?

- What kinds of activity will attract support?

- How many events do we need to reach our target?

- How much advance notice will supporters need?

- What else is happening on and around that date: in this school? others? locally? nationwide? on TV?

- Who will arrange the publicity? the main activity? refreshments? music? insurance? cloakrooms? creche?

- Who will liaise with the school? organise a volunteer rota for the day itself? co-ordinate all planning?

- Are we charging enough to make a profit?

Figure 12.4: Checklist for a fund-raising event

Sponsorship

Sponsorship can be at two levels, community or business. The former normally participates in sponsored events, while the latter means inviting financial or other support in return for commercially valuable advertising, publicity, goodwill or association (Knight, 1993, p. 92). Community sponsorship is generally associated with sponsored events: a walk, a swim, a musical performance. Each can be difficult to organise, and safety for the participants must be a priority.

Business sponsorship requires careful analysis and preparation. Resource managers need to consider: what is being offered? are the benefits to the sponsor tangible? Large sums will only be paid for large benefits. As Knight (1993, p. 93) states, thorough research is needed:

> Which companies or businesses might be interested in this kind of sponsorship? How profitable are they? What personal contacts already exist? (A good network of contacts is often the foundation for successful fund raising.) Who will make the decisions on this kind of request? (Always go to the top.) A reasonable request at the right time is better than a good one at the wrong time.

Subscriptions

Termly, or yearly, subscriptions will yield very little; parents often object to contributing towards their child's education in this manner.

Deeds of covenant

This approach requires a charitable trust: donations made in this way are tax free. A deed of covenant is a legally binding document by which a donor promises to pay the same donation each year for a period of at least four years out of their income. Because the charity itself does not need to pay tax, it can reclaim the tax paid on the donation. Additional funds can be added from special events and income on investment from the capital. Resource managers need to seek specialist advice about how to set up a covenant scheme, and how to become a registered charity.

Gift Aid

Gift Aid is a tax benefit, which is easier to operate than a deed of covenant. When a donor makes a single gift in one year of £250 or more for a charitable purpose, the school can reclaim the basic rate tax on the gift.

Lottery

Bell (1996, p. 19) comments:

> Whatever critics say, the lottery is undoubtedly a national success story in Britain. [. . .] What better way to demonstrate the nation's commitment to education than to tie it up with something which is seen as successful and fun?

Bell discusses the merits of the Georgia state lottery that pumps extra funds into education. Indeed, it is written into the Georgia state constitution that lottery proceeds are divided into three educational areas: funding for college scholarships, the expansion of the pre-kindergarten programme and investment in new technology. Each has been successful (p. 19):

> The power of lottery advertising to promote educational messages would be considerable and at a time when our aspirations for education must be higher, the lottery could provide a ready-made means of advertising all the good things there are to say about education. So in future, 'It could be you' may not just mean the pointing finger of lottery good fortune, but rather the possibility of enhanced educational opportunity.

The following advice is taken from the *Schools Funding Update* (Vol. 1, No.10, available from Pitman Publishing). It describes the process of a physical education (PE) teacher applying to the Sports Council for lottery funds.

Step 1: The idea

The first step for any school with an idea for a project is to contact someone with experience. S/he evaluates the project by paying a visit to the school. From there, if s/he thinks the project is going to go forward s/he will consult with the officers within the County Council. At this stage s/he has to be convinced that the project will meet the Sports Council's criteria (demonstrate community use). If the school doesn't meet the criteria s/he will be blunt and tell them so. 'I have to be hard-nosed about it and advise schools that if the project doesn't meet the criteria then there's no point in applying.' The whole process is very time consuming so there's little point in putting together a bid that s/he knows won't be successful. If this is the case then s/he will suggest that the school applies to the Foundation for Sports and the Arts (FSA).

When seeking out Lottery funding LEAs are looking to form a professional relationship with schools. They aren't trying to play 'big brother'. 'What we are trying to do is work together with the school to say this will make it difficult to apply or you need to overcome these hurdles.'

Step 2: Involving the architects

If the project is going to meet the criteria and it has the matched funding required then the school is in a position to move forward. The next step involves instructing the Architect's Department to carry out a feasibility study to see if the project will actually physically fit onto the school site.

LEAs have to be confident in the viability of a project because feasibility studies are expensive. Sports Development Officers have to be fairly cost-effective in what they ask their colleagues in the Architect's Department to get involved with.

Even at this point it is still not certain that the Council is going to put an application to the Sports Council. What the Council is saying is that they are taking a look at the feasibility of applying. 'It's very important to take these cautious steps,' says the head of PE, '. . . because statistically, on a national level it has been proved that applications from schools are quite hard to bring to fruition. This is because a lot of schools are going at it from the perspective of what the school needs rather than what the community needs.' For example, the school may need a sports hall, but the Sports Council aren't allowed to fund what is the statutory responsibility of the LEA.

Step 3: Project development

If the Architects give the go-ahead (i.e. if the project will physically fit onto the school site) then the school is ready to move on to the project development stage. There is a need to highlight the role Local Borough Councils should play in all this. Until education started to branch out into the community, the provider of leisure facilities in any area was the Local Borough Council. If a school is going to provide genuine community educational opportunities then they are going to have to work with these people.

It is important that the school's project fits in with the development strategy of the County and Borough. For example, schools may meet the funding and the feasibility criteria but when the applicant speaks to a colleague at Borough level, they may tell him/her that, strategically, they don't need a sports hall/astro-turf pitch. If this is the case then the fund-raiser is going to have great difficulty in claiming to the Sports Council that the project is strategically necessary. For the fund-raiser it is a question of dovetailing all these needs. The school may want a sports hall but if it's not needed in the community then the Sports Council aren't going to fund it.

One of the things that should be completed very early on is a document outlining what sports facilities there are in the County. The local authority report was intended to provide schools with information to support their submission for funding from such bodies as the National Lottery and the FSA in their planning for developing community use. The document identifies specific sports facilities needing development or improvement on school sites in order to enable and promote greater community use. However, within these many priorities, it is possible to highlight specific areas needing development.

Step 4: Filling in the form

Once the feasibility study has been done and a good deal of the research into the project has taken place, but before an application goes to the Sports Council, the local authority funding officer asks schools to fill out a form, peculiar to the County Council, that is basically a way of interrogating the soundness of a project. The form is a proposal for National Lottery funding and most people will be horrified at its length. However, once schools have filled this form out the Lottery form becomes a piece of cake as the information from the former is written onto the latter.

The form is a bit like an Income Tax form in that it has guidance notes. What it seeks to do is see if the school has thought about the project – what's the school community education policy? what's the present feel of community education? and so on. You then start to get into the financial side, with questions about the anticipated management structure, the governors, staffing (who will take bookings, who will open and close the facilities, who will clean the building).

All these questions have to be answered. Also, the school will need to break down the cost of the project – where the contributions are coming from, i.e. the contribution from the Sports Council, County Council, the school, so they can see what the actual capital cost is going to be.

This process goes on and on until you get to the point where the school is developing a very simple business plan. Some of the questions can be answered by the local authority funding officer, some by the Leisure Officer at Borough level. It is very much a collaborative approach to filling out the form. The form does seem too long, but if you are asking for £0.5 million you have to go about it in a professional and thorough way, making sure you cover every possible area.

The fund-raiser then takes the form and sends it round to the relevant officers, both at County and District level, for their comments. If there are any comments then the local authority funding officer will take them up with the people concerned. It's very important that everyone is consulted when you are claiming to be strategic as a County Council.

Step 5: Making an application

Having done all of the above the school can then move on to the application stage. Again, the fund-raiser will work with schools to fill in the form and then it's a question of sitting back and waiting the 14 weeks for an answer. However, the process doesn't end there because schools are in constant liaison with the Architect's Department right up to the project's completion.

Step 6: Success

If you were successful in your application to the Sports Council the project would go out to tender and the acceptance of these tenders would take another six weeks. The contract would then be completed and the builders would agree when they are going to start. It could take anything between 10 months and a year before building starts on a major capital project. There may be smaller capital projects that happen much quicker, such as refurbishment of existing facilities (the minimum cost of a project the Sports Council can deal with is £5 000).

Local authority activities and grants

The LEA is only part of the local authority, which has other departments that provide grants for voluntary sector activities. Schools can work in partnership with such groups to develop workshops, sports activities or community events. The local authority could also advise schools of new activities. Training and Enterprise Councils (TECs) and many government-funded initiatives often work in partnership with local authorities.

Local authority discretionary grants may also support school and youth activities. Knight (1993, p. 93) advises:

Government grants available are not always well known and European Community grants are particularly complex, especially when a grant first becomes available.

Alternatively, trusts are reasonably well documented; information will be available from the local library and the *Directory of Social Change*.

Recycling

Recycling waste paper is both ecologically and financially sound. The TES (19 April 1996) reported that a Kent primary school saved £400 from their refuse collection bill and also collected a cheque from the recycling company who processed the waste paper.

Banking

A number of banks provide schools with the opportunity of banking, as reported in the TES. This enables pupils to save and schools to receive grants and curriculum materials.

Called to account: banking in schools

- *Yorkshire Bank, which set up the School Bank Scheme in 1974, has 4 000 branches in schools. It provides £50 to set up a mini branch and £50 marketing costs. It also offers curriculum materials, including videos on money matters, and grants of up to £100 for environmental projects.*

- *Barclays entered school banking six years ago and has 200 branches. It offers £1 for new accounts opened at a school bank. In April Barclays launched a PC based banking package for schools. It has three survival guides,* How to Do Better in Exams, Staying On *and* Leaving School.

- *Midland Bank has 830 mini-branches in schools. Children who want jobs in the banks are interviewed by a local branch manager. The bank sent schools 25 000 free copies of* How to Manage Your Money.

- *TSB has a wide network of school liaison officers, and provides* Moving On, *a resource pack including communications skills, and money management. It sponsors school athletics awards and Artsbound, which is subsidising schools beyond the M25 for trips to the National Gallery.*

- *NatWest has produced its wide-ranging* Face 2 Face With Finance *programme, involving talks, role play and work experience, in partnership with the NatWest Department for Education and Literacy at Warwick University. More than 2 370 schools are registered.*

Further advice

Further advice may also be found in:

- **The Education Funding Guide**, which is a new source book for schools seeking additional finance from European organisations, government, trusts and companies. It contains information on the grants offered to educational establishments by more than 200 charities, and information on the support provided to schools and colleges by 100 major companies with details of what they offer and how to apply. Published by the Directory of Social Change, 24 Stephenson Way, London NW1 2DP (£15.95, plus £2.50 postage).

- **Schools Funding Update**, which provides a monthly guide to income generation covering everything from government grants to sponsorship, competitions and awards for schools and teachers. It includes advice from schools and professional fund-raisers on innovative ways to make money and offers a money-back guarantee if it doesn't work for you. Pitman Publishing, 128 Long Acre, London WC2E 9AN, (£149.00 per annum, subscription hotline 01483 733884).

In sum, resource managers need to have the skill and ability required to manage opportunities that increase revenue as appropriate.

Summary

The responsibility for determining a school's fund-raising policy rests with the governing body. Headteachers or resource managers should not have sole control of the distribution of funds; a collegiate approach will produce the most positive results. Fund-raising may be considered to be undesirable by those who believe that schools should be funded by government.

Critically, resource managers need to set a realistic target for funding development. Funders will need to know and understand what schools are raising money for and how to plan to raise money. Once a target has been set, a group of interested individuals will need to form a committee to create a budget. All additional school funds should be treated with the same formality as central funding.

The school building is a source of income generation, as are the pupils, staff and members of the extended community. The school is often the largest resource in the area with premises, land, expertise and time; it is often the most under-utilised.

Schools may wish to establish partnerships with established grant or contract-funded voluntary organisations, or develop their own volunteer scheme. Central to volunteer help is management. Volunteers need to feel wanted and appreciated, so that the satisfaction they gain is more valuable than the time donated. Should you wish to raise funds from a business, you must be comfortable with what the donating company represents.

Major appeals are rooted in the private sector; in practice many less well-off LEA-maintained schools are now attempting to raise capital appeals for new buildings or to improve play and sports facilities. Establish a committee to manage the appeal.

Occasionally school fund-raisers forget the need to make money – some even forget to cover their costs. Others think of nothing but profit. Fund-raising should be fun, not overly time-consuming, and involve as much of the school community as is realistically possible. There will be the need for resource managers/fund-raisers to plan their fund raising strategy. All events should be organised by a competent and reliable organiser supported by an enthusiastic and reliable committee.

Sponsorship can be at two levels, community or business. The former normally participates in sponsored events, while the latter means inviting financial or other support in return for commercially valuable advertising, publicity, goodwill or association. Termly, or yearly, subscriptions will yield very little; parents often object to contributing towards their child's education in this manner. The LEA is only part of the local authority, which has other departments that provide grants for voluntary sector activities. Schools can work in partnership with such groups to develop workshops, sports activities or community events.

In sum, resource managers need to have the skill and ability required to manage opportunities that increase revenue as appropriate. Good luck!

Glossary

■ ■ ■

Academic year The school year, which runs from September until August.

Accounts Documents recording income and expenditure, for a particular accounting period.

Actual expenditure Record of real spending. This does not include expected or budgeted expenditure.

Aggregated Schools Budget Defined in section 33(4)(b) of the Act, it is the amount remaining following deduction of the General Schools Budget mandatory and discretionary exceptions.

Budget A statement or plan of expenditure for a particular period of time.

Budget heads The headings used when planning spending.

Budget share The amount a school receives that year as a result of a formula being applied to the Aggregated Schools Budget.

Budgetary control Monitoring expenditure and income against the planned budget.

Budgeting Preparation of estimated expenditure and income.

Capital expenditure Expenditure on major assets that will have long-term benefit, e.g. buildings.

Capitation Described the money allocated annually to schools for equipment before LMS. The amount was based on age and number of pupils.

Cash limit A method of controlling expenditure, by setting amount that cannot be increased regardless of effects of inflation.

Central administration Support provided for schools by the LEA including financial, legal and personnel support.

Committed expenditure A system within the budgetary control where a transaction is recorded at the time it arises. A spending commitment is recorded at the time of ordering and deleted when payment is made.

Constructive dismissal Termination of an employee's contract by the employee, with or without notice, due to action by the employer.

Contingency The amount set aside for future expenditure that may be unquantifiable or unforeseen.

Cost centre A unit against which expenditure and income is charged. A school is a cost centre, and may have a unique reference for use within the LEA's accountancy system.

County school A school provided by the LEA.

Delegated budget The school's budget share which is delegated to the governing body to control.

Delegation requirement The requirement under the Act to delegate a budget to all secondary schools and eligible primary schools (with over 200 pupils).

Depreciation The loss in value of an item due to age, wear and tear.

Discretionary exceptions Items that may be delegated to schools or held centrally if the LEA decides.

Earmarked funds Funds allocated for specific purposes.

Education support grants Funds earmarked by the government for specific projects, e.g. governor training and LEA inspection.

Exception Items of expenditure for which no provision is made in the school's budget share. Some may be mandatory exceptions, others may be discretionary exceptions.

Expenditure profile The pattern by which expenditure within a budget is expected to be incurred.

Fair dismissal Dismissal which meets the statutory tests in the employment legislation for deciding if dismissal is fair.

Final accounts Accounts relating to an accounting period.

Financial delegation A management strategy where management units are identified and allocated resources to control and manage against a set of objectives.

Financial regulations A document agreed by the LEA to provide a framework for conduct of its financial affairs.

Financial year The period from 1 April to 31 March

Formula The method by which the LEA distributes the Aggregated Schools Budget to schools.

General Schools Budget The total amount available in any one year to all schools covered by the scheme of delegation. It includes planned direct and indirect spending at both school and centre.

Governing body A body assigned responsibility for the conduct of a school.

Incentive allowances Additional amounts payable to teachers in accordance with rates and criteria laid down in the *School Teachers' Pay and Conditions Document*. Headteachers and deputy heads are not eligible.

Income Received or expected amounts due to an organisation.

Increment An enhancement to salary according to a particular salary scale in recognition of experience and skill gained in the previous year.

Incremental budgeting Preparation of a budget for one year based on previous budgets.

Industrial tribunal Courts with jurisdiction over claims made under the employees' rights aspects of employment legislation.

Inflation Increases in costs of purchasing goods and services or employing staff.

Job description A statement of duties attached to a post. The description of skills, abilities and experience required is the job specification.

Local education authority Part of the local government structure, responsible for running the state education service in that area.

Mandatory exceptions Items that are excepted from delegation to schools, and must be retained centrally by the LEA.

On costs Employee costs that are additional to those of the employee's salary. National Insurance contributions and superannuation are examples.

Open enrolment Requires schools to enrol pupils up to the school's physical capacity.

Outturn   Actual expenditure and income for a whole financial year.

Outturn prices   The average price of items purchased within a financial year.

Peripatetic teachers   Teachers that move between schools providing specialist tuition, for example in music.

Price base   Rates of pay and prices of goods or services at a particular date, often November.

Reserve fund   An amount funded by the budget in order to meet costs in the future. The fund may be for a specific purpose or for general purposes.

Resource allocation   The process of distributing funds to schools, according to a *formula*.

Safety net   A scheme to limit changes in the amount of resources a school receives year to year.

Scheme of delegation   Scheme in which budget shares are determined and the delegation of budget shares is operated.

Special agreement school   A school provided by a voluntary body which provides 15 per cent of the capital of the school cost. Teaching staff are employed by the LEA.

Specific grant   A grant towards the cost of specified goods or services. An expenditure which is grant aided is a mandatory exception.

Staff complement   The number of people working at the school.

Standard number   The number of places a school has, defined in section 15 of the 1980 Education Act which uses the 1979 entry figure as a baseline.

Standard subjective classification   The classification of types of income and expenditure defined by CIPFA.

Standing orders   Rules drawn up by the LEA for the conduct of business and proceedings.

Statemented pupil   A pupil who has a formal document of special educational needs, assessed under criteria in the 1981 Education Act.

Supply teacher   A teacher appointed to cover for temporarily absent staff.

Transitional period   The period of four years from April 1990 during which the formula for resource allocation may include elements designed to protect schools from major changes in resourcing.

Unfair dismissal   Dismissal failing to meet the specific statutory tests in the employment legislation for deciding if a dismissal is fair.

Virement   Transfer of budgetary provision from one expenditure heading to another.

Voluntary aided school   A school established by a voluntary body which provides 15 per cent of the capital cost of the school. Staff are generally employed by the governors.

Voluntary controlled school   A voluntary school which is neither a *voluntary aided school* nor a *special agreement school*. Its staff are employed by the LEA.

Zero-based budgeting   Preparation of a budget without considering previous plans and spending.

List of abbreviations

■ ■ ■

AGM	annual general meeting
APT&C	administrative, professional, technical and clerical (staff)
ASB	Aggregated Schools Budget
AWPU	age-weighted pupil unit
BEMAS	British Educational Management and Administration Society
C&AG	Comptroller and Auditor General
CCT	compulsory competitive tendering
CEO	Chief Education Officer (LEA)
CIMA	Chartered Institute of Management Accountants
CIPFA	Chartered Institute of Public Finance and Accountancy
CPD	continuous professional development
CTC	city technology college
DDP	department development plan
DES	Department of Education and Science
DFE	Department for Education
DFEE	Department for Education and Employment
DSO	direct service organisation
ERA	Education Reform Act 1988
FAS	Funding Agency for Schools
FSA	Foundation for Sports and the Arts
GM	grant maintained
GNVQ	General National Vocational Qualification
GSB	General Schools Budget
HEADLAMP	The Headteachers' Leadership and Management Programme
HMI	Her Majesty's Inspectors
HRM	human resource management
IIP	Investors In People
INSET	in-service training
IT	information technology
LEA	local education authority
LFM	local financial management
LGMB	Local Government Management Board
LMS	local management of schools
MIS	management information system
NAHT	National Association of Headteachers
NASUWT	National Association of School Masters and Union of Women Teachers
NCE	National Commission on Education
NFER	National Foundation for Education Research
NI	National Insurance
NPBEA	National Policy Board for Educational Administration (USA)
NPQH	National Professional Qualification for Headteachers
NPQSL	National Professional Qualification for Subject Leaders
NUT	National Union of Teachers
OFSTED	Office for Standards in Education

PC	personal computer
PERT	Programme Evaluation and Review Technique
PES	Public Expenditure Survey
PPBS	Planning Programming Budgeting System
PSB	Potential Schools Budget
PTA	parent–teacher association
PTR	pupil–teacher ratio
SAT	standard assessment test
SCAA	Schools Curriculum and Assessment Authority
SDP	school development plan
SEN	special educational needs
SENCO	special educational needs co-ordinator
SIMS	Schools Information Management System
SMT	senior management team
SSA	Standard Spending Assessment
TEC	Training and Enterprise Council
TES	Times Educational Supplement
TSS	Total Standard Spending
TTA	Teacher Training Agency
ZBB	zero-based budgeting

References

■ ■ ■

ACAS (1980) *Code of Practice No. 1, Disciplinary Practice and Procedures in Employment*, London: HMSO.

Adair, J. (1987) *Effective Teambuilding*, London: Pan.

Allan, P. (1990) 'The school development plan', in Gilbert, C. (ed.) (1990) *Local Management of Schools: A Guide for Governors and Teachers*, London: Kogan Page.

Alter, C. and Hage, J. (1993) *Organisations Working Together*, London: Sage.

Argyris, C. (1970) *Understanding Organisational Behaviour*, Homewood, Ill.: Dorsey Press.

Arkin, A. (1996) 'Patches of financial flabbiness', *Times Educational Supplement 2*, 15 March 1996, p. 8.

Armstrong, F. (1995) 'Integration Inequality in the UK', *International Directions in Education*, 3(2): 3.

Armstrong, L., Evans, B. and Page, C. (1993) *A Guide for Middle Managers*, Lancaster: Framework Press Educational.

Arnott, M.A., Bullock, A.D. and Thomas, H.R. (1992) *The Impact of Local Management on Schools. A Source Book. The First Report of the 'Impact' Project*, University of Birmingham: School of Education.

Ashford, D. (1974) 'The effects of central finance on the British local government system', *British Journal of Political Science*, 4: 705–22.

Association of County Councils Audit Commission (1989) *Losing an Empire, Gaining a Role*, Occasional Paper No. 10, December, London.

Association of County Councils Audit Commission (1993) *The Education Bill; Memorandum by the Local Authority Associations*, London.

Atkins, J. (1996) 'Towards a saner funding system', *Times Educational Supplement*, 26 July 1996, p. 13.

Audit Commission (1984a) *Code of Local Government Audit Practice for England and Wales*, London: HMSO.

Audit Commission (1984b) *Obtaining Better Value in Education: Aspects of Non-Teaching Costs in Secondary Schools*, London: HMSO.

Audit Commission (1986) *Towards Better Management of Secondary Education*, London: HMSO.

Audit Commission (1988) *The Local Management of Schools: A Note to LEAs*, Bristol: Audit Commission.

Audit Commission (1989a) *Losing an Empire: Finding a Role. The LEA of the Future*, London: HMSO.

Audit Commission (1989b) *Assessing Quality in Education*, London: HMSO.

Audit Commission (1991) *Rationalising Primary School Provision*, London: HMSO.

Audit Commission (1993) *Adding Up the Sums: Schools' Management of Their Finances and Comparative Information for Schools*, London: HMSO.

Audit Commission (1996) *Adding Up the Sums: 4*, London: HMSO.

Audit Commission/OFSTED (1993) *Keeping Your Balance: Standards for Financial Administration in Schools*, London: OFSTED.

Bagley, C., Woods, P. and Glatter, R. (1994) *Empowerment, Effectiveness and Marketing: The Engagement of Stakeholders in Education*. Paper presented at the British Educational Research Association and Annual Conference, Oxford, September.

Ball, S.J. (1987) *The Micropolitics of the School: Towards a Theory of School Organisation*, London: Routledge.

Ball, S.J. (1993) 'Education markets, choice and social class: the market as a class strategy in the UK and USA', *British Journal of Sociology of Education*, **14**(1): 3–20.

Barber, B. (1975) 'Command Performance', *Harper's Magazine* (April), New York.

Barber, M. (1996) *Times Educational Supplement*, 10 May 1996, p. 128.

Barber, M., Evans, A. and Johnson, M. (1995) *An Evaluation of the National Scheme of School Teacher Appraisal*, London: HMSO.

Bassey, M. (1996) 'Wherefore are thou paid more for Romeo?', *Times Educational Supplement*, 24 May 1996, p. 13.

Bell, D. (1996) 'More cash for schools? – you bet', *Times Educational Supplement*, 12 July 1996, p. 19.

Bell, L. (1992) *Managing Teams in Secondary Schools*, London: Routledge.

Bell, L., Halpin, D. and Neill, S. (1996) 'Managing self-governing primary schools in the locally maintained, grant-maintained and private sectors', *Educational Management and Administration*, **24**(3): 253–61.

Bennis, W. (1987) *Why Leaders Can't Lead*, San Francisco: Jossey Bass.

Blandford, S. (1997) *Middle Management in Schools*, London: Pitman Publishing.

Boaden, N. (1971) *Urban Policy Making*, London: Cambridge University Press.

Book Trust (1996) *School Spending on Books*, London: Book Trust.

Bottery, M. (1992) *The Ethics of Educational Management*, London: Cassell.

Bowe, R. and Ball, S. (1992) 'Doing what comes naturally: an exploration of LMS in a secondary school', in Wallace, G. (ed.), *Local Management of Schools: Research and Experience*, Clevedon: Multilingual Matters.

Bowe, R., Ball, S.J. and Gewirtz, S. (1994a) 'Parental choice, consumption and social theory: the operation of micro markets in education', *British Journal of Educational Studies*, **XXXXII**(1): 38–52.

Bowe, R., Ball, S.J. and Gewirtz, S. (1994b) 'Captured by the discourse? Issues and concerns in researching parental choice', *British Journal of Sociology of Education*, **15**(1): 63–78.

Bowles, G. (1989) 'Aspects of marketing and promotion', in Fidler, B. and Bowles, G. (eds), *Effective Local Management of Schools: A Strategic Approach*, Harlow: Longman (for BEMAS).

Braund, C. (1989) 'Aspects of income generation', in Fidler, B. and Bowles, G. (eds), *Effective Local Management of Schools: A Strategic Approach*, Harlow: Longman (for BEMAS).

Brighouse, T. (1990) quoted in Sutcliffe, J., *How to See All of the Wood Instead of the Trees*, TES, 16 February.

British Columbia Teachers' Federation (BCTF) (1996) *Guidelines for Education/Business*, Vancouver: BCTF.

Broadbent, J., Laughlin, R., Shearn, D. and Dandy, N. (1992) ' "It's a long way from teaching Susan to read". Some preliminary observations of a project studying the introduction of local management of schools', in Wallace, G. (ed.), *Local Management of Schools: Research and Experience*, Clevedon: Multilingual Matters.

Brockman, F.J. (1972) 'Problem budgeting: implications for secondary principals', *NAASP Bulletin*, **56**(366): 34–42, Virginia: NAASP.

Bullock, A.D. and Thomas, H. (1992) 'School size and local management funding formulae', *Educational Management and Administration*, **20**(1): 30–9.

Bullock, A.D. and Thomas, H. (1994a) *The Impact of Local Management on Schools: Final Report*, Birmingham: University of Birmingham/NAHT.

Bullock, A.D. and Thomas, H. (1994b) 'The political economy of local management of schools', in Tomlinson, S. (ed.), *Educational Reform and its Consequences*, London: IPPR/Rivers Oram.

Bullock, A.D. and Thomas, H. (1996) *Schools at the Centre?*, London: Routledge.

Burgess, R.G, Hockley, J., Phtiaka, H., Pole, C.J. and Sanday, A. (1992) *Thematic Report and Case Studies*, Sheffield: Sheffield City Council.

Burgess, T. and Travers, T. (1980) *Ten Billion Pounds*, London: Grant McIntyre.

Bush, T. and West-Burnham, J. (eds) (1994) *The Principles of Educational Management*, Harlow: Longman.

Bush, T., Coleman, M. and Glover, D. (1993) *Managing Autonomous Schools: The Grant-Maintained Experience*, London: Paul Chapman.

Caines, J. (1992) 'Improving education through better management: a view from the DES', in Simkins, T., Ellison, L. and Garrett, V. (eds), *Implementing Educational Reform. The Early Lessons,* Harlow: Longman (for BEMAS).

Caldwell, B.J. (1990) 'Educational reform through school-site management: an international perspective on restructuring in education', *Advances in Research and Theories of School Management and Educational Policy*, 1: 303–33.

Caldwell, B.J. (1993) 'Paradox and uncertainty in the governance of education', in Beare, H. and Lowe Boyd, W. (eds), *Restructuring Schools*, Lewes: Falmer Press.

Caldwell, B.J. (1996) 'Beyond the self-managing school', *BEMAS Annual Conference, Coventry 1996: Leadership Markets and Values: Educational Change in Context.*

Caldwell, B.J. and Spinks, J.M. (1988) *The Self-Managing School*, Lewes: Falmer Press.

Cambridgeshire County Council (1985) *Local Financial Management*, County Council Information Paper, Cambridge: Cambs CC.

Cambridgeshire County Council (1986) *Local Financial Management: A Pilot Scheme in Cambridgeshire,* Cambridge: Cambs CC.

Campion, D. (1996) 'Campaign tactics', *Times Educational Supplement,* 15 March 1996, p. 9.

Chambers, A.D. (1998) *Computer Auditing,* London: Pitman Publishing.

Chapman, J. (1990) 'School based decision-making and management: implications for school personnel', in Chapman, J. (ed.), *School Based Decision-Making and Management*, Lewes: Falmer Press.

Chartered Institute of Management Accountants (CIMA) (1994) *Management Accounting – Offical Terminology of the CIMA,* London: CIMA.

Chartered Institute of Public Finance and Accountancy (CIPFA) (1984) *Performance Indicators in the Education Service: A Consultative Document*, London: CIPFA.

Chartered Institute of Public Finance and Accountancy (CIPFA) (1988) *Performance Indicators for Educational Establishments*, CIPFA Statistical Information Service.

Chartered Institute of Public Finance and Accountancy (CIPFA) (1989) *Audit Implications of LMS,* London: CIPFA.

Chartered Institute of Public Finance and Accountancy (CIPFA) (1990a) *Councillors' Guide to Local Government Finance*, London: CIPFA.

Chartered Institute of Public Finance and Accountancy (CIPFA) (1990b) *Education Statistics: 1990–91 Estimates*, London: CIPFA.

Chartered Institute of Public Finance and Accountancy (CIPFA) (1990–91, 1991–92, 1992–93) *Education Estimates*, London: CIPFA.

Chartered Institute of Public Finance and Accountancy (CIPFA) and Local Government Training Board, SEO *et al.* (1990) *Local Management in Schools: A Practical Guide*, Second Edition, London: The LMS Initiative.

Coopers & Lybrand (1988) *The Local Management of Schools: A Report to the DES,* London: Coopers & Lybrand.

Coopers & Lybrand (1996) *The National Union of Teachers. The Funding of Education*, London: Coopers & Lybrand.

Cordingly, P. and Kogan, M. (1992) *Supporting Education: Matching National and Local Systems to Needs*, London: Jessica Kingsley.

Cotter, R. (1996) 'Benchmarking: perspectives and purposes', *BEMAS Annual Conference, Coventry 1996: Leadership Markets and Values: Educational Change in Context*.

Coulby, D. (1991) 'Introduction: the 1988 Education Act and themes of government policy', in Coulby, D. and Bash, L. (eds), *Contradiction and Conflict: The 1988 Education Act in Action*, London: Cassell.

Crawford, M. (1994) *The Primary School Secretary: A Key Part of the Learning Institution*. Paper presented at the BEMAS Annual Conference, Manchester, September 1994.

Davies, B. (1989) 'Budgetary and economic perspectives and their application in local management of schools', in Fidler, G. and Bowles, G. (eds), *Effective Local Management of Schools: A Strategic Approach*, Harlow: Longman (for BEMAS).

Davies, B. (1990) 'Resource management in schools', in Davies, B. *et al.* (eds), *Educational Management for the 1990s*, Harlow: Longman.

Davies, B. (1994) 'Managing resources', in Bush, T. and West-Burnham, J. (eds), *The Principles of Educational Management*, Harlow: Longman.

Davies, B. and Braund, C. (1989) *Local Management of Schools: An Introduction for Teachers, Governors and Parents*, Plymouth: Northcote House.

Davies, B. and Ellison, L. (1990) 'Management information', in Davies, B., Ellison, L., Osbourne, A. and West-Burnham, J. (eds), *Educational Management for the 1990s*, Harlow: Longman.

Davies, B. and Ellison, L. (1991) *Marketing the Secondary School*, Harlow: Longman.

Davies, B. and Ellison, L. (1992) *School Development Planning*, Harlow: Longman.

Davies, B. and West-Burnham, J. (1990) 'Marketing schools', in Davies, B. Ellison, L., Osbourne, A. and West-Burnham, J. (eds), *Educational Management for the 1990s*, Harlow: Longman.

Dean, C. (1996a) 'Move to get cash split for schools made public', *Times Educational Supplement*, 5 April 1996, p. 6.

Dean, C. (1996b) 'Head in cash crisis works for nothing', *Times Educational Supplement*, 24 May 1996, p. 3.

Dean, C. (1996c) 'GM school is £100,000 in the red', *Times Educational Supplement*, 7 June 1996, p. 7.

Department for Education (DFE) (1992) *Choice and Diversity – A New Framework for Schools*, London: HMSO.

Department for Education (DFE) (1993) *School Governors: A Guide to the Law*, London: DFE.

Department for Education (DFE) (1994) *Local Management of Schools*, Circular 2/94, London: DFE.

Department for Education and Employment (DFEE) and Welsh Office (1996a) *The Common Funding Formula*, Circular 9/96, London: HMSO.

Department for Education and Employment (DFEE) and Welsh Office (1996b) *A Discussion Paper: National Funding for GM Schools*, London: HMSO.

Department for Education and Employment (DFEE) and Welsh Office (1996c) *White Paper: Self-Government for Schools (A Summary)*, London: HMSO.

Department of Education and Science (DES) (1968) *Statistics of Education, Volume 1*, London: HMSO.

Department of Education and Science (DES) (1972) *Education: A Framework for Expansion* (White Paper), London: HMSO.

Department of Education and Science (DES) (1977a) *Education in Schools: A Consultative Document* (Cmd. 6869), London: HMSO.

Department of Education and Science (DES) (1977b) *A New Partnership for Our Schools* (The Taylor Report), London: HMSO.

Department of Education and Science (DES) (1977c) *Ten Good Schools: A Secondary School Enquiry*, HMI Series: Matters for Discussion 1, London: HMSO.

Department of Education and Science (DES) (1980a) *A Framework of the Curriculum*, HMI Series: Matters for Discussion, London: HMSO.

Department of Education and Science (DES) (1980b) *A View of the Curriculum*, London: HMSO.

Department of Education and Science (DES) (1981) *The School Curriculum*, London: HMSO.

Department of Education and Science (DES) (1983) *Teaching Quality* (White Paper, Cmd. 8836), London: HMSO.

Department of Education and Science (DES) (1984) *Slow Learners and Less Successful Pupils in Secondary Schools*, London: HMSO.

Department of Education and Science (DES) (1985a) *Better Schools* (White Paper), London: HMSO.

Department of Education and Science (DES) (1985b) *The Curriculum from 5 to 16*, London: HMSO.

Department of Education and Science (DES) (1985c) *Quality in Schools: Evaluation and Appraisal*, London: HMSO.

Department of Education and Science (DES) (1987a) *Financial Delegation to Schools: Consultation Paper*, London: DES.

Department of Education and Science (DES) (1987b) *Grant Maintained Schools: Consultation Paper*, London: HMSO.

Department of Education and Science (DES) (1987d) *The National Curriculum 5–16: A Consultation Document*, London: DES.

Department of Education and Science (DES) (1987e) *Admission of Pupils to Maintained Schools*, London: DES.

Department of Education and Science (DES) (1987, revised DFE, 1993) *School Teachers' Pay and Conditions Document*, London: HMSO.

Department of Education and Science (DES) (1988a) *Education Reform Act: Local Management of Schools*, London: HMSO.

Department of Education and Science (DES) (1988b) *Education Reform Act: Local Management of Schools,* Circular 7/88, London: HMSO.

Department of Education and Science (DES) (1988c) *Local Management of Schools*, London: HMSO.

Department of Education and Science (DES) (1988d) *Admission of Pupils to County and Voluntary Schools*, Circular 11/88, London: DES.

Department of Education and Science (DES) (1988e) *National Curriculum Task Group on Assessment and Testing: A Report,* London: DES.

Department of Education and Science (DES) (1988f) *School Teachers' Pay and Conditions Document 1988*, London: DES.

Department of Education and Science (DES) (1989) *Planning for School Development I: Advice to Governors, Headteachers and Teachers*, London: DES.

Department of Education and Science (DES) (1990a) *Burntwood School*. A report by HMI, 12–16 November. Reference 105/91/S2.

Department of Education and Science (DES) (1990b) *Aspects of Education in the USA: Teaching and Learning in New York City Schools: A Paper by Her Majesty's Inspectorate*, London: HMSO.

Department of Education and Science (DES) (1990c) *Planning for School Development II*, London: DES.

Department of Education and Science (DES) (1991a) *Local Management of Schools: Further Guidance*, Circular 9/91, London: DES.

Department of Education and Science (DES) (1991b) *Development Planning: A Practical Guide*, London: DES.

Department of Education and Science (DES) (1991c) *School Teacher Appraisal*, Circular 12/91, London: HMSO.

Department of Education and Science (DES) (1992) *School Governors: A Guide to the Law*, London: HMSO.

Downes, P. (ed.) (1988) *Local Financial Management in Schools*, Oxford: Blackwell.

Doyal, L. and Gough, I. (1991) *A Theory of Human Need*, London: Macmillan.

Drucker, P. (1980) *Managing in Turbulent Times*, London: Heinemann.

Drucker, P. (1990) *Managing the Non-Profit Organisation*, Oxford: Butterworth Heinemann.

Drucker, P. (1991) 'The new productivity challenge', *Harvard Business Review*, November/December.

Duried, C. (1992) *Management and Cost Accounting* (3rd edn), London: Chapman & Hall.

Earley, P. (1994) *School Governing Bodies: Making Progress?*, Slough: NFER.

Elliott, B. and Duffus, K. (1996) 'What has been happening to pay in the public service sector of the British economy?' *British Journal of Industrial Relations*, **34** (March 1996): 51–85, Oxford: Blackwell.

Elliott, J. (1981) 'How do parents judge schools?', in *School Accountability*, SSRC Cambridge Accountability Project, London: McIntyre.

Emmanuel, C., Otley, D. and Merchant, K. (1991) *Accounting for Management Control*, London: Chapman & Hall.

Esp, D. and Saran, R. (eds) (1994) *Effective Governors for Effective Schools – Roles and Relationships*, London: Pitman Publishing (for BEMAS).

Everard, K.B. (1986) *Developing Management in Schools*, Oxford: Blackwell.

Everard, K.B. and Morris, G. (1990) *Effective School Management* (2nd edn), London: Paul Chapman.

Everard, K.B. and Morris, G. (1996) *Effective School Management* (3rd edn), London: Paul Chapman.

Evetts, J. (1993) 'Local management and headship: changing the contexts for micro-politics', *Educational Review*, **45**(1): 53–66.

Fidler, B. (1989) 'Aspects of personal management', in Fidler, B. and Bowles, G. (eds), *Effective Local Management of Schools: A Strategic Approach*, Harlow: Longman (for BEMAS).

Fidler, B. and Bowles, G. (eds) (1989) *Effective Local Management of Schools: A Strategic Approach*, Harlow: Longman (for BEMAS).

Fidler, B. and Cooper, R. (eds) (1992) *Staff Appraisal and Staff Management in Schools and Colleges: A Guide to Implementation*, Harlow: Longman.

Fidler, B., Bowles, G. and Hart, J. (1991) *Planning Your School's Strategy: ELMS Workbook*, Harlow: Longman.

Fielden, J. (1986) 'Educational costing for troubled times', *Proceedings of the Eighth Annual Conference of BEMAS*, Sheffield City Polytechnic.

Fisher, P. (1996) 'How to get ahead without advertising', *Times Educational Supplement*, 14 June 1996, p. 13.

Foskett, N.H. (1996) 'Marketisation and cultural change in schools – an analytical framework', *BEMAS Annual Conference, Coventry 1996: Leadership Markets and Values: Educational Change in Context*.

Foster, K. (1996) 'Developing teachers as managers', *BEMAS Annual Conference, Coventry 1996: Leadership Markets and Values: Educational Change in Context*.

Fox, M. (1996) 'Tales of the unexpected', *Times Educational Supplement*, 23 August 1996, p. 15.

Francis, T. and Jackson, F. (eds) (1994) *The Public Service Yearbook*, London: Chapman and Hall.

Fullan, M. (1988) 'Research into educational evaluation', in Glatter (ed.), *Understanding School Management*, Milton Keynes: The Open University.

Fullan, M. (1991) *The New Meaning of Educational Change*, London: Cassell.

Fullan, M. (1993) *Change Forces*, Lewes: Falmer Press.

Furse, J. (1989) 'Marketing in a primary school', in Fidler, B. and Bowles, G. (eds), *Effective Local Management of Schools: A Strategic Approach*, Harlow: Longman (for BEMAS).

Gewirtz, S., Ball, S.J. and Bowe, R. (1995) *Markets, Choice and Equity in Education*, Buckingham: Open University Press.

Gilbert, C. (ed.) (1990a) *Local Management of Schools: A Guide for Governors and Teachers*, London: Kogan Page.

Gilbert, C. (1990b) 'Local management of schools: an introductory summary', in Gilbert, C. (ed.) *Local Management of Schools: A Guide for Governors and Teachers*, London: Kogan Page.

Glatter, R. (1994) 'Managing dilemmas in education: the tightrope walk of strategic choice in more autonomous institutions'. Paper presented at the *8th International Intervisitation Program in Educational Administration: Persistent Dilemmas in Administrative Preparation and Practice*, Toronto, Canada and Buffalo, USA, May.

Glatter, R. and Woods, P. (1994) 'The impact of competition and choice on parents and school', in Bartlett, W., Propper, C., Wilson, D. and Le Grand, J. (eds), *Quasi-markets in the Welfare State*, Bristol: SAUS.

Glatter, R., Johnson, D. and Woods, P. (1993) 'Marketing, choice and responses in education', in Smith, M. and Busher, H. (eds), *Managing Schools in an Uncertain Environment: Resources, Marketing and Power*, Sheffield: Sheffield Hallam University/ BEMAS.

Glatter, R., Preedy, M., Riches, C. and Masterton, M. (eds) (1988) *Understanding School Management*, Milton Keynes: Open University Press.

Glegg, A. (1996) 'Supping with the devil: fundraising, sponsorship and the public school system', *BEMAS Annual Conference, Coventry 1996: Leadership Markets and Values: Educational Change in Context*.

Glynn, J.J. (1993) *Public Sector Financial Control and Accounting* (2nd edn), Oxford: Blackwell Business.

Goldstein, H. (1980) 'Fifteen thousand hours: a review of its statistical procedures', *Journal of Child Psychology and Psychiatry*, 21: 364–6.

Gray, L. (1991) *Marketing Education*, Buckingham: Open University Press.

Greenfield, T. and Ribbins, P. (1993) *Greenfield on Educational Administration*, London: Routledge.

Guthrie, J.W., Garms, W.I. and Pierce, L.C. (1988) *School-based Leadership: Challenges and Opportunities*, Dubuque, IA: Wm C. Brown.

Halsey, G. (1993) 'The impact of local management on school management style', *Local Government Policy Making*, 19(5): 49–56.

Handy, C. (1993) *Understanding Organisations* (4th edn), Harmondsworth: Penguin.

Handy, C.B. and Aitken, R. (1986) *Understanding Schools as Organisations*, Harmondsworth: Penguin.

Hardman, J. and Levačić, R. (1994) The Impact of Competition on Secondary Schools: Factors Associated with Differential Market Success. Paper presented at the BEMAS Annual Conference, Oxford, September.

Hargreaves, D.H. (1995) 'Self-managing schools and development planning – chaos or control?', *School Organisation*, **15**(3): 215–17.

Hargreaves, D.H. and Hopkins, D. (1991) *The Empowered School: The Management and Practice of Development Planning*, London: Cassell.

Hargreaves, D.H., Hopkins, D., Leask, M., Connolly, M. and Robinson, P. (1989) *Planning for School Development*, London: DES.

Hart, J. (1993) *Successful Financial Planning and Management in Schools*, Harlow: Longman.

Hartley, H. (1979) 'Zero-based budgeting for schools', in Levačić, R. (ed.), *Financial Management in Education*, Milton Keynes: Open University Press.

Harvey-Jones, J.H. (1988) *Making it Happen*, London: Collins.

Hatch, J. (1989) 'Computer administration at St Peter's Primary School', in Fidler, B. and Bowles, G. (eds), *Effective Local Management of Schools: A Strategic Approach*, Harlow: Longman (for BEMAS).

Heads Legal Guide on Finance (1993).

Hill, D. (1988) *Local Financial Management. A Guide to the Financial Delegation of Budgets to Schools*, London: The Industrial Society.

Hill, D., Oakley Smith, B. and Spinks, J. (1990) *Local Management of Schools*, London: Paul Chapman.

Hirst, D. (1996) 'Local management of schools', *BEMAS Annual Conference, Coventry 1996: Leadership Markets and Values: Educational Change in Context*.

Hoare, S. (1996) 'All a load of valuable rubbish', *Times Educational Supplement*, 19 April 1996, p. 24.

Holmes, S.T. (1996) 'An investigation into the potential for a marketing culture in Australian schools', *BEMAS Annual Conference, Coventry 1996: Leadership Markets and Values: Educational Change in Context*.

Holt, K. (1990) 'Monitoring and evaluation: some thoughts', in Gilbert, C. (ed.), *Local Management of Schools: A Guide for Governors and Teachers*, London: Kogan Page.

House, E.R. (1973) 'The dominion of economic accountability', in House, E.R. (ed.), *School Evaluation: the Politics and Process*, London: McCutchon.

House of Commons Education Committee (1994) *2nd Report of the Education Committee, Session 1993–4*, London: HMSO.

Howson, J. (1982) 'Variations in local authority provision of education', *Oxford Review of Education*, 8(2): 187–98.

Hoy, W.K. and Miskel, C.G. (1989) 'Schools and their external environments', in Glatter, R. (ed.), *Educational Institutions and Their Environments: Managing the Boundaries*, Milton Keynes: Open University Press.

Hoy, W.K. and Miskel, C.G. (1991) *Educational Administration: Theory, Research and Practice* (4th edn), New York: McGraw-Hill.

Hoyle, E. (1980) 'Evaluation of the effectiveness of educational institutions', *Educational Administration* 8(2): 159–78.

Humphrey, C. and Thomas, H. (1994) 'An appraisal of change', in Caldwell, B. and Cooper, B. (eds), *Schools at the Centre: An International Perspective on School-Site Management*, New York: JAL.

Hutton, W. (1996) 'Look, listen and learn', *The Guardian*, 2 March 1996, p. 21.

ILEA (1987) *The ILEA Junior School Study*, London: ILEA.

Interim Advisory Committee on School Teachers' Pay and Conditions (1989) *Second Report* (The Chilver Report), London: HMSO.

Interim Advisory Committee on School Teachers' Pay and Conditions (1990) *Third Report*, London: HMSO.

Interim Advisory Committee on School Teachers' Pay and Conditions (1991) *Fourth Report*, London: HMSO.

Irvine, V.B. (1975) 'Budgeting: functional analysis and behavioural implications', in Rappaport, A. (ed.), *Information for Decision-Making, Quantitative and Behavioural Dimensions* (2nd edn), Englewood Cliffs, NJ: Prentice Hall.

Jones, B.M. (1995) *Local Government Financial Management*, Hemel Hempstead: ICSA.

Jones, R. and Pendlebury, M. (1996) *Public Sector Accounting* (4th edn), London: Pitman Publishing.

Kendall, M. and Stuart, A. (1979) *Advanced Theory of Statistics*, Vol. 2, 4th edn, Charles Griffin.

Knight, B. (1983) *Managing School Finance*, Oxford: Heinemann.

Knight B. (1987) 'Managing the honeypots', in Thomas, H. and Simkins, T. (eds), *Economics and the Management of Education: Emerging Themes*, Lewes: Falmer Press.

Knight, B. (1989a) *Managing School Time*, Harlow: Longman.

Knight, B. (1989b) *Local Management in Schools*, London: Longman/Peat Marwick McClintock.

Knight, B. (1992a) 'What price the National Curriculum', *Managing Schools Today*, **1**(2): 18–21.

Knight, B. (1992b) *Financial Management for Schools. The Thinking Manager's Guide*, London: Heinemann .

Knight, B. (1993) *Financial Management for Schools. The Thinking Manager's Guide*, London: Heinemann .

Knight, B., Morris, P. and Tapply, G. (1993) *Questions and Answers: Finance*, Heads Legal Guide, Kingston Upon Thames: Croner.

Kogan, M. (1986) *Education Accountability*, London: Hutchinson.

Kogan, M., Johnson, D., Packwood, T. and Whitaker, T. (1984) *School Governing Bodies*, London: Heinemann.

Kotler, P. (1984) *Marketing Management: Analysis, Planning and Control*, 5th edn, Englewood Cliffs, NJ: Prentice Hall.

LaGrand, J. (1991) *Equity and Choice: An Essay in Applied Social Policy*, London: HarperCollins.

LaGrave, J., Mole, R. and Swingler, J. (1994) 'Planning and managing your work', *B600 The Capable Manager*, Milton Keynes: Open Business School, The Open University.

Lancaster, D. (1989) 'Aspects of management information systems', Fidler, B. and Bowles, G. (eds), *Effective Local Management of Schools: A Strategic Approach*, Harlow: Longman (for BEMAS).

Levačić, R. (ed.) (1989a) *Financial Management in Education*, Milton Keynes: Open University Press.

Levačić, R. (1989b) 'Rules and formulae for allocating the spending of delegated budgets: a consideration of general principles', *Educational Management and Administration*, **17**(2): 79–90.

Levačić, R. (1990a) 'Public choice: the economics of politics', in Shackleton, L. (ed.), *New Thinking in Economics*, Aldershot: Edward Elgar.

Levačić, R. (1990b) 'Evaluating local management of schools: methodology and practice', *Financial Accountability and Management*, **6**(3): 209–27.

Levačić, R. (1992a) 'Local management of schools: aims, scope and impact', *Educational Management and Administration*, **20**(1): 16–29.

Levačić, R. (1992b) 'The LEA and its schools: the decentralised organisation and the internal market' in Wallace, G. (ed.), *Local Management of Schools: Research and Experience*, Clevedon: Multilingual Matters.

Levačić, R. (1992c) 'An analysis of differences between historic and formula school budgets: evidence from LEA submissions and from detailed study of two LEAs', *Oxford Review of Education*, **18**(1): 75–100.

Levačić, R. (1993a) 'Assessing the impact of formula funding on schools', *Oxford Review of Education*, **19**(4): 435–57.

Levačić, R. (1993b) 'Local management of schools as an organisational form: theory and application', *Journal of Education Policy*, **8**(2): 123–41.

Levačić, R. (1994) 'Improving student achievement by using value added of examination performance indicators', in Crawford, M., Kydd, L. and Parker, S. (eds), *Educational Management in Action: A Collection of Case Studies*, London: Paul Chapman.

Levačić, R. (1995) *Local Management of Schools: Analysis and Practice*, Buckingham: Open University Press.

Levačić, R. and Glover, D. (1994a) *The Efficiency of the School: An Examination of the Application of the OFSTED Inspection Framework*. Paper presented at the British Educational Management and Administration Society Annual Conference, Manchester, September.

Levačić, R. and Glover, D. (1994b) *OFSTED Assessment of Schools' Efficiency: An Analysis of 66 Secondary School Inspection Reports*, Milton Keynes: Open University Press.

Levačić, R. and Glover, D. (1996) 'Value for money: how schools are assessed by OFSTED' in Ouston, J., Earley, P. and Fidler, B. (eds), *OFSTED Inspections*, London: David Fulton.

Levačić, R. and Woods, P. (1994) 'New forms of financial co-operation', in Ranson, S. and Tomlinson, J. (eds), *School Co-operation: New Forms of Local Governance*, Harlow: Longman.

Lindsay, K. (1926) *Introduction in Social Progress and Educational Waste*, London: Routledge & Kegan Paul.

LMS Initiative, The (1988) *Local Management of Schools: A Practical Guide*, London: LMS Initiative.

LMS Initiative, The (1990) *Local Management in Schools: A Practical Guide* (2nd edn), London: LMS Initiative.

LMS Initiative, The (1992) *Local Management in Schools: A Study into Formula Funding and Management Issues*, London: LMS Initiative.

Local Government Management Board (1995) *Cost Centre Management: A Guide for Central Support Services*, Luton: LGMB.

McGregor, D. (1966) *Leadership and Motivation*, New York: MIT Press.

Maclure, J.S. (1989) *Education Re-formed – A Guide to the Education Reform Act* (2nd edn), London: Hodder & Stoughton.

McMahon, A., Bolam, R., Abbott, R. and Holly, P. (1984) *Guidelines for Review and Internal Development in Schools*, Harlow: Longman (for Schools Council).

Male, T. (1996) 'A critique of market forces approaches to systematic school reform', *BEMAS Annual Conference, Coventry 1996: Leadership Markets and Values: Educational Change in Context*.

Mant, A. (1983) *The Leaders We Deserve*, Oxford: Martin Robertson.

Marconi, H.R. and Seigal, G. (1989) *Behavioural Accounting*, Ohio: South Western.

Marren, E. and Levačić, R. (1994) 'Senior management, classroom teacher and governor responses to local management of schools', *Education Management and Administration*, **22**(1): 39–53.

Maslow, A.H. (1943) 'A theory of human motivation', *Psychological Review*, **50**(4): 370–96.

Maychell, K. (1994) *Counting the Cost: The Impact of LMS on Schools' Patterns of Spending*, Slough: NFER.

Mercer, D. and Mole, R. (1994) 'Operations and Marketing', *B600: The Capable Manager*, Milton Keynes: The Open University.

Minzberg, H. (1994) *The Rise and Fall of Strategic Planning*, London: Prentice-Hall.

Moisan, C. (1990) 'Local management of schools', in Gilbert, C. (ed.), *Local Management of Schools: A Guide for Governors and Teachers*, London: Kogan Page.

Mole, R. and Parkinson, A. (1994a) 'Understanding accounts and costs', *B600: The Capable Manager*, Milton Keynes: The Open University.

Mole, R. and Parkinson, A. (1994b) 'Budgeting and performance', *B600: The Capable Manager*, Milton Keynes: The Open University.

Morris, R. (1994) *The Functions and Roles of Local Education Authorities*, Slough: Education Management Information Unit, NFER .

Morris, R., Reid, E. and Fowler, J., (1993) *Education Act 93: A Critical Guide*, London: AMA.

Mountfield, A. (1993) *School Fundraising – What You Need to Know: A Guide to the Law and Good Practice for Parents, Teachers, Governors, and all Trustees of School Voluntary Funds*, London: Directory of Social Change.

Mullins, L.J. (1993) *Management and Organisational Behaviour* (3rd edn), London: Pitman Publishing.

National Association of Head Teachers (NAHT) (1989) *Guide to the Education Reform Act 1988*, London: NAHT.

National Association of Head Teachers (NAHT) (1991) 'The management of finance 2: basic budget management', in *NAHT Guide to School Management*, Harlow: Longman.

National Association of School Masters and Union of Women Teachers (NASUWT) (1993) *LMS – A Guide for Governors* (3rd edn), London: NASUWT.

National Audit Office (1994) *Value for Money in Grant-Maintained Schools: A Review of Performance*, London: HMSO.

National Commission on Education (NCE) (1995) *Learning to Succeed*, London: Paul Hamlyn Foundation.

National Commission on Education (NCE) (1996) *Success Against the Odds*, London: Routledge.

National Foundation for Education Research (NFER) (1996) *Comparative Costs: Perspectives on Primary–Secondary Differences*, Slough: NFER.

National Governors' Association (1986) *Time for Results: The Governors' 1991 Report on Education*, Washington, DC: NGA.

National Leadership Network (1991) *Developing Leaders for Restructuring Schools: New Habits of Mind and Heart*, Washington, DC: US Dept of Education.

National Policy Board for Educational Administration (NPBEA) (1993) *Principals for Our Changing Schools: Knowledge and Skill Base*, Virginia: NPBEA.

National Union of Teachers (NUT) (1989) *LMS: The Staffing Implications*, London: NUT Publication.

National Union of Teachers (NUT) (1996) *The Funding of Education: A Summary of the Coopers and Lybrand Proposals*, London: NUT Publication.

Nicholson, E.A.J. (1986) 'The effects of financial autonomy of the school as an organisation'. Unpublished BPhil(Ed) dissertation, University of Birmingham.

Nightingale, D. (1990) *Local Management of Schools at Work in the Primary School*, Lewes: Falmer Press.

Office for Standards in Education (OFSTED) (1993) *Standards and Quality in Education,* London: HMSO.

Office for Standards in Education (OFSTED) (1994) *Handbook for the Inspection of Schools,* London: HMSO.

Office for Standards in Education (OFSTED)/Audit Commission (1993) *Keeping Your Balance: Standards for Financial Administration in Schools,* London: OFSTED.

Oldroyd, D. and Hall, V. (1990) *Management Self-Development for Staff in Secondary Schools,* Bristol: NDCEMP.

Oxfordshire County Council (1979) *Starting Points in Self Evaluation,* Oxford: Oxford CC Education Department.

Parkinson, A. (1994) 'Sessions 1–3', in Mole, R. and Parkinson, A. (1994a) 'Understanding accounts and costs', *B600: The Capable Manager,* Milton Keynes: The Open University.

Peers School (1988) *The School Book: Life at a Comprehensive School,* Oxford: Peers School Books.

Pendlebury, M., Jones, R. and Karbhari, Y. (1992) 'Accounting for executive agencies in the UK government', *Financial Accountability and Management,* 8(1): 35–48.

Primary Majority Group (1988) *The Primary Majority Current Issues in Primary Education,* Manchester: Primary Majority Group.

Pugh, M. (1990) 'Headteachers, their governors and the local management of schools', in Gilbert, C. (ed.), *Local Management of Schools: A Guide for Governors and Teachers,* London: Kogan Page.

Rafferty, F. (1994) 'Many more heads leave jobs', *Times Educational Supplement,* 2 September.

Rafferty, F. (1996) 'Savings still possible insist auditors', *Times Educational Supplement,* 2 March, p. 6.

Ranson, S. (1992) *The Role of Local Government in Education,* Harlow: Longman.

Ranson, S. (1994) *The New System of Government for Education,* Swindon: ESRC.

Ranson, S. and Travers, T. (1994) 'Education', in Jackson, P. and Lavender, M. (eds), *The Public Services Yearbook 1994,* London: CIPFA Public Finance Foundation/Chapman & Hall.

Robbins, D (1990) 'The changing face of county hall', in Gilbert, C. (ed.), *Local Management of Schools: A Guide for Governors and Teachers,* London: Kogan Page.

Rosenthal, D. (1996) 'Spending on books at crisis point', *Times Educational Supplement,* 21 June, p. 7.

Rutter, M., Maughan, B., Mortimore, P. and Ouston, J. (1979) *Fifteen Thousand Hours: Secondary Schools and Their Effects on Children,* Shepton Mallet: Open Books.

Scheerens, J. (1992) *Effective Schooling: Research, Theory and Practice,* London: Cassell.

School Management Task Force (1990) *Developing Schools Management – The Way Forward,* London: HMSO.

School Teachers' Review Body (1992) *First Report,* London: HMSO.

School Teachers' Review Body (1993) *Second Report,* London: HMSO.

School Teachers' Review Body (1994) *Third Report,* London: HMSO.

School Teachers' Review Body (1995) *Fourth Report,* London: HMSO.

Scott, P. (1989) 'Accountability, responsiveness and responsibility', in Glatter, R. (ed.), *Educational Institutions and their Environments: Managing the Boundaries,* Milton Keynes: Open University Press.

Sheffield City Council Education Department (1992) *Resourcing Sheffield Schools,* Sheffield: Sheffield City Council.

Shipman, M.D. (1979) *In-School Evaluation*, London: Heinemann.

Simkins, T. (1986) 'Patronage markets and collegiality: reflections on the allocation of finance in secondary schools', *Educational Management and Administration* **14**(1): 17–30.

Simkins, T. (1987) 'Economics and the management of schools', in Thomas, H. and Simkins, T. (eds), *Economics and the Management of Education: Emerging Themes*, Lewes: Falmer Press.

Simkins, T. (1995) 'The equity consequences of educational reform', *Educational Management and Administration*, **23**(4): 221–32.

Skelton, M., Reeves, G. and Playfoot, D. (1991) *Development Planning for Primary Schools*, Windsor: NFER/Nelson.

Solihull MBC (1979) *Evaluating the School: A Guide for Secondary Schools in the Metropolitan Borough of Solihull*, Solihull: Education Department.

Spencer, R. (1996) *Times Educational Supplement*, 24 May, p. 3.

Spicer, B.J. (1990) 'Programme budgeting – a way forward in school management', in Chapman, J. (ed.), *School Based Decision-Making and Management*, Lewes: Falmer Press.

Spinks, J.M. (1990) 'Collaborative decision-making at the school level', in Chapman, J. (ed.), *School Based Decision-Making and Management*, Lewes: Falmer Press.

Taylor, F. (1990) 'Governors and the local management of schools', in Gilbert, C. (ed.), *Local Management of Schools: A Guide for Governors and Teachers*, London: Kogan Page.

Thomas, G. (1990) *Setting up LMS: A Study of LEAs' Submissions to the DES*, Milton Keynes: Open University Learning Materials.

Thomas, G. (1991) *The Framework for LMS: A Study of LEAs' Approved Local Management of Schools Schemes*, Milton Keynes: Open University Learning Materials.

Thomas, H. (1987) 'Efficiency and opportunity in school finance autonomy', in Thomas, H. and Simkins, T. (eds), *Economics and the Management of Education: Emerging Themes*, Lewes: Falmer Press.

Thomas, H. (1989) *Local Management of Schools in Action*, London: Cassell.

Thomas, H. (1996) 'Efficiency, equity and exchange in education', *Educational Management and Administration*, **24**(1): 31–47.

Thomas, H. and Martin, J. (1996) *Managing Resources for School Improvement. Creating a Cost-effective School*, London: Routledge.

Thomas, H., Kirkpatrick, G. and Nicholson, E. (1989) *Financial Delegation and the Local Management of Schools: Preparing for Practice*, London: Cassell.

Times Educational Supplement (TES) (1996a) 19 April.

Times Educational Supplement (TES) (1996b) 10 May, p. 18.

Times Educational Supplement (TES) (1996c) 'Opinion', 19 April, p. 16.

Times Educational Supplement Survey (1996) 'Classes of 35 no big deal anymore', *Times Educational Supplement*, 6 September, p. 6.

Tuckman, B.W. (1965) 'Development sequence in small groups', *Psychological Bulletin*, **63**(6): 384–99.

Walker, D. (1996) 'GM sector faces tougher audit rules', *Times Educational Supplement*, 26 January.

Wallace, M. (1989) 'Towards a collegiate approach to curriculum management in primary and middle schools', in Preedy, M. (ed.), *Approaches to Curriculum Management*, Milton Keynes: Open University Press.

Warwick, B. (1983) *Decision-Making*, London: The Industrial Society.

West-Burnham, J. (1990) 'Human resource management in schools', in Davies, B. Ellison, L., Osbourne, A. and West-Burnham, J. (eds), *Educational Management for the 1990s*, Harlow: Longman.

West-Burnham, J. (1992) *Managing Quality in Schools*, Harlow: Longman.

West-Burnham, J. (1994a) 'Strategy, policy and planning', in Bush, T. and West-Burnham, J. (eds), *The Principles of Educational Management*, Harlow: Longman.

West-Burnham, J. (1994b) 'Inspection, evaluation and quality assurance' in Bush, T. and West-Burnham, J. (eds), *The Principles of Educational Management*, Harlow: Longman.

Whitty, G., Edwards, T. and Gewirtz, S. (1993) *Specialisation and Choice in Urban Education: The City Technology Experiment*, London: Routledge.

Williams, E. (1996) 'Higher rates of interest', *Times Educational Supplement*, 10 May, p. 18.

Williams, V. (1981) *Leadership – A Developing Perspective*, Oxford: OUDES Occasional Paper.

Williams, V. (1985) *Accountability in Education: Public Confidence and Professional Development?*, Oxford: OUDES Occasional Paper.

Williams, V. (1989) 'Schools and their communities: issues in external relations', in Sayer, J. and Williams, V. (eds), *Schools and External Relations: Managing the New Partnerships*, London: Cassell.

Williams, V. (1995) *Towards Self-Managing Schools: A Secondary School's Perspective*, London: Cassell.

Woods, P. (1994) *Parents and Choice in Local Competitive Arenas: First Findings From the Main Phase of the PASCI Study*. Paper presented at the American Educational Research Association Annual Conference, New Orleans, April.

Woods, P., Bagley, C. and Glatter, R. (1994) 'Dynamics of competition: the effects of local competitive arenas on schools'. Paper presented at the *CEDAR International Conference: Changing Educational Structures, Policy and Practice*, University of Warwick, March 1994.

Young, P. (1989) 'Performance indicators', in Fidler, B. and Bowles, G. (eds), *Effective Local Management of Schools: A Strategic Approach*, Harlow: Longman (for BEMAS).

Index

■ ■ ■